AN AUTOBIOGRAPHY

SOLOMON MAIMON

AN AUTOBIOGRAPHY

Translated from the German by
J. Clark Murray

Introduction by
Michael Shapiro

UNIVERSITY OF ILLINOIS PRESS

URBANA AND CHICAGO

First Illinois paperback, 2001
Introduction © 2001 by the Board of Trustees
of the University of Illinois

Library of Congress Cataloging-in-Publication Data
Maimon, Salomon, 1754–1800.
[Lebensgeschichte. English]
Solomon Maimon : an autobiography / translated
from the German by J. Clark Murray ; introduction
by Michael Shapiro.
p.   cm.
Previously published: London ; Boston : A. Gardner,
1888. With new introd.
Includes bibliographical references.
ISBN 0-252-06977-3 (pbk. : alk. paper)
1. Maimon, Salomon, 1754–1800. 2. Jewish philoso-
phers—Germany—Biography. 3. Judaism—Europe,
Eastern—History—18th century. I. Title.
B3068.A32   2001
181'.06—dc21   00-048839
                  [B]

P 5 4 3 2 1

CONTENTS

INTRODUCTION

Michael Shapiro

———

AUTOBIOGRAPHY is by no means a traditional Jewish literary form. Most modern autobiographies derive directly or indirectly from *The Confessions* of Jean-Jacques Rousseau (1712–78), a work influenced by *The Confessions* of St. Augustine (354–480) and published posthumously between 1782 and 1789. The earliest known autobiography of a European Jew was written in 1690–91 by Glückel of Hameln (1646–1724). It was intended not as personal testimony about the state of her psyche or soul but to assuage her grief after the loss of her husband and to teach her descendants "from what sort of people you have sprung" (ix). She records much detail of the commercial and communal life of her day, and she is particularly acute in describing the negotiations that led to the marriages of each of her twelve children. She also includes stories of all kinds that appealed to her lively sense of the vagaries of human nature and the mysteries of providence. Her writing was never intended for publication, and it is only by chance that copies of the original manuscript were later discovered, leading to its publication in 1896.

In 1792–93, a full century after Glückel wrote and just a few years after Rousseau's *Confessions* appeared in print, Solomon Maimon (ca. 1752–1800) published the first modern Jewish autobiography. Following the French memoirist, whom he acknowledges in the epigraph to chapter 8 (where he refers to "A theft *à la Rousseau*" [54] that he committed as a child), but totally unlike Glückel, Maimon focuses squarely on his own intellectual development.

Maimon's book anticipated countless life histories and memoirs produced by other assimilated Jews, as well as countless Jewish versions of the bildungsroman, the kind of novel about the growth and development of a young man that has been extremely popular for the past two hundred years. Like many such works, Maimon's *Autobiography* also collapses a complex historical process covering several generations into a single lifetime.

For Maimon and many others, the journey to full development of one's human potential was both geographic and cultural. To become the person he eventually became, Maimon had to leave the provincial world of backwardness, ignorance, and religious orthodoxy and find a place in the urban or cosmopolitan world of enlightenment, rationality, and secular learning. One finds this archetypal pattern throughout non-Jewish and Jewish literature of the past two centuries—for example, in the fictionalized migrations of Hardy's or Balzac's heroes from the countryside to towered cities and urban salons, or in the transformations of Abraham Cahan's David Levinsky from shtetl orphan to New York clothing tycoon and Albert Memmi's alter ego from Tunisian Jewish-Arab to Parisian intellectual. Among non-Jewish and Jewish memoirists, similar journeys in geographic and cultural space are commonplace: one thinks of Willie Morris's odyssey from Mississippi to Manhattan, as well as Marc Chagall's from Vitebsk to Paris (and beyond and back) and Jacob Epstein's from the Lower East Side of New York to London. Physical distance is often the least significant factor, as Norman Podhoretz puts it in the opening sentence of *Making It:* "One of the longest journeys in the world is the journey from Brooklyn to Manhattan—or at least from certain neighborhoods in Brooklyn to certain parts of Manhattan" (3).

Maimon was the first Jewish writer to chronicle this journey from East to West—in this case from Polish Lithuania to Berlin—and to articulate its significance for Jewish history. For the Jews of western Europe, the East was the past. It was a world in which Jewish communities were surrounded by a hostile Christian majority and suffered severe economic restrictions. Living within their own communal structures informed by rabbinic orthodoxy, Jews spoke Yiddish with one another, educated their male children in one-room schools called *hederim,* and sent the most intellectually promising of them to *yeshivot,* or religious academies, where the curriculum consisted almost exclusively of the Talmud and other rabbinic commentaries. In the West, Jews were forsaking Yiddish for German and later for French, English, and the languages of their host nations. They were beginning a process of "civic emancipation," abandoning their own communal structures in exchange for freer participation, if not full membership, in the nation at large. The process also included reshaping Jewish theology and ritual to resemble more closely the religious practices of their neighbors and the adoption of "civilized"—that is, western European—manners and standards of social conduct. Emancipated Jews also sought, for their children and sometimes even for themselves, full access to all branches of modern secular learning.

Writing in German for an audience of Germans and German-speaking Jews, Maimon quite consciously invokes this master trope of Before and After, of moving from darkness into light as he journeyed from the East to the West. For him, Polish Lithuania was medieval, a place where Jews lived in terror—whether of decadent aristocrats thrashing them at will and seeking their women as sexual objects or of zealously anti-Semitic clerics and peasants raising charges of ritual murder of Christians. It was a land where their economic survival was precarious and where their own traditional social, religious, and educational forms had ossified. It was a place where the brightest boys became Talmudic scholars or at least rabbis and where, as in Maimon's case, they were ordained and married as early as their "eleventh year" (74, 89), were fathers as early as their fourteenth, and found employment only within the religious establishment or as private tutors in the homes of wealthy families. It was a world that for the most part was shut off from Western classical and modern languages and from the branches of knowledge recorded and transmitted in those languages.

To someone like Maimon, who thirsted for access to secular knowledge, Berlin seemed the antithesis of Polish Lithuania. Under the leadership of Moses Mendelssohn (1729–86), the Jewish intelligentsia of Berlin was rapidly absorbing the values of the Enlightenment, known in Hebrew as the *haskala* and its adherents as *maskilim*. Central to their program was the replacement of Judeo-German, or Western Yiddish, with German, along with such ancillary practices as the pursuit of secular learning, the adoption of modern Western dress, and the shaving of beards and the cutting of forelocks. Mendelssohn and his disciples also prepared the way for religious reform by trying to establish Judaism on a rational basis, though in his personal life he remained traditionally observant. (His detractors point out that most of his children converted to Christianity and that none of his grandchildren were raised as Jews.)

Mendelssohn associated with Gotthold Lessing and other leading non-Jewish thinkers of the German *Aufklärung,* or Enlightenment. He also led the way in the study of philosophy, the primary area of rational discourse, while others of his circle became prominent in such fields as medicine and law. In return for putting themselves through what John Murray Cuddihy has called "the ordeal of civility," Jews were to be officially tolerated, if not accepted without prejudice, in all branches of society. George Mosse and other historians have described how throughout the nineteenth century German-speaking Jews struggled to achieve *Bildung,* to fashion themselves into cultured citizens and be accepted as such by their neighbors. Some remained loyal to traditional or reformed forms of Judaism, while others became Christian. In retrospect, one might argue that this ideal was never fully realized in Germany or Austria even in the best of times. After the Nazis came to power in 1933, it was shattered once and for all.

Maimon, who took that surname in Germany, wanted his readers to appreciate how far he had come from his origins in Polish Lithuania, near the town of Mir on the Niemen River. His birthplace has been identified as either Niewiz or Sukoviboeg, and the year of his birth as either 1752, 1753, or 1754. His casual way with place-names, dates, and often the names of people, usually identified by initials if at all, indicates a desire to stress the general pattern of his life over the specific details—a typical Enlightenment reluctance, as Samuel Johnson phrased it, to "number the streaks of the tulip" (49). That general pattern, of course, is the flowering of his intellect once he transplanted himself to the West. To highlight this contrast with his origins, Maimon underscores his innate intelligence and his intellectual curiosity. He reports that as a child he used twisted rods to construct an armillary sphere, a kind of astronomical model, from a description and diagram he found in a Hebrew book on astronomy. He taught himself to read German more or less phonetically when he noticed the alphabetical use of Roman letters to label signatures, or clusters of pages, in Hebrew books, guessing that their sounds resembled the sounds of letters occupying analagous positions in the Hebrew alphabet. His knowledge of Yiddish, a language spoken by Jews, derived from Middle High German and written in Hebrew letters, evidently enabled him to identify many words as cognate. As a young man, he walked long distances to borrow books.

At the age of twenty-five, no longer able to resist the lure of the West, Maimon left home and family for Berlin via Königsberg and Stettin. He arrived on foot at the Rosenthaler Gate only to be refused admittance by the Jewish authorities. The source of the problem was his possession of a copy of *Moreh Nevukhim* (Guide for the perplexed) by Moshe (Moses) ben Maimon, or Maimonides (1135–1204), and his claim to be preparing a new edition and commentary of the work, which was considered subversive in some orthodox circles. Turned away from Berlin, Maimon wandered as a beggar for some months until he surfaced in Posen, where the chief rabbi was a native of his own region. This compassionate and generous man recognized Maimon as a Talmudic prodigy, financed his rehabilitation to regular society, and helped him find work as a tutor. Two years after his first attempt, Maimon returned to Berlin, this time by coach, and so avoided the interrogation of pedestrians at the Rosenthaler Gate. He soon found his way among the Jewish intelligentsia, who secured employment for him as a tutor, protected him from expulsion, and introduced him to Mendelssohn, who encouraged him to study philosophy and other subjects and often received him at home.

Here the master trope becomes complicated, for Maimon was not simply absorbed or transformed by Berlin but in many ways resisted "the ordeal of civility." For one thing, aside from tutoring, which was neither secure nor especially rewarding, Maimon had no way of earning a living and often had to depend on the generosity of patrons. When friends encouraged him to establish himself in a profession or occupation, he rejected medicine out of hand. After studying pharmacy for three years, mostly in a theoretical sort of way, he refused to practice it. Rather than becoming a good burgher—that is, a productive and self-sufficient member of the Berlin Jewish community—he preferred the freedom to read, think, and study philosophy. Eventually, mostly in the 1790s, he found work editing and writing both in Hebrew and German. He lived for the last six years of his life on the Silesian estate of a Christian nobleman named Adolf von Kalkreuth.

For Maimon, the assimilated Jews of Berlin and later of other German and Dutch cities were not as appreciative of his talents and desires as he had hoped, perhaps because he regularly tested the limits of their Enlightenment commitment to tolerance. Like many intellectuals of his time, he embraced a rationalistic approach to religion often labeled as natural, as distinguished from revealed, which he would not moderate or disguise. He frequently antagonized patrons, employers, and friends by refusing to recite the blessing over wine and spurning most ritualistic practices. As he explains in his *Autobiography,* "Moses, as well as the prophets who followed him, sought constantly to inculcate that the end of religion is not *external ceremonies,* but the knowledge of the true God as the sole incomprehensible cause of all things, and the practice of virtue in accordance with the prescriptions of reason" (184). For Maimon, the ritualistic aspects of Judaism, or any other religion, were inconsistent with Enlightenment doctrines of natural theology. Gershon Greenberg summarizes this view:

> According to Maimon, Judaism begins with the Sinai covenant between man and the metaphysical idea of unidentified ultimate cause. At first silent, the covenant is soon expressed by the symbol of the supreme being's name, by the covenant, by the system of Mosaic law, and then by the Temple. Originally intended to capture the silent moment and make it available in history, the symbols eventually turn opaque and block the original ex-

perience from expression. The obstacles become solidi-
fied as a result of the quest for power over access to
them by rabbis and mystics. Their control must be
removed, so that the original encounter with the
metaphysical idea may be liberated and reconnected to
history through transparent, rational symbols. Maimonides' Guide is the perfect vehicle. (480–81)

When Maimon felt the Jewish community of Berlin
had become inhospitable to him, he tried other cities in
Germany and Holland. On two occasions he felt his situation had become desperate and attempted drastic mea-
sures. Once he nearly committed suicide, but he claims
that his body resisted his mind's directive to hurl himself
into a canal. In a second and perhaps parallel incident, he
tried to obliterate his Jewish identity by converting to
Christianity. He did not do so out of religious conviction
but rather out of the belief that, as Heinrich Heine quipped
a generation later, the baptismal certificate was the ticket
of admission to European culture. Unlike Heine, Maimon
was rejected as a candidate for conversion when he admitted, rather ingenuously, that he had no more belief in
Christian principles of faith than he did in Jewish ones.
When all was lost, he observed, Judaism at least did not
require him to suspend his rational faculties.

If Maimon's religious principles were too enlightened
for the Jewish communities he enountered, in other ways
he managed to offend the Jewish intelligentsia by reject-

ing current fashions of polite society. He initially took relatively little interest in belles lettres, for example, which he evidently felt was more frivolous than philosophy, much as the rabbis he fled viewed anything less than the study of sacred texts to be *bittl Torah*, or a waste of time, which could be spent on such texts. He even suggests that the reading of poetry led him to bad company and dissolute practices, cost him the esteem of friends in Berlin, and resulted in a period of self-imposed exile.

Maimon's personal habits also fell short of Enlightenment standards of behavior and actually seem to have appalled his contemporaries, even his friends. J. Clark Murray, whose translation of the *Autobiography* is here reprinted, felt obliged to add a "Concluding Chapter" not *by* Maimon but *about* him, a summary of recollections culled from a volume entitled *Maimoniana.* These observations include details of Maimon's slovenliness, alcoholism, unwillingness to seek gainful employment, naïveté, thriftlessness, lack of disciplined work habits, and absent-mindedness. Also noted are an irritability that occasionally vented itself in violent outbursts in Yiddish, especially when he lost at chess, and a discomfort in social situations that expressed itself as shyness, curtness, or rudeness. Samuel Hugo Bergman, the author of a scholarly monograph on Maimon's philosophical works, offers a more gracious evaluation: "His strength was not in the management of his life but in the critical operations of his mind" (2).

While Maimon probably never lost the Yiddish accent
that branded him as an *ostjude,* he did make a serious effort to learn proper German and to fill other gaps in his
education. Upon the advice of friends, and with their support, he attended a gymnasium, or secondary school, in
Altona near Hamburg from 1783 to 1785. He seems not to
have chafed as much as other men of thirty might have
in such surroundings, for he evidently enjoyed the leisure
to read and think, as well as to learn some Latin, English,
and French even as he improved his German. Two extant
certificates issued by school officials attest to his character
and accomplishments. One of them contains the earliest
reference to him by the surname Maimon. For earlier writings, in Hebrew, he had used his given and patronymic
names, Shlomo (Solomon) ben (son of) Yehoshua (Joshua),
as was the traditional practice among Jews in eastern Europe. In choosing the surname Maimon he proclaimed
himself to be the intellectual heir of Maimonides, the celebrated scholar who had attempted a synthesis of Judaism and Aristotelean philosophy, just as Solomon Maimon
may have seen himself as attempting a synthesis of Judaism and the work of such modern philosophers as Benedict
de Spinoza and Gottfried Leibniz. As Liliane Weissberg
concludes, identifying with Maimonides was actually a
move toward modernity for Maimon: "The difference between 'Ben Joshua' and 'Maimon' is the difference between
orthodox religion and free spirit, between tradition and

Enlightenment, between East and West, and between past and present" (110).

The ability to write standard German, along with his excellent command of Hebrew, opened Maimon's way to several publishing projects in the late 1780s and early 1790s. On the Hebrew side, he wrote *Ta'alumot Hakhma* (Secret of wisdom), a work on the principles of physics; and *Givat Hamore* (Heights of the teacher), his commentary on Maimonides's *Guide*. He also translated Mendelssohn's *Morgenstunden* (Morning hours) into Hebrew and wrote for *Ha-Ma'assef* (The collector), the leading Hebrew-language periodical of the German *haskala*. He even completed the manuscript of a mathematics textbook intended for distribution in eastern Europe, a project commissioned and then abandoned by Mendelssohn's circle and for which, despite an appeal to Mendelssohn himself, Maimon was never paid.

The ten-year period between 1790 and his death in 1800 was an extremely productive one for Maimon. He published a number of works in German, including a philosophical lexicon, commentaries on Aristotle, Francis Bacon, and Sir Isaac Newton, and a text on logic, as well as many essays on a wide variety of topics in books and philosophical journals. Adding the German works to his Hebrew writings, Weissberg finds that Maimon's bibliography amounts to twelve books and fifty-eight articles (111). Perhaps the most significant of his German publications during this period was the *Versuch über die Transcenden-talphilosophie* (Essay on the transcendental philosophy), published in Berlin in 1790, which was a response to Kant's *Kritik der reinen Vernunft* (Critique of pure reason). Maimon explains how a member of Mendelssohn's circle sent the manuscript to Kant, whose reply Maimon quotes at some length. Initially irritated at being disturbed, Kant came to realize "not only that none of my opponents had understood me and the main problem so well, but that very few could claim so much penetration as Herr Maimon in profound inquiries of this sort" (282). Sander L. Gilman quotes Kant's letter to another philosopher in which he takes quite a different tone, belittling Maimon's contribution as "typical of Jews who like to better themselves on others' costs" (128). Historians of philosophy endorse the first of Kant's evaluations rather than his anti-Semitic way of saying "Touché." They generally cite Maimon as someone who thoroughly mastered the basic principles of Kant's system, synthesized it with that of Leibniz and Spinoza, and prepared the way for its further development by Johann Fichte and other neo-Kantians (Atlas 15).

Early in the last decade of his life, Maimon turned to autobiography. His first efforts appeared in veiled form as a sequence of unsigned articles in volume 9 of the *Magazin zur Erfahrungsseelenkunde* (Journal for the practical knowledge of psychology), founded and edited by Karl Philipp Moritz, with Maimon himself helping to edit the final volumes. These extracts were called "Fragmente aus Ben Josuas Lebensgeschichte" (Fragments from Ben Joshua's autobiography) and were written in the third person about a man named Ben Josua, which is the Germanized form of Maimon's patronymic Hebrew surname. The first fragment covers his early life and ends with his settling in Berlin, while the second installment, more impersonally, focuses on Jewish history and his experience with Chasidism. The shift from personal narration to analysis anticipates rhetorical strategies in the *Autobiography*.

Maimon recast these fragments and embedded them in his extended autobiographical work, *Salomon Maimons Lebensgeschichte von ihm selbst erzählt* (Solomon Maimon's autobiography told by himself), edited by Moritz and published in two volumes in 1792–93. Here Maimon wrote in the first person. Volume 1 covers his early life and education, his decision to go west to seek enlightenment, and his first journey to Berlin, as well as long treatises on the history of Judaism and on religious mysteries. Volume 2 continues to trace his intellectual development and offers accounts of his relations with various patrons and intellectuals in Berlin and other German and Dutch cities. It too features self-contained treatises, one of which is a German version of his commentary on Maimonides's *Guide;* another is an allegorical philosophical tale called "Der lustige Ball" (The joyful ball), in which several suitors vie for the hand of Miss Metaphysics, who finally allows herself to be led off by a masked stranger, perhaps Kant or even Maimon himself.

Most of Maimon's German editors omitted some or all of the treatises or confined them to appendixes, thus emphasizing the narrative flow of the events of his life history over the passages in which Maimon demonstrates his intellectual prowess. Mara Wade convincingly argues that the seemingly digressive treatises are an integral part of the rhetorical design of the work as a whole, a design that is seriously compromised if they are sequestered at the end or omitted. The historical treatises in volume 1, she contends, contextualize Maimon's life within the long history of the Jewish religion, something not readily available to the non-Jewish reader, just as the treatises on the hierarchical structure of Poland and the conditions under which the Jews lived, both topics unfamiliar to Jewish and non-Jewish readers, provide a social context for Maimon's decision to migrate to Germany. In them Maimon not only demonstrates that he was an Enlightenment intellectual but relates how he came to be one.

Following the example of most German editors, Murray includes some but not all of the supposedly digressive material in his translation, characterizing what he omits as "'padding'" (xiv). Moses Hadas slightly modernized Murray's Victorian prose and pared his source down by more than half to a slim picaresque tale. Murray, in fact, preserves enough of the historical and philosophical material to corroborate Wade's claim that Maimon designed his autobiography with great care and was in full control of his material: "By framing his autobiography with a series of discourses about Judaism and philosophy, Solomon is claiming for himself a place in the philosophical world of the German Enlightenment comparable to that of Maimonides in the medieval world" (188). He demonstrates that he not only made it *to* Berlin but *in* Berlin.

In both narrative and analytical sections, Maimon sometimes goes out of his way to display his mastery of Westernized categories of discourse. For instance, in chapter 3 he recalls asking his father about the origin of God and then debating whether God, who is eternal, can be said to have an origin. Maimon the adult raises the ante by explaining epistemological differences between the ways the understanding and the imagination comprehend objects. This philosophical problem, he contends, is the same one he addressed in his response to Kant, which he tells us he first presented to a Professor Garve while living in Breslau. In one stroke he has superimposed an image of himself as assimilated German intellectual on top of that of his image as the little Jewish prodigy, a foreshadowing of what was to come.

Maimon often uses Westernized discursive categories by way of analogy to clarify things for his readers. "Cabbala," he declares, "is nothing but an expanded Spinozism" (105), and he goes on to lay bare the conceptual structure of this branch of Jewish mysticism. He explains the history of Judaism itself through the mediation of Spinoza and Leibniz, and he compares the penitential adherents of the early Chasidic movement, whom he labels The Pious, with ancient Greek Stoics, Cynics, and Epicureans. Moreover, Maimon's exposition of such complex and abstruse topics as the historical development of Judaism or the inner logic of Talmudic reasoning is thoroughly Westernized in its presentation, organization, methodology, and style.

For the modern reader, the so-called digressive materials do more than certify Maimon's membership in the Berlin intelligentsia. These sections on Judaism and Jewish life supply one of the earliest and most trenchant of the many *maskilic* critiques of the eastern European orthodox rabbinate. Maimon is especially incisive on the inadequacies of the educational system, which relies on the teaching of Hebrew without textbooks or dictionaries, discourages the teaching of secular subjects, and rewards the exercise of rote memory and ingenuity, especially when put to the service of disputatiousness. He is critical of the rabbis for their entrenched backwardness, although he praises them for their high standards of personal morality and their crucial role in maintaining cohesive Jewish communities. As impatient as he is with Talmudic exegesis, he nonetheless assures his readers that the Talmud itself contains none of the nonsense attributed to it by some Christian commentators. He is equally critical of the rabbinate's leading adversaries, the new Chasidim, whom he castigates as idlers for seeking God through merriment rather than textual study and the disciplines of vigils and fasts, and he demystifies the movement's faith in shrewd men who pass for charismatic healers and miracle workers.

The modern reader will also learn much from Maimon about the rapidly changing life of assimilated Jews in Germany and Holland in the late eighteenth century. Maimon arrived in the West at the moment when the first modern assimilated Jewish communities were being formed out of a coalition of the Westernized intelligentsia and the liberal bourgeoisie. He devotes all of chapter 24, in addition to incidental observations, to a description of Mendelssohn, the key figure in this socio-intellectual formation. Maimon praises his "worthy friend" (221) for his wide learning, for the depth and acuity of his intellect, for his deep knowledge of human nature, for his self-control and tolerance, and for his generosity of mind and spirit. In the view of Mendelssohn's biographer, Alexander Altmann, such generosity produced a "steadying influence" on this "somewhat exasperating genius" (364, 362). Maimon mildly questions Mendelssohn's originality of mind and points up an apparent inconsistency between the latter's belief in the importance of Jewish observance for the cohesiveness of the community and his unwillingness to see the impious excommunicated, but he charitably ascribes this inconsistency to Mendelssohn's reluctance to see another Jew suffer. It is a sharply observed portrait of a key figure in the development of modern Jewish life and the only portrait of another human being in the entire autobiography.

One wonders whether Murray understood the significance of Maimon's work for the field of modern Jewish
history, given that this was a field remote from his own
interests and background (*Dictionary of Canadian Biography* 24 [1998]: 778–79). The two make an odd couple, indeed. In Hollywood parlance, one might say that Mr.
Chipps has met the *maskilic luftmensch* (literally, "air-
man"), a trickster with no visible means of support. Murray
was born in Scotland in 1836 and educated in theology at
the universities of Glasgow, Edinburgh, Heidelberg, and
Göttingen. In 1862 he became professor of mental and
moral philosophy at Queen's College in Kingston, now
Ontario. From 1872 until his retirement in 1903, he held
the John Frothingham Chair of Mental and Moral Philosophy at McGill University in Montreal.

Murray was known for his liberal civic-mindedness, especially on issues relating to women students. His interest in philosophy was practical rather than abstract and by
current academic standards might seem eclectic or dilet-
tantish. He tried to develop from various philosophers, as
well as from English and Scots literature, a sense of what
it took to lead an exemplary life. He was remembered by
former students as an energetic and open-minded teacher,
whose classrooms were arenas of lively and untrammeled
debate.

Murray wrote a short piece on Maimon's *Autobiography*
for the July 1885 issue of the *British Quarterly Review*, no

doubt shortly after he discovered a copy of the book in a secondhand store in Toronto. He most likely encountered Maimon's philosphical writings while studying Kant, and he was delighted to come across the very book purchased by one of the characters in George Eliot's *Daniel Deronda,* as he notes in his own introduction. What may have impressed Murray the most about Maimon was his self-transformation from Polish rabbi to German philosopher. If the earnest Scots schoolmaster rapped the knuckles of this wily, rootless Jewish philosopher for deficiencies in personal conduct, he nevertheless awarded him high marks in philosophy and Jewish history.

English readers owe Murray a large debt for his rendering of Maimon's saga of his journey, as it was lived and constructed, and another one to Willis Regier and Judith McCulloh of the University of Illinois Press for their decision to reprint this work.

WORKS CITED

Altmann, Alexander. *Moses Mendelssohn: A Biographical Study.* London: Littman Library of Jewish Civilization, 1998 (first published by the University of Alabama Press, 1973).

Atlas, Samuel. *From Critical to Speculative Idealism: The Philosophy of Solomon Maimon.* The Hague: Martinus Nijhoff, 1964.

Bergman, Samuel Hugo. *The Philosophy of Solomon Maimon.* Trans. Noah J. Jacobs. Jerusalem: Magnes Press, 1967.

Cuddihy, John Murray. *The Ordeal of Civility: Freud, Marx, Lévi-Strauss, and the Jewish Struggle with Modernity.* New York: Basic Books, 1974.

Gilman, Sander L. *Jewish Self-Hatred: Anti-Semitism and the Hidden Language of the Jews.* Baltimore: Johns Hopkins University Press, 1986.

Glückel of Hameln. *The Memoirs.* Trans. Marvin Lowenthal. New York: Schocken, 1977.

Greenberg, Gershon. "Solomon Maimon." In *The Blackwell Companion to Jewish Culture.* Ed. Glenda Abramson. Oxford: Blackwell, 1989.

Hadas, Moses, ed. *Solomon Maimon: An Autobiography.* New York: Schocken, 1947.

Johnson, Samuel. *Rasselas.* Great Neck, N.Y.: Barron's Education Series, 1962.

Moss, George. *German Jews beyond Judaism.* Bloomington: Indiana University Press, 1985.

Podhoretz, Norman. *Making It.* New York: Random House, 1967.

Wade, Mara. "Enlightenment and Self-Fashioning in the German Vernacular: Salomon Maimon's Autobiography." *Lessing Yearbook* 24 (1997): 175–98.

Weissberg, Liliane. "1792–93: Salomon Maimon Writes His Lebensgeschichte (Autobiography), a Reflection on His Life in the (Polish) East and the (German) West." In *Yale Companion to Jewish Writing and Thought in German Culture, 1096–1996.* Ed. Sander L. Gilman and Jack Zipes. New Haven, Conn.: Yale University Press, 1997. 108–15.

TRANSLATOR'S PREFACE.

ONE effect of *Daniel Deronda* was to make known to a wide circle of readers the vitality of Judaism as a system which still holds sway over the mental as well as the external life of men. During the few years which have passed since the publication of that great fiction, the interest in modern Judaism has continued to grow. It is but a short time since the Western world was startled by the outbreak of an ancient feeling against the Jews, which had been supposed to be long dead, at least in some of the quarters where it was displayed. The popular literature of the day also seems to indicate that the life of existing Jewish communities is attracting a large share of attention in the reading world. The charming pictures which Emil Franzos has drawn of Jewish life in the villages of Eastern Galicia, are not only popular in Germany, but some have been reproduced in a cheap form in New York to meet the demand of German Americans, and some have also been translated into English. The interest of English readers in the same subject is further shown by the recent translation of Kompert's *Scenes from the Ghetto*, as well as by Mr. Cumberland's still more recent and powerful romance of *The Rabbi's Spell*. Among students of philosophical literature a fresh interest has been awakened in the history of Jewish thought by the revival of the question in reference to the sources of Spinoza's philosophy. The affinities of this system with the familiar tendencies of Cartesian speculation have led the historians of philosophy generally to represent the former as simply an inevitable development of the latter, while the affinities of Spinozism with the unfamiliar speculations of earlier Jewish thinkers have been almost entirely ignored.

In these circumstances a special interest may be felt in the life of one of the most remarkable Jews of modern times—a life which forms one of the most extraordinary biographies in the history of literature.

Readers of *Daniel Deronda* may remember that, in his search among the Jews of London for some one who could throw light on the sad story of Mirah, the hero of the novel was attracted one day to a second-hand bookshop, where his eye fell on "that wonderful bit of autobiography—the life of the Polish Jew, Solomon Maimon." There are few men so remarkable as Maimon who have met with so little recognition in English literature. Milman, in his *History of the Jews*, refers once * to the autobiography as "a curious and rare book," but apparently he knew it only from some quotations in

---

* Vol. iii., p. 370, note.

Franck's *La Cabbale*.   Among English metaphysical
writers the only one who seems to have studied the
speculations of Maimon is Dr. Hodgson.*   Even the
new edition of the *Encyclopedia Britannica* gives no
place to Maimon among its biographies.   And yet he is
a prominent figure among the metaphysicians of the
Kantian period.   Kuno Fischer, in his *Geschichte der
Neueren Philosophie*,† devotes a whole chapter to the
life of Maimon, while the contemporary critics of Kant
are dismissed with little or no biographical notice.
Fischer's sketch is just sufficient to whet curiosity for
fuller details ; but, amid the dearth of rare literature in
Colonial libraries, I certainly never expected to come,
in a Canadian town, upon " a curious and rare book " of
last century, which was known even to the learned Milman only through some quotations from a French
author.   One day, however, in Toronto, in order to
while away an unoccupied hour, I was glancing, like
Daniel Deronda, over the shelves of a second-hand
bookseller, when I was attracted by a small volume, in
a good state of preservation, with "S. Maimon's Lebensgeschichte " on the back ; and on taking it down I
found it to be the veritable autobiography which I had
been curious to see.

Some account of the work was given in an article in

---

* See the Preface to his *Philosophy of Reflection*, pp. 16-18.
† Vol. v., chap. 7.

the *British Quarterly Review* for July, 1885; but I thought that a complete translation would probably be welcomed by a considerable circle of English readers. The book has many attractions. If the development of the inner life of man can ever be characterised as a romance, the biography of Maimon may, in the truest sense, be said to be one of the most romantic stories ever written. Perhaps no literature has preserved a more interesting record of a spirit imprisoned within almost insuperable barriers to culture, yet acquiring strength to burst all these, and even to become an appreciable power in directing the course of speculation. The book, however, is much more than a biography; it possesses historical interest. It opens up what, to many English readers, must be unknown efforts of human thought, unknown wanderings of the religious life. The light, which it throws upon Judaism especially, both in its speculative and in its practical aspects, is probably, in fact, unique. For the sketches, which the book contains, of Jewish speculation and life were made at a time when the author had severed all vital connection with his own people and their creed; and they are therefore drawn from a point of view outside of Jewish prejudices: but they are penned by one who had been brought up to believe the divine mission of his people, as well as the divine authority of their religion; and the criticism of his old faith is generally tempered by that kindly sympathy, with which the heart is apt to be warmed on lingering over the companionships and other associations of earlier years. Maimon's account of Jewish philosophy and theology acquires an additional value from the fact, that he was caught in the full tide of the Kantian movement, and he was thus in a position to point out unexpected affinities between many an old effort of speculative thought among the Jews and the philosophical tendencies of modern Christendom.

Since writing the above-mentioned article for the *British Quarterly Review*, I learnt that a volume of *Maimoniana* had been issued in 1813 by an old friend of our philosopher, Dr. Wolff*; and through the kindness of a friend in Leipsic, I was enabled, after some delay, to procure a copy. It is a small volume of 260 pages, and adds extremely little to our knowledge of Maimon. Nearly one third is simply a condensation of the autobiography ; and the remainder shows the author with the opportunities indeed, but without the faculty, of a Boswell. He has preserved but few of the felicities of Maimon's conversation ; and what he has preserved loses a good deal of its flavour from his want of the lively memory by which Boswell was able to reproduce the peculiar mannerisms of Johnson's talk. Still I have

---

* The volume bears the somewhat quaint title in full :—*Maimoniana, oder Rhapsodien Zur Charakteristik Salomon Maimon's.* Aus Seinem Privatleben gesammelt von Sabattia Joseph Wolff, M.D. Berlin, gedruckt bei G. Hayn, 1813.

culled from the little volume a few notes for illustration of the autobiography, and I am indebted to it for most of the materials of the concluding chapter. All my additions are indicated by "*Trans.*" appended.

The translation gives the whole of the biographical portion of the original. There are, however, ten chapters which I have omitted, as they are occupied entirely with a sketch of the great work of Maimonides,—the *Moreh Nebhochim*, or *Guide of the Perplexed.* Owing to their somewhat loose connection* with the rest, these chapters excite just the faintest suspicion of "padding;" and at all events there is no demand for such a sketch in English now, when our literature has been recently enriched by Dr. Friedländer's careful translation of the whole work.

In the performance of my task I have endeavoured to render the original as literally as was consistent with

---

* The only logical connection is the fact, that the writings of Maimonides formed the most powerful influence in the intellectual development of Maimon. In illustration of this he writes :—" My reverence for this great teacher went so far, that I regarded him as the ideal of a perfect man, and looked upon his teachings as if they had been inspired with Divine Wisdom itself. This went so far, that, when my passions began to grow, and I had sometimes to fear lest they might seduce me to some action inconsistent with those teachings, I used to employ, as a proved antidote, the abjuration, ' I swear, by the reverence which I owe my great teacher, Rabbi Moses ben Maimon, not to do this act.' And this vow, so far as I can remember, was always sufficient to restrain me." *Lebensgeschichte*, Vol. ii., pp. 3-4.

readable English.   Only in one or two passages I have
toned down the expression slightly to suit the tastes of
our own time ; but even in these I have not been
unfaithful to the author's meaning.

In the spelling of Hebrew and other foreign words I
have never, without some good reason, interfered with
the original.   But as Maimon is not always consistent
with himself in this respect, I have felt myself at liberty
to disregard his usage by adopting such forms as are
more familiar, or more likely to be intelligible, to an
English reader.

AN AUTOBIOGRAPHY

SOLOMON MAIMON.

INTRODUCTION.

THE inhabitants of Poland may be conveniently divided into six classes or orders :—the superior nobility, the inferior nobility, the half-noble, burghers, peasantry and Jews.

The superior nobility consist of the great landowners and administrators of the high offices of government. The inferior nobility also are allowed to own land and to fill any political office ; but they are prevented from doing so by their poverty. The half-noble can neither own land, nor fill any high office in the State ; and by this he is distinguished from the genuine noble. Here and there, it is true, he owns land ; but for that he is in some measure dependent on the lord of the soil, within whose estate his property lies, inasmuch as he is required to pay him a yearly tribute.

The burghers are the most wretched of all the orders. They are not, 'tis true, in servitude to any man ; they also enjoy certain privileges, and have a jurisdiction of their own. But as they seldom own any property of value, or follow rightly any profession, they always remain in a condition of pitiable poverty.

The last two orders, namely the peasantry and the Jews, are the most useful in the country. The former occupy themselves with agriculture, raising cattle, keeping bees,—in short, with all the products of the soil. The latter engage in trade, take up the professions and handicrafts, become bakers, brewers, dealers in beer, brandy, mead and other articles. They are also the only persons who farm estates in towns and villages, except in the case of ecclesiastical properties, where the reverend gentlemen hold it a sin to put a Jew in a position to make a living, and accordingly prefer to hand over their farms to the peasants. For this they must suffer by their farms going to ruin, as the peasantry have no aptitude for this sort of employment ; but of course they choose rather to bear this with Christian resignation.

In consequence of the ignorance of most of the Polish landlords, the oppression of the tenantry, and the utter want of economy, most of the farms in Poland, at the end of last century,* had fallen into such a state of decay, that a farm, which now yields about a thousand Polish gulden, was offered to a Jew for ten ; but in consequence of still greater ignorance and laziness, with all that advantage even he could not make a living off the

---

* That is, of course, the seventeenth. —*Trans.*

farm. An incident, however, occurred at this time, which gave a new turn to affairs. Two brothers from Galicia, where the Jews are much shrewder than in Lithuania, took, under the name of *Dersawzes* or farmers-general, a lease of all the estates of Prince Radzivil, and, by means of a better industry as well as a better economy, they not only raised the estates into a better condition, but also enriched themselves in a short time.

Disregarding the clamour of their brethren, they increased the rents, and enforced payment by the sub-lessees with the utmost stringency. They themselves exercised a direct oversight of the farms ; and wherever they found a farmer who, instead of looking after his own interests and those of his landlord in the improvement of his farm by industry and economy, spent the whole day in idleness, or lay drunk about the stove, they soon brought him to his senses, and roused him out of his indolence by a flogging. This procedure of course acquired for the farmers-general, among their own people, the name of tyrants.

All this, however, had a very good effect. The farmer, who at the term had hitherto been unable to pay up his ten gulden of rent without requiring to be sent to jail about it, now came under such a strong inducement to active exertion, that he was not only able to support a family off his farm, but was also able to pay, instead of ten, four or five hundred, and sometimes even a thousand gulden.

The Jews, again, may be divided into three classes:—
(1) the illiterate workingpeople, (2) those who make
learning their profession, and (3) those who merely devote themselves to learning without engaging in any remunerative occupation, being supported by the industrial
class. To the second class belong the chief rabbis,
preachers, judges, schoolmasters, and others of similar
profession. The third class consists of those who, by
their pre-eminent abilities and learning, attract the regard
of the unlearned, are taken by these into their families,
married to their daughters, and maintained for some
years with wife and children at their expense. Afterwards,
however, the wife is obliged to take upon herself the
maintenance of the saintly idler and the children (who
are usually very numerous); and for this, as is natural,
she thinks a good deal of herself.

There is perhaps no country besides Poland, where
religious freedom and religious enmity are to be met with
in equal degree. The Jews enjoy there a perfectly free
exercise of their religion and all other civil liberties; they
have even a jurisdiction of their own. On the other
hand, however, religious hatred goes so far, that the name
of Jew has become an abomination; and this abhorrence,
which had taken root in barbarous times, continued to
show its effects till about thirteen years ago. But this
apparent contradiction may be very easily removed, if it
is considered that the religious and civil liberty, conceded
to the Jews in Poland, has not its source in any respect

for the universal rights of mankind, while, on the other hand, the religious hatred and persecution are by no means the result of a wise policy which seeks to remove out of the way whatever is injurious to morality and the welfare of the State. Both phenomena are results of the political ignorance and torpor prevalent in the country. With all their defects the Jews are almost the only useful inhabitants of the country, and therefore the Polish people found themselves obliged, for the satisfaction of their own wants, to grant all possible liberties to the Jews ; but, on the other hand, their moral ignorance and stupor could not fail to produce religious hatred and persecution.

CHAPTER I.

My Grandfather's Housekeeping.

MY grandfather, Heimann Joseph, was farmer of some villages in the neighbourhood of the town of Mir, in the territory of Prince Radzivil.* He selected for his residence one of these villages on the river Niemen, called Sukoviborg, where, besides a few peasants' plots, there was a water-mill, a small harbour, and a warehouse for the use of the vessels that come from Königsberg, in Prussia. All this, along with a bridge behind the village, and on the other side a drawbridge on the river Niemen, belonged to the farm, which was then worth about a thousand gulden, and formed my grandfather's *Chazakah.*† This farm, on account of the warehouse and the great traffic, was very lucrative. With sufficient industry and economical skill, *si mens non laeva fuisset*, my grandfather should have been able, not only to support his family, but even to gather wealth. The bad

---

* Maimon himself nowhere mentions the date or place of his birth ; but Wolff says that he was born at Nesvij, in Lithuania, about the year 1754 (*Maimoniana*, p. 10). *Trans.*

† This word is explained below, at the beginning of the next chapter.

constitution of the country, however, and his own want of all the acquirements necessary for utilising the land, placed extraordinary obstacles in his way.

My grandfather settled his brothers as tenants under him in the villages belonging to his farm. These not only lived continually with my grandfather under the pretence of assisting him in his manifold occupations, but in addition to this they would not pay their rents at the end of the year.

The buildings, belonging to my grandfather's farm, had fallen into decay from age, and required therefore to be repaired. The harbour and the bridge also had become dilapidated. In accordance with the terms of the lease the landlord was to repair everything, and put it in a condition fit for use. But, like all the Polish magnates, he resided permanently in Warsaw, and could therefore give no attention to the improvement of his estates. His stewards had for their principal object the improvement rather of their own condition than of their landlord's property. They oppressed the farmers with all sorts of exactions, they neglected the orders given for the improvement of the farms, and the moneys intended for this purpose they applied to their own use. My grandfather indeed made representations on the subject to the stewards day after day, and assured them that it was impossible for him to pay his rent, if everything was not put into proper condition according to the lease. All this, however, was of no avail. He always received promises indeed, but the promises were never fulfilled. The result was not only the ruin of the farm, but several other evils arising from that.

As already mentioned, there was a large traffic at this place ; and as the bridges were in a bad state, it happened not infrequently that these broke down just when a Polish nobleman with his rich train was passing, and horse and rider were plunged into the swamp. The poor farmer was then dragged to the bridge, where he was laid down and flogged till it was thought that sufficient revenge had been taken.

My grandfather therefore did all in his power to guard against this evil in the future. For this purpose he stationed one of his people to keep watch at the bridge, so that, if any noble were passing, and an accident of this sort should happen, the sentinel might bring word to the house as quickly as possible, and the whole family might thus have time to take refuge in the neighbouring wood. Every one thereupon ran in terror out of the house, and not infrequently they were all obliged to remain the whole night in the open air, till one after another ventured to approach the house.

This sort of life lasted for some generations. My father used to tell of an incident of this sort, which happened when he was still a boy of about eight years. The whole family had fled to their usual retreat. But my father, who knew nothing of what had happened, and was playing at the back of the stove, stayed behind alone. When the angry lord came into the house with his suite, and found nobody on whom he could wreak his vengeance, he ordered every corner of the house to be searched, when my father was found at the back of the stove. The nobleman asked him if he would drink brandy, and, on the boy refusing, shouted: "If you will not drink brandy, you shall drink water." At the same time he ordered a bucketful of water to be brought, and forced my father, by lashes with his whip, to drink it out. Naturally this treatment brought on a quartan fever, which lasted nearly a whole year, and completely undermined his health.

A similar incident took place when I was a child of three years. Every one ran out of the house; and the housemaid, who carried me in her arms, hurried forth. But as the servants of the nobleman who had arrived ran after her, she quickened her steps, and in her extreme haste let me fall from her arms. There I lay whimpering on the skirt of the wood, till fortunately a peasant passing by lifted me up and took me home with him. It was only after everything had become quiet again, and the family had returned to the house, that the maid remembered having lost me in the flight, when she began to lament and wring her hands. They sought me everywhere, but could not find me, till at last the peasant came from the village and restored me to my parents.

It was not merely the terror and consternation, into which we used to be thrown on the occasion of such a flight; to this was added the plundering of the house when deprived of its inhabitants. Beer, brandy, and mead were drunk at pleasure; the spirit of revenge even went so far at times, that the casks were left to run out; corn and fowls were carried off; and so forth.

Had my grandfather, instead of seeking justice from a more powerful litigant, rather borne the injustice, and built the bridge in question at his own expense, he would have been able to avoid all these evils. He appealed, however, persistently to the terms of his lease, and the steward made sport of his misery.

And now something about my grandfather's domestic economy. The manner of life, which he led in his house, was quite simple. The annual produce of the arable lands, pasture-lands, and kitchen-gardens, belonging to the farm, was sufficient, not only for the wants of his own family, but also for brewing and distilling. He could even, besides, sell a quantity of grain and hay. His bee-hives were sufficient for the brewing of mead. He had also a large number of cattle.

The principal food consisted of a poor kind of corn-bread mixed with bran, of articles made of meal and milk, and of the produce of the garden, seldom of flesh-meat. The clothing was made of poor linen and coarse stuff. Only the women made in these matters a slight exception, and my father also, who was a scholar, required a different sort of life.

Hospitality was here carried very far. The Jews in

this neighbourhood are continually moving about from place to place; and as there was a great traffic at our village, they were frequently passing through it, and of course they had always to stop at my grandfather's inn. Every Jewish traveller was met at the door with a glass of spirits; one hand making the *salaam*,* while the other reached the glass. He then had to wash his hands, and seat himself at the table which remained constantly covered.

The support of a numerous family along with this hospitality would have had no serious effect in impairing my grandfather's circumstances, if at the same time he had introduced a better economy in his house. This, however, was the source of his misfortune.

My grandfather was in trifles almost too economical, and neglected therefore matters of the greatest importance. He looked upon it, for example, as extravagance to burn wax or tallow candles; their place had to be supplied with thin strips of resinous pine, one end of which was stuck into the chinks of the wall, while the other was lit. Not unfrequently by this means fires were occasioned, and much damage caused, in comparison with which the cost of candles was not worth taking into consideration.

The apartment, in which beer, spirits, mead, herrings, salt and other articles were kept for the daily account of

---

* The customary Jewish salutation.

the inn, had no windows, but merely apertures, through
which it received light.   Naturally this often tempted the
sailors and carriers who put up at the inn to climb into
the apartment, and make themselves drunk gratuitously
with spirits and mead.   What was still worse, these
carousing heroes, from fear of being caught in the act,
often took to flight, on hearing the slightest noise, without waiting to put in the spigot, sprang out at the holes
by which they had come in, and let the liquor run as long
as it might.   In this way sometimes whole casks of
spirits and mead ran out.

The barns had no proper locks, but were shut merely
with wooden bolts.   Any one therefore, especially as the
barns were at some distance from the dwelling-house,
could take from them at pleasure, and even carry off
whole waggonloads of grain.   The sheepfold had, all
over, holes, by which wolves (the forest being quite near)
were able to slink in, and worry the sheep at their convenience.

The cows came very often from the pasture with empty
udders.   According to the superstition which prevailed
there, it was said in such cases, that the milk had been
taken from them by witchcraft,—a misfortune, against
which it was supposed that nothing could be done.

My grandmother, a good simple woman, when tired
with her household occupations, lay down often in her
clothes to sleep by the stove, and had all her pockets
full of money, without knowing how much.   Of this the

housemaid took advantage, and emptied the pockets of half their contents. Nevertheless my grandmother seldom perceived the want, if only the girl did not play too clumsy a trick.

All these evils could easily have been avoided of course by repairing the buildings, the windows, the window-shutters and locks, by proper oversight of the manifold lucrative occupations connected with the farm, as also by keeping an exact account of receipts and disbursements. But this was never thought of. On the other hand, if my father, who was a scholar, and educated partly in town, ordered for himself a rabbinical suit, for which a finer stuff was required than that in common use, my grandfather did not fail to give him a long and severe lecture on the vanity of the world. " Our forefathers," he used to say, " knew nothing of these newfashioned costumes, and yet were devout people. You must have a coat of striped woolen cloth,* you must have leather hose, with buttons even, and everything on the same scale. You will bring me to beggary at last ; I shall be thrown into prison on your account. Ay me, poor unfortunate man ! What is to become of me ? "

My father then appealed to the rights and privileges of the profession of a scholar, and showed moreover that,

---

* The original is " ein Kalamankenes Leibserdak,"—a provincialism which, I believe, is substantially rendered in this translation.— *Trans.*

in a well-arranged system of economy, it does not so much matter whether you live somewhat better or worse, and that even my grandfather's misfortunes arose, not from extravagant consumption in housekeeping, but rather from the fact that he allowed himself by his remissness to be plundered by others. All this however was of no avail with my grandfather. He could not tolerate innovations. Everything therefore had to be left as it was.

My grandfather was held in the place of his abode to be a rich man, which he could really have been if he had known how to make use of his opportunities ; and on this account he was envied and hated by all, even by his own family, he was abandoned by his landlord, he was oppressed in every possible way by the steward, and cheated and robbed by his own domestics as well as by strangers. In short, he was *the poorest rich man* in the world.

In addition to all this there were still greater misfortunes, which I cannot here pass over wholly in silence. The pope, that is, the Russian clergyman in this village, was a dull ignorant blockhead, who had scarcely learned to read and write. He spent most of his time at the inn, where he drank spirits with his boorish parishioners, and let his liquor always be put down to his account, without ever a thought of paying his score. My grandfather at last became tired of this, and made up his mind to give him nothing more upon credit. The fellow naturally took this very ill, and therefore resolved upon revenge.

For this he found at length a means, at which indeed humanity shudders, but of which the Catholic Christians in Poland were wont to make use very often at that time. This was to charge my grandfather with the murder of a Christian, and thus bring him to the gallows. This was done in the following way : A beaver-trapper, who sojourned constantly in this neighbourhood to catch beavers on the Niemen, was accustomed at times to trade in these animals with my grandfather ; and this had to be done secretly, for the beaver is game preserved, and all that are taken must be delivered at the manor. The trapper came once about midnight, knocked and asked for my grandfather. He showed him a bag which was pretty heavy to lift, and said to him with a mysterious air, " I have brought you a good big fellow here." My grandfather was going to strike a light, to examine the beaver, and come to terms about it with the peasant. He however said, that this was unnecessary, that my grandfather might take the beaver at any rate, and that they would be sure to agree about it afterwards. My grandfather, who had no suspicion of evil, took the bag just as it was, laid it aside, and betook himself again to rest. Scarcely, however, had he fallen asleep again, when he was roused a second time with a loud noise of knocking.

It was the clergyman with some boors from the village, who immediately began to make search all over in the house. They found the bag, and my grandfather already trembled for the issue, because he believed nothing else than that he had been betrayed at the manor on account of his secret trade in beavers, and he could not deny the fact.   But how great was his horror, when the bag was opened, and, instead of a beaver, there was found a corpse !

My grandfather was bound with his hands behind his back, his feet were put into stocks, he was thrown into a waggon, and brought to the town of Mir, where he was given over to the criminal court.   He was made fast in chains, and put into a dark prison.

At the trial my grandfather stood upon his innocence, related the events exactly as they had happened, and, as was reasonable, demanded that the beaver-trapper should be examined too.   He, however, was nowhere to be found, was already over the hills and far away.   He was sought everywhere.   But the blood-thirsty judge of the criminal court, to whom the time became tedious, ordered my grandfather three times in succession to be brought to torture.   He, however, continued steadfast in his assertion.

At last the hero of the beavers was found.   He was examined; and as he straightway denied the whole affair, he also was put to the test of torture.   Thereupon at once he blabbed the whole story.   He declared that, some time before, he had found this dead body in the water, and was going to bring it to the parsonage for burial.   The parson however had said to him, " There is plenty of time for the burial. You know that the Jews are a hardened race, and are therefore damned to all eternity. They crucified our Lord Jesus Christ, and even yet they seek Christian blood, if only they can get hold of it for their passover, which is instituted as a sign of their triumph. They use it for their passover-cake. You will therefore do a meritorious work, if you can smuggle this dead body into the house of the damned Jew of a farmer. You must of course clear out, but your trade you can drive anywhere."

On this confession the fellow was whipped out of the place, and my grandfather set free; but the pope remained pope.

For an everlasting memorial of this deliverance of my grandfather from death, my father composed in Hebrew a sort of epopee, in which the whole event was narrated, and the goodness of God was sung. It was also made a law, that the day of his deliverance should be celebrated in the family every year, when this poem should be recited in the same way as the Book of Esther at the festival of Haman.*

---

* Till quite recently it had been almost forgotten that one of the commonest manifestations of fanaticism against the Jews, especially in Eastern Europe, was to charge them with the murder of Christian children for the use of some horrid religious rite, and that scarcely ever was the dead body of a child found in the neighbourhood of a Jewish community without some outburst of this cruel suspicion, ending in an indiscriminate massacre of the Jews by the infuriated

mob. It is a singularly creditable proof of the liberal government
of Stephen Batory,—one of the ablest monarchs who ever sat on
the throne of Poland,—that, so long ago as 1576, he issued an edict
prohibiting the imputation of this crime to the Jews, as being
utterly inconsistent with the principles of their religion. Yet, in
spite of this enactment, the fanatical suspicion continued to display
itself at frequent intervals. Milman supposed it had been finally
quelled by the ukase of the Russian Government in 1835, which
went in the same direction as the earlier prohibition of the Polish
king (*History of the Jews*, vol. iii., p. 389). What would have
been his astonishment, had he lived to learn that, half a century
after he thought it extinguished, this ancient delusion was to revive,
that an Hungarian court was to spend thirty one days in the solemn
trial of a Jewish family on the charge of sacrificing a Christian girl
in their synagogue, that a learned professor in the Imperial and
Royal University of Prague was to write in defence of the charge,
and that the trial was to form the subject of an extensive contro-
versial literature in the language of the most learned nation in the
world ! An interesting account of this famous trial at Tisza Eszlar,
as well as of the literature connected with it, will be found in an
article by Dr. Wright, on *The Jews and the Malicious Charge of
Human Sacrifice* in the *Nineteenth Century*, for November, 1883.
—*Trans.*

CHAPTER II.

First Reminiscences of Youth.

IN this manner my grandfather lived for many years in the place where his forefathers had dwelt ; his farm had become, as it were, a property of the family. By the Jewish ceremonial law the *Chazakah*, that is, the right of property in an estate, is acquired by three years' possession ; and the right is respected even by Christians in this neighbourhood. In virtue of this law no other Jew could try to get possession of the farm by a *Hosaphah*, that is, an offer of higher rent, if he would not bring down upon himself the Jewish excommunication. Although the possession of the farm was accompanied with many hardships and even oppressions, yet it was from another point of view very lucrative. My grandfather could not only live as a well-to-do man, but also provide richly for his children.

His three daughters were well dowered, and married to excellent men. His two sons, my uncle Moses and my father Joshua, were married likewise ; and when he became old, and enfeebled by the hardships to which he had been exposed, he gave over the management of the house to his two sons in common. These were of different temperaments and inclinations, my uncle Moses being of strong bodily constitution, but inferior intelligence, while my father was the opposite ; and consequently they could not work together well. My grandfather therefore gave over to my uncle another village, and kept my father by himself, although from his profession as a scholar my father was not particularly adapted for the occupations of household-management. He merely kept accounts, made contracts, conducted processes at law, and attended to other matters of the same sort. My mother, on the other hand, was a very lively woman, well disposed to all sorts of occupations. She was small of stature, and at that time still very young.

An anecdote I cannot avoid touching on here, because it is the earliest reminiscence from the years of my youth. I was about three years old at the time. The merchants, who put up constantly at the place, and especially the *shaffers*, that is, the nobles who undertook the navigation, the purchase and delivery of goods, for the higher nobility, were extremely fond of me on account of my liveliness, and made all sorts of fun with me. These merry gentlemen gave my mother, on account of her small stature and liveliness, the nickname of *Kuza*, that is, a young filly.* As I heard them often call her by this

---

* It seems that Maimon gives a euphemistic explanation of this word, as I am told its real meaning makes much more intelligible its extreme offensiveness to his mother. — *Trans.*

name, and knew nothing of its meaning, I also called her *Mama Kuza*. My mother rebuked me for this, and said, " God punishes any one who calls his mother *Mama Kuza*." One of these *Shaffers*, Herr Piliezki, used every day to take tea in our house, and enticed me to his side by giving me at times a bit of sugar. One morning while he was drinking his tea, when I had placed myself in the usual position for receiving the sugar, he said he would give it to me only on condition that I should say *Mama Kuza*. Now as my mother was present, I refused to do it. He made a sign therefore to my mother to go into an adjoining room. As soon as she had shut the door, I went to him and whispered into his ear, *Mama Kuza*. He insisted however that I should say it out loud, and promised to give me a piece of sugar for each time that it was spoken. Accordingly I said, " Herr Piliezki wants me to say *Mama Kuza ;* but I will not say *Mama Kuza*, because God punishes any one who says *Mama Kuza*." Thereupon I got my three pieces of sugar.

My father introduced into the house a more refined mode of life, especially as he traded with Königsberg in Prussia, where he procured all sorts of pretty and useful articles. He provided himself with tin and brass utensils ; we began to have better meals, to wear finer clothes, than before ; I was even clad in damask.

CHAPTER III.

Private Education and Independent Study.

In my sixth year my father began to read the Bible with
me. " In the beginning God created the heaven and
the earth." Here I interrupted my father, and asked,
" But, papa, who created God ? "

" God was not created by any one," replied my father ;
" He existed from all eternity."

" Did he exist ten years ago ?" I asked again.

" O yes," my father said, " He existed even a hundred
years ago."

" Then perhaps," I continued, " God is already a
thousand years old ?"

" Silence ! God was eternal."

" But," I insisted, " He must surely have been born at
some time."

" You little fool," said my father, " No ! He was for
ever and ever and ever."

With this answer I was not indeed satisfied ; but I
thought " Surely papa must know better than I, and with
that I must therefore be content."

This mode of representation is very natural in early youth, when the understanding is still undeveloped, while the imagination is in full bloom. The understanding seeks merely to grasp, the imagination to grasp all round.* That is to say, the understanding seeks to make the origin of an object conceivable, without considering, whether the object, whose origin is known, can also be actually represented by us or not. The imagination, on the other hand, seeks to gather into a complete image something, the origin of which is to us unknown. Thus, for example, an infinite series of numbers, which progresses according to a definite law, is for the understanding an object, to which by this law definite qualities are attached, and an object just as good as a finite series, which progresses according to the same law. For the imagination, on the other hand, the latter indeed is an object ; but not the former, because it cannot grasp the former as a completed whole.

A long time afterwards, when I was staying in Breslau, this consideration suggested to me a thought, which I expressed in an essay that I laid before Professor Garve, and which, though at the time I knew nothing of the Kantian philosophy, still constitutes its foundation. I explained this somewhat in the following way :—The metaphysicians necessarily fall into self-contradiction.

---

* The original runs : " Der Verstand sucht bloss zu *fassen,* die Einbildungskraft aber zu *umfassen.*"—*Tr.*

According to the confession of Leibnitz himself, who in this appeals to the experiment of Archimedes with the lever, the Law of Sufficient Reason or Causality is a principle of experience. Now, it is quite true that in experience everything is found to have a cause ; but for the very reason, that *every* thing has a cause, nothing can be met with in experience which is a *first* cause, that is, a cause which has no cause to itself. How then can the metaphysicians infer from this law the existence of a first cause ?

Afterwards I found this objection more particularly developed in the Kantian philosophy, where it is shown that the Category of Cause, or the form of hypothetical judgments used in reference to the objects of nature, by which their relation to one another is determined *a priori*, can be applied only to objects of experience through an *a priori* schema. The first cause, which implies a complete infinite series of causes, and therefore in fact a contradiction, since the infinite can never be complete, is not an object of the understanding, but an idea of reason, or, according to my theory, a fiction of the imagination, which, not content with the mere knowledge of the law, seeks to gather the multiplicity, which is subject to the law, into an image, though in opposition to the law itself.

On another occasion I read in the Bible the story of Jacob and Esau ; and in this connection my father quoted the passage from the Talmud, where it is said, " Jacob

and Esau divided between them all the blessings of the
world. Esau chose the blessings of this life, Jacob, on
the contrary, those of the future life; and since we are
descended from Jacob, we must give up all claim to temporal blessings." On this I said with indignation,
" Jacob should not have been a fool; he should rather
have chosen the blessings of this world." Unfortunately
I got for answer, "You ungodly rascal!" and a box on
the ear. This did not of course remove my doubt, but
it brought me to silence at least.

The Prince Radzivil, who was a great lover of the
chase, came one day with his whole court to hunt in the
neighbourhood of our village. Among the party was his
daughter who afterwards married Prince Rawuzki. The
young princess, in order to enjoy rest at noon, betook
herself with the ladies of her court, the servants in waiting
and the lackeys, to the very room, where as a boy I was
sitting behind the stove. I was struck with astonishment
at the magnificence and splendour of the court, gazed
with rapture at the beauty of the persons and at the
dresses with their trimmings of gold and silver lace; I
could not satisfy my eyes with the sight. My father
came just as I was out of myself with joy, and had broken
into the words, " O how beautiful!" In order to calm
me, and at the same time to confirm me in the principles
of our faith, he whispered into my ear, " Little fool, in
the other world the *duksel* will kindle the *pezsure* for us,"
which means, In the future life the princess will kindle

C

the stove for us. No one can conceive the sort of feeling which this statement produced in me. On the one hand, I believed my father, and was very glad about this future happiness in store for us ; but I felt at the same time pity for the poor princess who was going to be doomed to such a degrading service. On the other hand, I could not get it into my head, that this beautiful rich princess in this splendid dress should ever make a fire for a poor Jew. I was thrown into the greatest perplexity on the subject, till some game drove these thoughts out of my head.

I had from childhood a great inclination and talent for drawing. True, I had in my father's house never a chance of seeing a work of art, but I found on the title-page of some Hebrew books woodcuts of foliage, birds and so forth. I felt great pleasure in these woodcuts, and made an effort to imitate them with a bit of chalk or charcoal. What however strengthened this inclination in me still more was a Hebrew book of fables, in which the personages who play their part in the fables—the animals—were represented in such woodcuts. I copied all the figures with the greatest exactness. My father admired indeed my skill in this, but rebuked me at the same time in these words, " You want to become a painter ? You are to study the Talmud, and become a rabbi. He who understands the Talmud, understands everything."

This desire and faculty for painting went with me so

far, that when my father had settled in H——, where there was a manor-house with some beautifully tapestried rooms, which were constantly unoccupied because the landlord resided elsewhere, and very seldom visited the place, I used to steal away from home whenever I could, to copy the figures on the tapestries. I was found once in mid-winter half-frozen, standing before the wall, holding the paper in one hand (for there was no furniture in this apartment), and with the other hand copying the figures off the wall. Yet I judge of myself at present, that, if I had kept to it, I should have become a *great*, but not an *exact*, painter, that is to say, I sketched with ease the main features of a picture, but had not the patience to work it out in detail.

My father had in his study a cupboard containing books. He had forbidden me indeed to read any books but the Talmud. This, however, was of no avail: as he was occupied the most of his time with household affairs, I took advantage of the opportunity thus afforded. Under the impulse of curiosity I made a raid upon the cupboard and glanced over all the books. The result was, that, as I had already a fair knowledge of Hebrew, I found more pleasure in some of these books than in the Talmud. And this result was surely natural. Take the subjects of the Talmud, which, with the exception of those relating to jurisprudence, are dry and mostly unintelligible to a child—the laws of sacrifice, of purification, of forbidden meats, of feasts, and so forth—in which the oddest rabbinical conceits are elaborated through many volumes with the finest dialectic, and the most absurd questions are discussed with the highest efforts of intellectual power ; for example, how many white hairs may a red cow have, and yet remain a *red* cow ; what sorts of scabs require this or that sort of purification ; whether a louse or a flea may be killed on the Sabbath, —the first being allowed, while the second is a deadly sin ;—whether the slaughter of an animal ought to be executed at the neck or the tail ; whether the highpriest put on his shirt or his hose first ; whether the *Jabam*, that is, the brother of a man who died childless, being required by law to marry the widow, is relieved from his obligation if he falls off a roof and sticks in the mire. *Ohe jam satis est!* Compare these glorious disputations, which are served up to young people and forced on them even to disgust, with history, in which natural events are related in an instructive and agreeable manner, with a knowledge of the world's structure, by which the outlook into nature is widened, and the vast whole is brought into a well-ordered system ; surely my preference will be justified.

The most valuable books in the collection were four. There was a Hebrew chronicle under the title of *Zemach David*,* written by a sensible chief rabbi in Prague,

---

* That is, *The Branch* (or *Offspring*) *of David*.　See Jeremiah xxiii. 5 ; xxxiii. 15 ; Isaiah xi. 1.—*Trans.*

named Rabbi David Gans. He was also the author of the astronomical book spoken of in the sequel, and he had had the honour of being acquainted with Tycho Brahe, and of making astronomical observations with him in the Observatory at Copenhagen. There were besides, a Josephus, which was evidently garbled, and a History of the Persecutions of the Jews in Spain. But what attracted me most powerfully was an astronomical work. In this work a new world was opened to me, and I gave myself up to the study with the greatest diligence. Think of a child about seven years of age, in my position, with an astronomical work thrown in his way, and exciting his interest. I had never seen or heard anything of the first elements of mathematics, and I had no one to give me any direction in the study : for it is needless to say, that to my father I dared not even let my curiosity in the matter be known, and, apart from that, he was not in a position to give me any information on the subject. How must the spirit of a child, thirsting for knowledge, have been inflamed by such a discovery ! This the result will show.

As I was still a child, and the beds in my father's house were few, I was allowed to sleep with my old grandmother, whose bed stood in the above-mentioned study. As I was obliged during the day to occupy myself solely with the study of the Talmud, and durst not take another book in my hand, I devoted the evenings to my astronomical inquiries. Accordingly after my grandmother had gone to bed, I put some fresh wood on the fire, made for the cupboard, and took out my beloved astronomical book. My grandmother indeed scolded me, because it was too cold for the old lady to lie alone in bed ; but I did not trouble myself about that, and continued my study till the fire was burnt out.

After I had carried this on for some evenings, I came to the description of the celestial sphere and its imaginary circles, designed for the explanation of astronomical phenomena. This was represented in the book by a single figure, in connection with which the author gave the reader the good advice, that, since the manifold circles could not be represented in a plane figure except by straight lines, he should, for the sake of rendering them more clearly intelligible, make for himself either an ordinary globe or an armillary sphere. I therefore formed the resolution to make such a sphere out of twisted rods ; and after I had finished this work, I was in a position to understand the whole book. But as I had to take care lest my father should find out how I had been occupied, I always hid my armillary sphere in a corner behind the cupboard before I went to bed.

My grandmother, who had on several occasions observed that I was wholly absorbed in my reading, but now and then lifted my eyes to look at a number of circles formed of twisted rods laid on one another, fell into the greatest consternation over the matter ; she believed nothing less than that her grandson had lost his wits. She did not delay, therefore, to tell my father, and point out to him the place where the magical instrument was kept. He soon guessed what was the meaning of this. Accordingly he took the sphere in his hand, and sent for me. When I came, he asked me, " What sort of plaything is this ? "

" It is a *Kadur*,* " I replied.

" What does it mean ? " he asked.

I then explained to him the use of all the circles for the purpose of making the celestial phenomena intelligible. My father, who was a good rabbi indeed, but had no special talent for science, could not comprehend all that I endeavoured to make comprehensible. He was especially puzzled, by the comparison of my armillary sphere with the figure in the book, to understand how out of straight lines circles should be evolved ; but one thing he could see,—that I was sure of my business. He therefore scolded me, it is true, because I had transgressed his command to meddle with nothing beyond the Talmud ; but still he felt a secret pleasure, that his young son, without a guide or previous training, had been able by himself to master an entire work of science. And with this the affair came to an end.

---

* The Hebrew word for a globe.

CHAPTER IV.

Jewish Schools—The Joy of being released from them causes a stiff foot.

My brother Joseph and I were sent to Mir to school. My brother, who was about twelve years old, was put to board with a schoolmaster of some repute at that time, by name Jossel. This man was the terror of all young people, " the scourge of God ; " he treated those in his charge with unheard of cruelty, flogged them till the blood came, even for the slightest offence, and not infrequently tore off their ears, or beat their eyes out. When the parents of these unfortunates came to him, and brought him to task, he struck them with stones or whatever else came to hand, and drove them with his stick out of the house back to their own dwellings, without any respect of persons. All under his discipline became either blockheads or good scholars. I, who was then only seven years old, was sent to another schoolmaster.

An anecdote I must here relate, which shows on the one side great brotherly love, and on the other may be viewed as expressing the condition of a child's mind, that sways between the hope of lightening an evil, and the fear of increasing it. One day as I came from school, my eyes were all red with weeping, for which there was doubtless good cause. My brother observed this, and asked the reason. At first I showed some hesitation in answering ; but at last I said, " I weep because we dare not tell tales out of school." My brother understood me very well, was extremely indignant at my teacher, and was going to read him a lesson on the subject. I begged him however not to do it, because in all probability the teacher would take his revenge on me for telling tales out of school.

I must now say something of the condition of the Jewish schools in general. The school is commonly a small smoky hut, and the children are scattered, some on benches, some on the bare earth. The master, in a dirty blouse sitting on the table, holds between his knees a bowl, in which he grinds tobacco into snuff with a huge pestle like the club of Hercules, while at the same time he wields his authority. The ushers give lessons, each in his own corner, and rule those under their charge quite as despotically as the master himself. Of the breakfast, lunch, and other food sent to the school for the children, these gentlemen keep the largest share for themselves. Sometimes even the poor youngsters get nothing at all ; and yet they dare not make any complaint on the subject, if they will not expose themselves to the vengeance of these tyrants. Here the children are imprisoned from morning to night, and have not an hour

to themselves, except on Friday and a half-holiday at
the Newmoon.

As far as study is concerned, the reading of Hebrew
at least is pretty regularly learned. On the other hand,
with the mastery of the Hebrew language very seldom is
any progress made. Grammar is not treated in the
school at all, but has to be learnt *ex usu*, by translation
of the Holy Scriptures, very much as the ordinary man
learns imperfectly the grammar of his mother-tongue by
social intercourse. Moreover there is no dictionary of
the Hebrew language. The children therefore begin at
once with the explanation of the Bible. This is divided
into as many sections as there are weeks in the year, in
order that the Books of Moses, which are read in the
synagogues every Saturday, may be read through in a
year. Accordingly every week some verses from the
beginning of the section proper to the week are explained
in school, and that with every possible grammatical
blunder. Nor can it well be otherwise. For the Hebrew
must be explained by means of the mother-tongue. But
the mother-tongue of the Polish Jews is itself full of
defects and grammatical inaccuracies ; and as a matter
of course therefore also the Hebrew language, which is
learned by its means, must be of the same stamp. The
pupil thus acquires just as little knowledge of the
language, as of the contents, of the Bible.

In addition to this the Talmudists have fastened all
sorts of extraordinary conceits on the Bible. The

ignorant teacher believes with confidence, that the Bible cannot in reality have any other meaning than that which these expositions ascribe to it; and the pupil must follow his teacher's faith, so that the right understanding of words necessarily becomes lost. For example, in the first Book of Moses it is said, "Jacob sent messengers to his brother Esau, etc." Now, the Talmudists were pleased to give out, that these messengers were angels. For though the word *Malachim* in Hebrew denotes messenger as well as angels, these marvel-mongers preferred the second signification, because the first contains nothing marvellous. The pupil therefore holds the belief firm and fast, that Malachim denotes nothing but angels; and the natural meaning of messengers is for him wholly lost. A correct knowledge of the Hebrew language and a sound exegesis can be attained only gradually by independent study and by reading grammars and critical commentaries on the Bible, like those of Rabbi David Kimchi * and Aben Esra; but of these very few rabbis make use.

---

* This rabbi belonged to a family of eminent linguists. The father, Joseph Kimchi, was one of the numerous Jews who were obliged to flee from Spain to escape the cruel persecutions of the Mohades about the middle of the twelfth century. He left two sons who both followed his favourite studies. The elder, Moses, has the credit of having educated his younger and more illustrious brother, David, whose Hebrew grammar and dictionary continued in general use among scholars for centuries. Kimchi is said to have been powerfully influenced, not only by Maimonides, but also

As the children are doomed in the bloom of youth to such an infernal school, it may be easily imagined with what joy and rapture they look forward to their release. We, that is, my brother and I, were taken home to the great feasts; and it was on a trip of this sort, that the following incident happened, which in relation to me was very critical. My mother came once before Whitsuntide to the town where we were at school, in order to purchase sundry articles required for the house. She then took us home with her. The release from school, and the sight of the beauty of nature which at this season displays its best attire, threw us into such ecstasy, that we fell upon all sorts of wanton fancies. When we were not far from home, my brother sprang out of the carriage, and ran forward on foot. I was going to imitate his daring leap, but unfortunately had not sufficient strength. I fell down therefore with violence on the carriage, so that my legs came between the wheels, and one of these passed over my left leg, which was thereby pitiably crushed. I was carried home half-dead. My foot became cramped, and I was wholly unable to move it.

A Jewish doctor was consulted, who had not indeed regularly studied and graduated at a university, but had acquired his medical knowledge merely by serving with

---

by Aben Esra, who preceded him by nearly a century, and who was one of the most learned scholars, as well as one of the most versatile authors, of his time. (Jost's *Geschichte des Judenthums,* vol. ii., pp. 419-423 ; and vol. iii , pp. 30-31).—*Trans.*

a physician and reading some medical books in the Polish language, who was nevertheless a very good practical physician, and effected many successful cures. He said that at present he was provided with no medicines,—the nearest apothecary's shop was about twenty miles* distant,—and consequently he could prescribe nothing in the ordinary method, but that meanwhile a simple domestic remedy might be applied. The remedy was, to kill a dog and thrust into it the cramped foot ; this, repeated several times, was to give certain relief. The prescription was followed with the desired result, so that after some weeks I was able to use the foot again, and by degrees I completely recovered.

I think it would not be at all amiss, if medical men gave more attention to such domestic remedies, which are used with good results in districts where there are no regular physicians or apothecaries' shops ; they might even make special journeys with this end in view. I know many a case of this sort, which can be in nowise explained away. This however in passing. I return to my story.

---

* That is, about 100 English miles.—*Trans.*

CHAPTER V.

My Family is driven into Misery, and an old Servant loses by his
great Faithfulness a Christian Burial.

My father, who, as already mentioned, traded with
Königsberg in Prussia, had once shipped in a vessel of
Prince Radzivil's some barrels of salt and herrings which
he had bought there.   When he came home and was
going to fetch his goods, the agent, Schachna, absolutely
refused to let him take them.   My father then showed
the bill of lading, which he had got on the shipment of
the goods ; but the agent tore it out of his hands, and
threw it into the fire.   My father found himself therefore
compelled to carry on a long and costly suit, which he
had to delay till the following year, when he would again
make a journey to Königsberg.   Here he obtained a
certificate from the custom-house, showing that he had
shipped the said goods in a vessel of Prince Radzivil's
under the direction of Herr Schachna.   On this certificate the agent was summoned before the court, but
found it convenient not to make an appearance ; and
my father gained the suit in the first, second, and third
instances.   In spite of this, however, as a consequence
of the wretched administration of justice in Poland at

the time, my father had no power to execute this decision, and therefore from this successful suit he did not even recover the costs.

To this was added the further result, that by this suit he made Herr Schachna an enemy who persecuted him now in every possible way. This the cunning scoundrel could accomplish very well, as by all sorts of intrigues he had been appointed by Prince Radzivil steward of all his estates situated in the district of Mir. He resolved therefore on my father's ruin, and only waited for a convenient opportunity to carry out his revenge.

This he found soon ; and indeed a Jew, who was named after his farm Schwersen, and was known as the biggest scoundrel in the whole neighbourhood, offered him a hand. This fellow was an ignoramus, did not even understand the Jewish language, and made use therefore of Russian. He occupied himself mainly in examining the farms in the neighbourhood, and he knew how to get possession of the most lucrative among them by offering a higher rent and bribing the steward. Without troubling himself in the least about the laws of the *Chazakah*,* he drove the old legal farmers from their possessions, and enriched himself by this means. He thus lived in wealth and fortune, and in this state reached an advanced age.

The scoundrel had already for a long time had his eye

---

* See above, p. 14.—·*Trans.*

on my grandfather's farm, and waited merely for a favourable opportunity and a plausible pretext to get possession of it himself. Unfortunately my granduncle Jacob, who lived in another village belonging to my grandfather's farm, had been obliged to become a debtor of the scoundrel to the amount of about fifty rix-dollars. As he could not clear off the debt at the time when it was due, his creditor came with some servants of the manor, and threatened to seize the cauldron, in which my granduncle's whole wealth consisted. In consternation he loaded a waggon secretly with the cauldron, drove with all haste to my grandfather's, and, without letting any of us know, hid it in the adjoining marsh behind the house. His creditor, however, who followed on his heels, came to my grandfather's, and made search all over, but could find the cauldron nowhere. Irritated at this unsuccessful stroke, and breathing vengeance against my grandfather who, he believed, had prevented his success, he rode to the town, carried to the steward an imposing present, and offered for my grandfather's farm double the rent, besides an annual voluntary present to the steward.

This gentleman, joyous over such an offer, and mindful of the disgrace which my father, a Jew, had brought upon him, a Polish noble, by the above-mentioned suit, made on the spot a contract with the scoundrel, by which he not only gave over to him this farm with all the rights pertaining to it even before the end of my grandfather's lease, but also robbed my grandfather of all he had,—his barns full of grain, his cattle, etc.,—and shared the plunder with the new farmer.

My grandfather was therefore obliged with his whole family to quit his dwelling-place in mid-winter, and, without knowing where he should settle again, to wander about from place to place. Our departure from this place was very affecting. The whole neighbourhood lamented our fate. An old and faithful servant of eighty years, named Gabriel, who had carried in his arms even my grandfather as a child, insisted on going with us. Representations were made to him on the severity of the season, our unfortunate situation, and the uncertainty in which we ourselves were placed as to our future destiny. But it was of no avail. He placed himself on the road before the gate, by which our waggons had to pass, and lamented so long that we were obliged to take him up. He did not however travel with us long: his advanced age, his grief over our misery, and the severe season gave him soon the finishing stroke. He died when we had gone scarcely two or three miles ; and as no Catholic or Russian community would allow him burial in their churchyard—he was a Prussian and a Lutheran—he was buried at our expense in the open field.

D

CHAPTER VI.

New Abode, new Misery—The Talmudist.

WE wandered about therefore in the country, like the Israelites in the wilderness of Arabia, without knowing where or when we should find a place of rest: At last we came to a village which belonged to two landlords. The one part was already leased; but the landlord of the other could not lease his, because he had still to build a house. Weary of wandering in winter-time with a whole family, my grandfather resolved to take a lease of this house, which was still to be built, along with its appurtenances, and meanwhile, till the house was ready, to make shift as well as he could. Accordingly we were obliged to take up our quarters in a barn. The other farmer did all in his power to prevent our settlement in the place; but it was of no avail. The building was finished, we took possession, and began to keep house.

Unfortunately however everything went backward here; nothing would succeed. An addition came to our misfortunes in my mother's illness. Being of a very lively temperament and disposed to a life of activity, she found here the weariness of having nothing to do. This, with her anxiety about the means of subsistence, threw her into a state of melancholy, which developed at last into insanity. In this condition she remained for some months. Everything was tried for her benefit, but without success. At last my father hit upon the idea of taking her to a celebrated doctor at Novogrod, who made a specialty of curing mental disorders.

The method of cure employed by this specialist is unknown to me, because I was at the time too young to wish or be able to institute inquiries on the subject ; but so much I can declare with certainty, that in the case of my mother, as well as most of his patients afflicted with the same malady, the treatment was followed with success. My mother returned home fresh and healthy, and from that time she never had an attack of the same sort.

Immediately after this I was sent to school at Iwenez, about fifteen miles from our abode, and here I began to study the Talmud. The study of the Talmud is the chief object of a learned education among our people. Riches, bodily advantages, and talents of every kind have indeed in their eyes a certain worth, and are esteemed in proportion ; but nothing stands among them above the dignity of a good Talmudist. He has the first claim upon all offices and positions of honour in the community. If he enters an assembly,—he may be of any age or rank,—every one rises before him most respectfully, and the most honourable place is assigned to him. He is director of the conscience, lawgiver and judge of the common man. He, who does not meet such a scholar with sufficient respect, is, according to the judgment of the Talmudists, damned to all eternity. The common man dare not enter upon the most trivial undertaking, if, in the judgment of the scholar, it is not according to law. Religious usages, allowed and for bidden meats, marriage and divorce are determined not only by the rabbinical laws which have already accumulated to an enormous mass, but also by special rabbinical judgments which profess to deduce all special cases from the general laws. A wealthy merchant, farmer or professional man, who has a daughter, does everything in his power to get a good Talmudist for his son-in-law. As far as other matters are concerned, the scholar may be as deformed, diseased, and ignorant as possible, he will still have the advantage over others. The future father-in-law of such a phoenix is obliged, at the betrothal, to pay to the parents of the youth a sum fixed by previous agreement ; and besides the dowry for his daughter, he is further obliged to provide her and her husband with food, clothing, and lodging, for six or eight years after their marriage, during which time the interest on the dowry is paid, so that the learned son-in-law may continue his studies at his father-in-law's expense. After this period he receives the dowry in hand, and then he is either promoted to some learned office, or he spends his whole life in learned leisure. In either case the wife undertakes the management of the household and the conduct of business; and she is content if only in return for all her toils she becomes in some measure a partaker of her husband's fame and future blessedness.

The study of the Talmud is carried on just as irregularly as that of the Bible. The language of the Talmud is composed of various Oriental languages and dialects; there is even many a word in it from Greek and Latin. There is no dictionary, in which you can turn up the expressions and phrases met with in the Talmud; and, what is still worse, as the Talmud is not pointed, you cannot even tell how such words, that are not pure Hebrew, are to be read. The language of the Talmud, therefore, like that of the Bible, is learned only through frequent translation; and this constitutes the *first* stage in the study of the Talmud.

When the pupil has been directed for some time in translation by the teacher, he goes on to the independent reading or explanation of the Talmud. The teacher gives him a limited portion of the Talmud, containing within itself a connected argument, as a task in exposition, which he must perform within a fixed time. The particular expressions and forms of speech occurring in the passage must either be known by the pupil from his former lessons, or the teacher, who here takes the place of a dictionary, explains them to him. But the tenor and the entire connection of the prescribed passage the pupil is required to bring out himself; and this constitutes the *second* stage in the study of the Talmud.

Two commentaries, which are commonly printed along with the text, serve as the chief guides at this point. The author of the one is Rabbi Solomon Isaac,* a man gifted with grammatical and critical knowledge of language, with extensive and thorough Talmudic insight, and with an uncommon precision of style. The other is known by the title of *Tosaphoth (Additions)*, and is the work of several rabbis. Its origin is very remarkable. A number of the most famous rabbis agreed to study the Talmud in company. For this purpose each selected a separate portion, which he studied by himself till he believed that he had fully comprehended it, and retained it in memory. Afterwards all the rabbis met, and began to study the Talmud in company according to the order of its parts. As soon as the first part had been read out, thoroughly explained, and settled according to the Talmudic Logic, one of the rabbis produced, from the part of the Talmud with which he was most familiar, anything that appeared to contradict this passage. Another then adduced, from the part which he had made thoroughly his own, a passage which was able to

---

* Solomon ben Isaac, as he is more correctly named, or Raschi, as he is also called, was an eminent Talmudic scholar of Troyes in the latter half of the eleventh century. It was his son-in-law, Meir, and the three sons of Meir, who may be said to have begun the Tosaphoth, referred to in the text.—*Trans.*

remove this contradiction by means of some distinction or some qualification unexpressed in the preceding passage. Sometimes the removal of such a contradiction occasioned another, which a third rabbi disclosed, and a fourth laboured to remove, till the first passage was explained harmoniously by all, and made perfectly clear. It may easily be imagined, what a high degree of subtlety is required to reduce the Talmud to first principles, from which correct inferences may be drawn after an uniform method ; for the Talmud is a voluminous and heterogeneous work, in which even the same subject often turns up in different passages, where it is explained in different ways.

Besides these two there are several other commentaries which treat the subject further, and even make corrections on the two just mentioned. Indeed, every rabbi, if he possesses sufficient acuteness, is to be viewed as a living commentary on the Talmud. But the highest effort of the mind is required to prepare a selection from the Talmud or a code of the laws deducible from it. This implies not only acuteness, but also a mind in the highest degree systematic. Herein our Maimonides undoubtedly deserves the first rank, as may be seen from his code, *Jad Hachazekah.*

The *final* stage in the study of the Talmud is that of disputation. It consists in eternally disputing about the book, without end or aim. Subtlety, loquacity, and impertinence here carry the day. This sort of study was formerly very common in the Jewish high schools ; * but in our times along with the schools it has also fallen into decay. It is a kind of Talmudic scepticism, and utterly incompatible with any systematic study directed to some end.

---

* As it was at one time throughout all Christendom, and probably under every civilisation at a certain stage of its history.—*Trans.*

CHAPTER VII.

Joy endureth but a little while.

AFTER this digression on the study of the Talmud I return to my story. As already mentioned, I was sent to school at Iwenez. My father gave me a letter to the chief rabbi of this place, who was a relation of ours, requesting him to give me in charge to an able teacher, and to give some attention to the progress of my studies. He gave me however in charge to a common schoolmaster, and told me I was to visit him every Sabbath in order that he might examine me himself. This injunction I punctually followed; but the arrangement did not continue long; for at one of these examinations I began to dispute about my lessons and suggest difficulties, when, without replying to them, the chief rabbi asked me if I had stated these difficulties to my teacher also.

" Of course," I replied.

" And what did he say ? " asked the chief rabbi.

" Nothing to the point," I replied, " except that he enjoined silence on me, and said, ' A youngster must not be too inquisitive ; he must see to it merely that he understands his lesson, but must not overwhelm his teacher with questions.' "

"Ah!" said the chief rabbi, "your teacher is altogether too easy, we must make a change. I will give you instruction myself. I will do it merely out of friendship, and I hope that your father will have as little to say against it as your former teacher. The fee which your father pays for your education, will be given to your teacher without deduction."

In this way I got the chief rabbi for a teacher. He struck out a way of his own with me. No weekly lessons repeated till they are impressed on the memory, no tasks which the pupil is obliged to perform for himself, and in which the course of his thoughts is very often arrested for the sake of a single word or a figure of speech, which has little to do with the main subject. His method distinguished itself from all this. He made me explain something from the Talmud *ex tempore* in his presence, conversed with me on the subject, explained to me so much as was necessary to set my own mind in activity, and by means of questions and answers turned my attention away from all side-issues to the main subject, so that in a short time I passed through all the three above-mentioned stages in the study of the Talmud.

My father, to whom the chief rabbi gave an account of his plan with me and of my progress, went beside himself with joy. He returned his warmest thanks to this excellent man for putting himself to so much trouble with me out of mere friendship, and that notwithstanding his delicate state of health, for he was consumptive. But this joy did not last long ; before a half year was ended, the chief rabbi had to betake himself to his fathers, and I was left like a sheep without a shepherd.

This was announced to my father, who came and fetched me home. Not, however, to H———, from which I had been sent to school, but to Mohilna, about six miles from H———, whether my father had meanwhile removed. This new change of abode had taken place in the following way.

Mohilna is a small hamlet in the territory of Prince Radzivil four miles from Nesvij, his residence. The situation of this place is excellent. Having the river Niemen on one side, and on the other a large quantity of the best timber for ships, it is adapted equally for trade and for shipbuilding. Moreover the district in itself possesses great fertility and amenity. These facts could not escape the attention of the Prince. The farmer or *arendant* of the place, whose family for some generations had been in possession of this lucrative farm, and had become rich by means of the shipbuilding trade, and the numerous fine products of the district, took all possible pains to prevent these great advantages from being observed, in order that he might be able to enjoy them alone without being disturbed. But it happened once that the prince was travelling through the place, and was so taken with its beauty, that he resolved to make a town of it. He sketched a plan for this, and made an announcement that the place was to be a *Slabode ;* that is, every one was to be at liberty to settle in the place, and drive any kind of trade, and was even to be free from all taxes for the first six years. For a long time, however, this plan was never carried out, owing to all sorts of intrigues on the part of the arendant, who went so far as even to bribe the advisers of the prince to turn his attention away from the subject.

My father, who saw clearly that the miserable farm of H—— could not support him and his family, and had been obliged to remain there hitherto only from want of a better abode, rejoiced very much at the announcement, because he hoped that Mohilna would offer him a place of refuge, especially as the arendant was a brother-in-law of my uncle. In this connection he made a journey to the place with my grandfather, had a conversation with the arendant, and opened to him his proposal to settle in Mohilna with his consent. The arendant, who had feared that, on the announcement of the prince's wish, people would stream in from all sides, and press him out of his possession, was delighted that at least the first who settled there was not a stranger, but related to his family by marriage. He therefore not only gave his consent to the proposal, but even promised my father all possible assistance. Accordingly my father removed with his whole family to Mohilna, and had a small house built for himself there; but till it was ready, the family were obliged once more to take up their quarters in a barn.

The arendant, by whom at first we were received in a friendly manner, had unfortunately meanwhile changed his mind, and found that his fear of being pressed out of his possession by strangers was wholly without ground, inasmuch as already a considerable time had passed since the announcement of the prince's wish, and yet nobody had presented himself besides my father. The prince, as a Polish chief and *Voivode* in Lithuania, was constantly burdened too much with State affairs in Warsaw, to be able to think on the carrying out of his plan himself ; and his subordinates could be induced by bribes to frustrate the whole plan. These considerations showed the arendant that the new-comer could not only be spared, but was even a burden, inasmuch as he had now to share with another what he had before held in possession alone. He sought therefore to restrict my father, and to disturb him in his settlement, as much as possible. With this view he built for himself a splendid house, and succeeded in obtaining a command from the prince, in accordance with which none of the new-comers should enjoy the rights of a burgher till he had built a similar house. My father saw himself therefore compelled to waste his little fortune, which was indispensably required for the new arrangements, wholly and solely on this useless building.

CHAPTER VIII.

The Pupil knows more than the Teacher—A theft *à la Rousseau,*
    which is discovered — "The ungodly provideth, and the
    righteous putteth it on."

My father's condition had thus externally an improved
appearance, but so much the more doubtful did it appear internally on that account.   My mother, notwithstanding her unwearied activity, was able to make only
a very sorry provision for the family.   Accordingly my
father was obliged to seek, in addition to his other duties,
a position as teacher, in which he carried on my education ; and I must confess that in this connection I gave
him, on the one hand, much joy, but, on the other hand,
not a little vexation.   I was then indeed only about
nine years old ; still, I could not only understand the
Talmud and its commentaries correctly, but I even took
delight in disputing about it, and in this I felt a childish
pleasure in triumphing over my honest father, whom I
thereby threw into no small perplexity.

The arendant and my father lived together like neighbours ; that is, they envied and hated each other.   The
former looked on my father as a vagrant, who had forced
himself upon him, and disturbed him in his undivided

possession of the advantages of the place. My father took the arendant for a wealthy blockhead, who, against the consent which he had granted, which my father might have dispensed with altogether and had sought merely from the love of peace, endeavoured in every way to restrict him and to narrow his rights, notwithstanding the fact that he received actual advantages from his settlement. For from this time Mohilna had acquired a sort of independence, by means of which the arendant was spared many expenses and depreciations. There was also a small synagogue erected, and my father took the position of chief rabbi, preacher, and director of the conscience, as he was the only scholar in the place. He lost, indeed, no opportunity of representing all this to the arendant, and making complaints of his conduct; but unfortunately this was of little use.

I must take this opportunity of mentioning the only theft which I ever perpetrated in my life. I often went to the house of the arendant, and played with his children. Once, when I entered a room and found no one there, it being summer and the people of the house all busy out of doors, I spied in an open closet a neat little medicine-box which appeared to me uncommonly charming. When I opened it, I found, to my very great sorrow, some money in it; for it belonged to one of the children of the house. I could not resist the desire to carry off the little box; but to take the money seemed to me in the highest degree shameful. But when I considered that the theft would be all the more easily discovered if I put the money out, full of fear and shame I took the box as it was and thrust it in my pocket. I went home with it, and buried it very carefully. The night following I could not sleep, and was disquieted in conscience, especially on account of the money. I resolved, therefore, to take it back; but in regard to the little box, I could not conquer myself: it was a work of art, the like of which I had never seen before. The next day I emptied the box of its contents, slunk with them into the room already mentioned, and waited for an opportunity when nobody was there. I was already engaged in smuggling the money into the closet; but I had so little skill in doing this without noise and with the necessary despatch, that I was caught in the act, and forced to a confession of the whole theft. I was obliged to dig up again the valuable work of art,— it must have cost about a quarter of a groschen,—to return it to its owner, little Moses, and to hear myself called *thief* by the children of the house.

Another incident, which happened to me and had a comical issue, was the following. The Russians had been quartered for some time in Mohilna, and as they obtained new mountings, they were allowed to sell the old. My eldest brother Joseph and my cousin Beer applied to Russian acquaintances of theirs, and received in a present some brass buttons, which, being considered a fine decoration, they got sewed on to their hose instead

of the wooden buttons they had before. I also was delighted with the decoration; but as I had not the skill
to furnish myself by my own diligence, I was compelled
to make use of force. I applied, therefore, to my father,
and demanded that Joseph and Beer should be required
to share their buttons with me. My father, who, indeed,
was extremely fair, but still was fond of me above everything, said that the buttons were, of course, the rightful
property of their owners, but that, as these had more
than they required for their own wants, it was but fair
that they should give me some of those that they did
not require. To my commendation and their confusion
he added the passage of the Bible, "The ungodly pro-
videth, and the righteous putteth it on."* This decision
had to be carried out in spite of the protest of Joseph
and Beer; and I had the pleasure of also shining in
brass buttons on my hose.

Joseph and Beer however could not get over their loss.
They complained loudly of the impious wrong which had
been done to them. My father, who wished to get rid
of the affair, told them therefore, that, as the buttons had
been already sewed on to Solomon's hose, they must not
use force, but that, if they could get them back again by

---

* This seems to be Job xxvii. 17, which in our Authorised Version runs:—"He (a wicked man) may prepare it (raiment), but
the just shall put it on." Maimon seems to render it from memory:
—"Der Gottlose schafft sich an, und der Fromme bekleidet sich
damit."—*Trans.*

stratagem, they were at liberty to do so. Both were
pleased with this decision. They came to me, looked at
my buttons, and both at once exclaimed in astonishment,
"Oh! what is that we see? Buttons sewed on to cloth
hose with linen instead of hemp thread! They must be
taken off at once." While they were speaking, they took
off all the buttons, and went off with joy over their successful stratagem. I ran after them, and demanded that
they should sew the buttons on again; but they laughed
me to scorn. My father said to me smiling at this,
"Since you are so credulous, and allow yourself to be
deceived, I cannot help you any longer; I hope you will
be wiser in the future." With this the affair came to an
end. I was obliged to content myself with wooden
buttons, and to have often repeated to my mortification
by Joseph and Beer, the biblical passage, which my
father had used to my advantage, "The ungodly pro-
videth, and the righteous putteth it on."

CHAPTER IX.

Love Affairs and Matrimonial Proposals—The Song of Solomon may be used in Matchmaking—A new *Modus Lucrandi*—Smallpox.

In my youth I was very lively, and had in my nature a good deal that was agreeable. In my passions I was violent and impatient. Till about my eleventh year, as I had the benefit of a very strict education, and was kept from all intercourse with women, I never traced any special inclination towards the fair sex. But an incident produced in me a great change in this respect.

A poor, but very pretty, girl about my own age was taken into our house as a servant. She charmed me uncommonly. Desires began to stir in me, which till this time I had never known. But in accordance with the strict rabbinical morals, I was obliged to keep on my guard against looking on the girl with attentive gaze, and still more against speaking with her, so that I was able only now and then to throw at her a stolen glance.

It happened once however that the women of the house were going to bathe, which by the usage of the country they are accustomed to do two or three times a week. By chance my instinct drove me without reflection towards the place where they bathed; and there I suddenly perceived this beautiful girl, as she stepped out of the steam-bath and plunged into the river flowing by. At this sight I fell into a sort of rapture. After my feelings had calmed down again, being mindful of the strict Talmudic laws, I wished to flee. But I could not; I remained standing, as if rooted in the spot. As I dreaded however lest I might be surprised here, I was obliged to return with a heavy heart. From that time I became restless, was sometimes beside myself; and this state continued till my marriage.

Our neighbour, the arendant, had two sons and three daughters. The eldest daughter, Deborah, was already married. The second, Pessel, was about my age; the peasantry of the place professed to find even a certain resemblance in our features, and therefore, in accordance with all the laws of probability, conjectured that there would be a match between us. We formed also a mutual affection. But by ill luck the youngest daughter, Rachel, had to fall into a cellar and dislocated one of her legs. She herself, indeed, completely recovered, but the leg remained somewhat crooked. The arendant then started a hunt after me; he was absolutely determined to have me for a son-in-law. My father was quite agreeable, but he wished to have for his daughter-in-law the straight-legged Pessel rather than Rachel of the crooked leg. The arendant however declared that this was impracticable, inasmuch as he had fixed on a rich husband for the elder, while the youngest was destined for me ; and as my father was unable to give me anything, he was willing to provide for her richly out of his own fortune. Besides a considerable sum which he agreed to give as a portion, he was willing in addition to make me a joint-heir of his fortune, and to provide me with all necessaries the whole of my life. Moreover he promised to pay my father a fixed sum immediately after the betrothal, and not only to leave him undisturbed in his rights, but also to try and promote his domestic happiness in every possible way. The feuds between the two families were to cease from this time, and a league of friendship was to unite them for the future into one family.

Had my father lent an ear to these representations, he would without doubt have established the fortune of his house, and I should have lived with a spouse, who, it is true, had a crooked leg, but (as I found out some time afterwards when I was tutor in her family) was in other respects an amiable woman. I should thus have been freed from all cares in the midst of good fortune, and I should have been able to apply myself without hindrance to my studies. But unhappily my father rejected this proposal with scorn. He was absolutely determined to have Pessel for his daughter-in-law ; and since this, as already mentioned, was impracticable, the feuds between the two families broke out afresh. But as the arendant was rich, and my father was a poor man, the latter was necessarily always the loser.

Some time afterwards another matrimonial proposal for me turned up. Mr. L—— of Schmilowitz, a learned and at the same time a rich man, who had an only daughter, was so enchanted with my fame, that he chose me for his son-in-law without having seen me before. He began by entering into correspondence with my father on the subject, and left it to him to prescribe the conditions of the union. My father answered his letter in lofty style, made up of Biblical verses and passages from the Talmud, in which he expressed the conditions briefly by means of the following verses from the Canticles, "The thousand gulden are for thee, O Solomon, and the two hundred for those who keep his fruits." * Consent was given to everything.

My father accordingly made a journey to Schmilowitz, saw his future daughter-in-law, and had the marriage-contract drawn in accordance with the terms agreed upon. Two hundred gulden were paid to him on the spot. With this, however, he was not content, but insisted that in his letter he had been obliged to limit himself to two hundred gulden merely for the sake of the

---

* Evidently viii., 12, rendered in our Authorised Version, "Thou, O Solomon, must have a thousand (pieces of silver), and those that keep the fruit thereof two hundred." Maimon translates apparently from memory, "Die tausend Gulden sind für dich, Salomo, und die Zweihundert für die, die seine Früchte bewahren." In my rendering of this the pronoun "his" must be understood in its old English latitude as either neuter or masculine.—*Trans.*

beautiful verse which he did not wish to spoil; but he would not enter into the transaction at all unless he received for himself twice two hundred gulden (fifty thalers in Polish money). They had therefore to pay him two hundred gulden more, and to hand over to him the so-called little presents for me, namely, a cap of black velvet trimmed with gold lace, a Bible bound in green velvet with silver clasps, etc. With these things he came home full of joy, gave me the presents, and told me that I was to prepare myself for a disputation to be held on my marriage day, which would be in two months' time.

Already my mother had begun to bake the cakes she was expected to take with her to the wedding, and to prepare all sorts of preserves; I began also to think about the disputation I was to hold, when suddenly the mournful news arrived that my bride had died of smallpox. My father could easily reconcile himself to this loss, because he thought to himself that he had made fifty thalers by his son in an honourable way, and that now he could get fifty thalers for him again. I also, who had never seen my bride, could not particularly mourn her loss; I thought to myself, "The cap and the silver-clasped Bible are already mine, and a bride will also not be awanting long, while my disputation can serve me again." My mother alone was inconsolable about this loss. Cakes and preserves are of a perishable nature and will not keep long. The labour which my mother had expended was therefore rendered fruitless by this fatal accident ; and to this must be added, that she could find no place to keep the delicious cakes from my secret attacks.

CHAPTER X.

I become an object of contention, get two wives at once, and am
kidnapped at last.

MEANWHILE the domestic circumstances of my father
became every day worse. He saw himself, therefore,
compelled to make a journey to the town of Nesvij, and
apply for a position as teacher there, whither I also had
to follow him. Here he opened under favourable conditions a school of his own, in which he could employ
me as assistant.

A widow, celebrated for her superior talents, as well
as for her Xanthippe-like character, kept a public-house
at the extremity of one of the suburbs. She had a
daughter who yielded to her in none of the above-
mentioned qualities, and who was indispensable to her
in the management of the house. Madam Rissia, (this
was the widow's name), excited by my constantly increasing reputation, fixed on me as a husband for her
daughter Sarah. Her family represented to her the
impossibility of carrying out this plan ; first, my father's
pride, and the demands which he would therefore make,
and which she could never satisfy ; then my fame, which
had already excited the attention of the most prominent

and wealthy people of the town; and finally, the moderate character of her own fortune, which was far from sufficient to carry out such a proposal. All these representations, however, were of no avail with her. She had once for all taken it into her head, to have me for a son-in-law, let it cost her what it might; and she thought, the devil would needs be in it, if she could not get the young man.

She sent a proposal to my father, let him have no rest the whole time he was in the town, discussed the matter with him herself on various occasions, and promised to satisfy all his demands. My father, however, sought to gain time for deliberation, and to put off the question for a while. But the time came when we were to return home. My father went with me to the widow's house, which was the last on our road, in order to wait for a conveyance which started from that place. Madam Rissia made use of the opportunity, began to caress me, introduced my bride, and asked me how I was pleased with her. At last she pressed for a decisive answer from my father. He was still always holding back, however, and sought in every possible way to represent the difficulties connected with the subject.

While they were thus treating with one another, suddenly there burst into the room the chief rabbi, the preacher, and the elders of the place, with many of the most respectable people. This sudden appearance was brought about without any magic in the following way.

These gentlemen had been invited to a circumcision at the house of a prominent man in this very suburb. Madam Rissia, who knew this very well, sent her son at once to the house with an invitation to the whole company to come, immediately after rising from table, to a betrothal at her house. They came therefore half intoxicated ; and as they believed nothing else than that all the preliminaries of the marriage—contract had been settled, and that nothing was awanting but to write out and subscribe the contract, they sat down to table, set my father in the midst, and the chief rabbi began to dictate the contract to the scribe of the community.

My father assured them that on the main point nothing had yet been decided, and that still less had the preliminary articles been settled. The chief rabbi fell into a passion at this, for he supposed that it was only a quibble, and that his sacred person and the whole honourable company were being made sport of. He turned therefore to the company, and said with a haughty air, "Who is this Rabbi Joshua, who makes himself of so much consequence?" My father replied, "The Rabbi is here superfluous. I am, 'tis true, a common man ; but I believe, no man can dispute my right to care for the welfare of my son, and to place his future happiness on a firm footing."

The chief rabbi was greatly offended with the ambiguity of the expression, " The Rabbi is here superfluous." He saw clearly that he had no right to lay down laws to my father in the matter, and that it was a piece of rashness on the part of Madam Rissia to invite a company to a betrothal before the parties were agreed on the preliminary articles. He began therefore to strike a lower tone. He represented to my father the advantages of this match, the high ancestry of the bride, (her grandfather, father, and uncle, having been learned men, and chief rabbis), her personal attractions, and the willingness and ability of Madam Rissia to satisfy all his demands.

My father, who in fact had nothing to say against all this, was compelled to yield. The marriage-contract was made out, and in it Madam Rissia made over to her daughter her public-house with all its belongings as a bridal portion, and came under an obligation also to board and clothe the newly-married couple for six years. Besides I received as a present the entire work of the Talmud with its appurtenances, together worth two or three hundred thalers,* and a number of other gifts. My father came under no obligation at all, and in addition received fifty thalers in cash. Very wisely he had refused to accept a bill for this sum ; it had to be paid to him before the betrothal.

---

* The bulk of the gift explains its costliness. " The Babylonian Talmud is about four times as large as that of Jerusalem. Its thirty-six treatises now cover, in our editions, printed with the most prominent commentaries (Rashi and Tosafoth), exactly 2947 folio leaves in twelve folio volumes." (E. Deutsch's *Literary Remains*, p. 41).—*Trans.*

After all this had been arranged, there was a capital entertainment, and the brandy bottle was vigorously plied. The very next day my father and I went home. My mother-in-law promised to send after us as soon as possible the so-called little presents and the articles of clothing for me, which in the hurry she had not been able to get ready. Many weeks however passed without our hearing or seeing anything of these. My father was perplexed about this ; and as the character of my mother-in-law had long been suspicious to him, he could think nothing else than that this intriguing woman was seeking some subterfuge to escape from her burdensome contract. He resolved therefore to repay like with like.

The following circumstance strengthened him in this resolve. A rich arendant, who used to bring spirits to Nesvij for sale, and to lodge in our house on his journey through Mohilna, likewise cast his eye upon me. He had an only daughter, for whom he fixed on me in his thoughts as a husband. He knew however what difficulties he would have to overcome, if he were to treat on the subject directly with my father. He chose therefore an indirect way. His plan was to make my father his debtor ; and as his critical circumstances would make it impossible for him to clear off the debt, he expected to force him, as it were, to consent to this union with the view of wiping out the debt by means of the amount stipulated for the son. He offered my father therefore some barrels of spirits on credit, and the offer was accepted with delight.

As the date of payment approached, Hersch Dukor (this was the name of the arendant) came and reminded my father. The latter assured him, that at the moment he was not in a position to clear off the debt, and begged him to have patience with him for some time yet. "Herr Joshua," said the arendant, "I will speak with you quite frankly on this matter. Your circumstances are growing daily worse; and if no fortunate accident occurs, I do not see any possibility of your being able to clear off your debt. The best thing for us both therefore is this. You have a son, and I have a daughter who is the sole heiress of all my property. Let us enter into an alliance. By this means not only will your debt be wiped out, but a sum to be fixed by yourself will be paid in addition, and I shall take a general care to improve your circumstances so far as lies in my power."

No one could be more joyous over this proposal than my father. Immediately a contract was closed, in which the bride's dowry, as well as the required presents, was decided in accordance with my father's suggestion. The bill for the debt, which amounted to fifty thalers in Polish money, was returned to my father, and torn on the spot, while fifty thalers in addition were paid to him.

Thereupon my new father-in-law went on to Nesvij to collect some debts there. Unfortunately he had to lodge at my former mother-in-law's. She, being a great prattler, told him of her own accord about the good match which her daughter had made. "The father of the bridegroom," said she, "is himself a great scholar, and the bridegroom is a young man of eleven years, who has scarcely his equal."

"I also," replied the arendant, "have, thank God, made a good choice for my daughter. You have perhaps heard of the celebrated scholar, Rabbi Joshua, in Mohilna, and of his young son, Solomon : he is my daughter's bridegroom."

Scarcely had these words been spoken, when she cried out, "That is a confounded lie. Solomon is my daughter's bridegroom ; and here, sir, is the marriage-contract."

The arendant then showed her his contract too ; and they fell into a dispute, the result of which was that Madam Rissia had my father summoned before the court to give a categorical explanation. My father, however, did not put in an appearance, although she had him summoned twice.

Meanwhile my mother died, and was brought to Nesvij for burial. My mother-in-law obtained from the court an attachment on the dead body, by which its interment was interdicted till the termination of the suit. My father therefore saw himself compelled to appear in court, my mother-in-law of course gained the suit, and I became again the bridegroom of my former bride. And now to prevent any similar reversal of her plans in the future, and to take from my father all occasion for it, my mother-in-law endeavoured to satisfy all his demands in accordance with her promise, clothed me from top to toe, and even paid my father for my board from the date of the betrothal to the marriage. My mother also was now buried, and we returned home again.

My second father-in-law came too, and called upon my father for the ratification of his contract. He however pointed out that it was null and void, as it contravened a previous contract, and had been made by him merely in the supposition that my mother-in-law had no intention of fulfilling hers. The arendant seemed to give an ear to these representations, to yield to necessity, and reconcile himself to his loss; but in reality he was thinking of some means to get me into his hands. Accordingly he rose by night, yoked his horses, took me in silence from the table on which I was sleeping, packed me with all despatch into his carriage, and made off with his booty out at the gate. But as this could not be accomplished without some noise, the people in the house awoke, discovered the theft, pursued the kidnapper, and snatched me out of his hand. To me the whole incident appeared at the time like a dream.

In this way my father was released from his debt, and got fifty thalers besides as a gratuity; but I was immediately afterwards carried off by my legal mother-in-law, and made the husband of my legal bride. I must of course confess that this transaction of my father's cannot be quite justified in a moral point of view. Only his great need at the time can in some measure serve as an excuse.

CHAPTER XI.

My Marriage in my Eleventh Year makes me the Slave of my
Wife, and procures for me Cudgellings from my Mother-in-
law—A Ghost of Flesh and Blood.

On the first evening of my marriage my father was not
present. As he told me at my departure that he had
still to settle some articles on my account, and therefore
I was to wait for his arrival, I refused, in spite of all the
efforts that were made, to appear that evening. Nevertheless the marriage festivities went on. We waited the
next day for my father, but still he did not come. They
then threatened to bring a party of soldiers to drag me
to the marriage ceremony; but I gave them for an
answer, that, if this were done, it would help them little,
for the ceremony would not be lawful except as a
voluntary act. At last, to the joy of all interested, my
father arrived towards evening, the articles referred to
were amended, and the marriage ceremony was performed.

Here I must mention a little anecdote. I had read
in a Hebrew book of an approved plan for a husband to
secure lordship over his better half for life. He was to

tread on her foot at the marriage ceremony ; and if both hit on the stratagem, the first to succeed would retain the upper hand. Accordingly, when my bride and I were placed side by side at the ceremony this trick occurred to me, and I said to myself, Now you must not let the opportunity pass of securing for your whole life-time lordship over your wife. I was just going to tread on her foot, but a certain *Je ne sais quoi*, whether fear, shame, or love, held me back. While I was in this irresolute state, all at once I felt the slipper of my wife on my foot with such an impression that I should almost have screamed aloud if I had not been checked by shame. I took this for a bad omen and said to myself, Providence has destined you to be the slave of your wife, you must not try to slip out of her fetters. From my faint-heartedness and the heroic mettle of my wife, the reader may easily conceive why this prophecy had to be actually realised.

I stood, however, not only under the slipper of my wife, but—what was very much worse—under the lash of my mother-in-law. Nothing of all that she had promised was fulfilled. Her house, which she had settled on her daughter as a dowry, was burdened with debt. Of the six years' board which she had promised me I enjoyed scarcely half a year's, and this amid constant brawls and squabbles. She even, trusting to my youth and want of spirit, ventured now and then to lay hands on me, but this I repaid not infrequently with compound interest. Scarcely a meal passed during which we did not fling at each other's head, bowls, plates, spoons, and similar articles.

Once I came home from the academy extremely hungry. As my mother-in-law and wife were occupied with the business of the public house, I went myself into the room where the milk was kept; and as I found a dish of curds and cream, I fell upon it, and began to eat. My mother-in-law came as I was thus occupied, and screamed in rage, "You are not going to devour the milk with the cream !" The more cream the better, thought I, and went on eating, without disturbing myself by her cry. She was going to wrest the dish forcibly from my hands, beat me with her fists, and let me feel all her ill-will. Exasperated by such treatment, I pushed her from me, seized the dish, and smashed it on her head. That was a sight ! The curds ran down all over her. She seized in rage a piece of wood, and if I had not cleared out in all haste, she would certainly have beat me to death.

Scenes like this occurred very often. At such skirmishes of course my wife had to remain neutral, and whichever party gained the upper hand, it came home to her very closely. "Oh !" she often complained, "if only the one or the other of you had a little more patience !"

Tired of a ceaseless open war I once hit upon a strat-agem, which had a good effect for a short time at least. I rose about midnight, took a large vessel of earthenware, crept with it under my mother-in-law's bed, and began to

speak aloud into the vessel after the following fashion:—
" O Rissia, Rissia, you ungodly woman, why do you treat
my beloved son so ill? If you do not mend your ways,
your end is near, and you will be damned to all eternity."
Then I crept out again, and began to pinch her cruelly ;
and after a while I slipped silently back to bed.

The following morning she got up in consternation,
and told my wife, that my mother had appeared to her
in a dream, and had threatened and pinched her on my
account. In confirmation she showed the blue marks on
her arm. When I came from the synagogue, I did not
find my mother-in-law at home, but found my wife in
tears. I asked the reason, but she would tell me nothing.
My mother-in-law returned with dejected look, and eyes
red with weeping. She had gone, as I afterwards learned,
to the Jewish place of burial, thrown herself on my
mother's grave, and begged for forgiveness of her fault.
She then had the burial place measured, and ordered a
wax-light as long as its circumference, for burning in the
synagogue. She also fasted the whole day, and towards
me showed herself extremely amiable.

I knew of course what was the cause of all this, but
acted as if I did not observe it, and rejoiced in secret
over the success of my stratagem. In this manner I
had peace for some time, but unfortunately it did not
last long. The whole was soon forgotten again, and on
the slightest occasion the dance went on as before. In
short, I was soon afterwards obliged to leave the house

altogether, and accept a position as a private tutor.   Only
on the great feast-days I used to come home.

CHAPTER XII.

The Secrets of the Marriage State—Prince Radzivil,* or what is not all allowed in Poland?

IN my fourteenth year I had my eldest son, David. At my marriage I was only eleven years old, and owing to the retired life common among people of our nation in those regions, as well as the want of mutual intercourse between the two sexes, I had no idea of the essential duties of marriage, but looked on a pretty girl as on any other work of nature or art, somewhat as on the pretty medicine-box that I stole. It was therefore natural that for a considerable time after marriage I could not have any thought about the fulfilment of its duties. I used to approach my wife with trembling as a mysterious object. It was therefore supposed that I had been bewitched at the time of the wedding; and under this supposition I was brought to a witch to be cured. She took in hand all sorts of operations, which of course had a good effect, although indirectly through the help of the imagination.

---

* Maimon gives merely the initial " R " of this name ; but as he has already (Chap. i.) told us that his prince was Radzivil, there is not much mystery in this artifice.—*Trans.*

My life in Poland from my marriage to my emigration, which period embraces the springtime of my existence, was a series of manifold miseries with a want of all means for the promotion of culture, and, necessarily connected with that, an aimless application of my powers, in the description of which the pen drops from my hands, and the painful memories of which I strive to stifle.*

The general constitution of Poland at the time ; the condition of our people in it, who, like the poor ass with the double burden, are oppressed by their own ignorance and the religious prejudices connected therewith, as well as by the ignorance and prejudices of the ruling classes ; the misfortunes of my own family ;—all these causes combined to hinder me in the course of my development, and to check the effect of my natural disposition.

The Polish nation, under which I comprehend merely

---

* This horror of memory tormented Maimon to the end of his days. " He dreamed often that he was in Poland again, deprived of all his books ; and Lucius metamorphosed into an ass was not in a more pitiable plight. 'From this agony,' said Maimon, 'I was usually aroused by a loud cry, and my joy was indescribable on finding that it was only a dream.'" (*Maimoniana*, p. 94). " He once received a visit from his brother, for whom he was deeply affected. Poor as he was himself, Maimon kept him a long while, gave him clothing and everything else that he could, besides procuring from some friends enough money to pay his travelling expenses. Above all, he told me, he was affected at letting his brother go back into the wilderness ; and if he had not had a wife and children at home, he would have tried to keep him beside himself." (*Ibid.*, p. 175).—*Trans.*

the Polish nobility, is of a very mixed kind. Only the very few have an opportunity of culture by means of upbringing, instruction, and well-directed travels, by which they can best promote at once their own welfare and that of their tenantry. Most of them, on the other hand, spend their lives in ignorance and immorality, and become the sport of their extravagant passions, which are ruinous to their tenants. They make a display with titles and orders, which they disgrace by their actions ; they own many estates which they do not understand how to manage, and they are at perpetual feud with one another, so that the kingdom must of necessity become the prey of its neighbours, who are envious of its greatness.

Prince Radzivil was, as Hettmann in Poland and Voivode in Lithuania, one of the greatest magnates, and as occupant of three inheritances in his family owned immense estates. He was not without a certain kindness of heart and good sense ; but, through neglected training and a want of instruction, he became one of the most extravagant princes that ever lived. From want of occupation, which was a necessary consequence of neglect in cultivating his tastes and widening his knowledge, he gave himself up to drinking, by which he was tempted to the most ridiculous and insane actions. Without any particular inclination for it he abandoned himself to the most shameful sensuality ; and without being cruel, he exercised towards his dependents the greatest cruelties.

He supported at great cost an army of ten thousand men, which was used for no purpose in the world except display; and during the troubles in Poland he took, without knowing why, the part of the Confederates. By this means he got himself encumbered with the friendship of the Russians, who plundered his estates, and plunged his tenants into the greatest destitution and misery. He himself was obliged several times to flee from the country, and to leave as booty for his enemies treasures which had been the gathering of many generations.

Who can describe all the excesses he perpetrated? A few examples will, I believe, be sufficient to give the reader some idea of them. A certain respect for my former prince does not allow me to consider his faults as anything but faults of temperament and education, which deserve rather our pity than our hatred and contempt.

When he passed through a street, which he commonly did with the whole pomp of his court, his bands of music and soldiers, no man, at the peril of his life, durst show himself in the street; and even in the houses people were by no means safe. The poorest, dirtiest peasant-woman, who came in his way, he would order up into his carriage beside himself.

Once he sent for a respectable Jewish barber, who, suspecting nothing but that he was wanted for some surgical operation, brought his instruments with him, and appeared before the prince.

" Have you brought your instruments with you ? " he was asked.

" Yes, Serene Highness," he replied.

" Then," said the prince, " give me a lancet, and I will open one of your veins."

The poor barber had to submit. The prince seized the lancet ; and as he did not know how to go about the operation, and besides his hand trembled as a result of his hard drinking, of course he wounded the barber in a pitiable manner. But his courtiers smiled their applause, and praised his great skill in surgery.

He went one day into a church, and being so drunk that he did not know where he was, he stood against the altar, and commenced to ——. All who were present became horrified. Next morning when he was sober, the clergy brought to his mind the misdeed he had committed the day before. " Eh ! " said the prince, " we will soon make that good." Thereupon he issued a command to the Jews of the place, to provide at their own expense, fifty stone of wax for burning in the church. The poor Jews were therefore obliged to bring a sin-offering for the desecration of a Christian Church by an orthodox Catholic Christian.

He once took it into his head to drive on the wall round the town. But as the wall was too narrow for a coach with six horses,—and he never drove in any other,

—his hussars were obliged, with much labour and peril of their lives, to carry the coach with their hands till he had driven round the town in this way.

Once he drove with the whole pomp of his court to a Jewish synagogue, and, without any one to this day knowing the reason, committed the greatest havoc, smashed windows and stoves, broke all the vessels, threw on the ground the copies of the Holy Scriptures kept in the ark, and so forth. A learned, pious Jew, who was present, ventured to lift one of these copies from the ground, and had the honour of being struck with a musket-ball by His Serene Highness' own hand. From here the train went to a second synagogue, where the same conduct was repeated, and from there they proceeded to the Jewish burial-place, where the buildings were demolished, and the monuments cast into the fire.

Can it be conceived, that a prince could show himself so malicious towards his own poor subjects, whom he was in a position to punish legally whenever they really did anything amiss? Yet this is what happened here.

On one occasion he took it into his head to make a trip to Mohilna, a hamlet belonging to him, which lay four short miles from his Residence. This had to be done with his usual suite and all the pomp of his court. On the morning of the appointed day the train went forth. First marched the army in order according to its usual regimental divisions,—infantry, artillery, cavalry, and so on. Then followed his bodyguard, Strelitzi, consisting of volunteers from the poor nobility. After them came his kitchen-waggons, in which Hungarian wine had not been forgotten. These were followed by the music of his janissaries, and other bands. Then came his coach, and last of all his satraps. I give them this name, because I can compare this train with no other than that of Darius in the war against Alexander. Towards evening His Serene Highness arrived at our public house in the suburb of the town which was His Serene Highness' Residence, Nesvij. I cannot say that he arrived in his own high person, for the Hungarian wine had robbed him of all consciousness, in which alone of course personality rests. He was carried into the house and thrown with all his clothes, booted and spurred, on to my mother-in-law's dirty bed, without giving it a supply of clean linen.

As usual, I had to take to flight. My Amazons, however, I mean my mother-in-law and my wife, trusted to their heroic mettle, and remained at home alone. Riot went on the whole night. In the very room where His Serene Highness slept, wood was chopped, cooking and baking were done. It was well known that, when His Serene Highness slept, nothing could waken his high person except perhaps the trumpet of the Judgment-Day. The next morning, when he wakened, and looked around, he scarcely knew whether to trust his eyes, when he found himself in a wretched public-house, thrown on to a dirty bed swarming with bugs. His valets, pages, and negroes

waited on his commands. He asked how he had come
there, and was answered, that His Serene Highness had
yesterday commenced a journey to Mohilna, but had
halted here to take rest, that his whole train had meanwhile gone on, and had undoubtedly arrived in Mohilna
by this time.

The journey to Mohilna was for the present given up,
and the whole train ordered back. They returned
accordingly to the Residence in the usual order and
pomp. But the prince was pleased to hold a great
banquet in our public-house. All the foreign gentlemen,
who happened to be in the place at the time, were
invited. The service used on the occasion was of gold,
and it is impossible adequately to realise the contrast
which reigned here in one house, between Asiatic splendour and Lappish poverty. In a miserable public-house,
whose walls were black as coal with smoke and soot,
whose rafters were supported by undressed round stems
of trees, whose windows consisted of some fragments of
broken panes of bad glass, and small strips of pine
covered with paper,—in this house sat princes on dirty
benches at a still dirtier table, and had the choicest
dishes and the finest wines served to them on gold plate.

Before the banquet the prince took a stroll with the
other gentlemen in front of the house, and by chance
observed my wife. She was then in the bloom of her
youth ; and although I am now separated from her, still
I must do her the justice to allow that—leaving, of course,

out of account all that taste and art contribute to the heightening of a person's charms, inasmuch as these had had no influence on her—she was a beauty of the first rank. It was therefore natural that she should please the prince. He turned to his companions, and said, "Really a pretty young woman! Only she ought to get a white chemise." This was a common signal with him, and meant as much as the throwing of a handkerchief by the Grand Sultan. When these gentlemen therefore heard it, they became solicitous for the honour of my wife, and gave her a hint to clear out as fast as possible. She took the hint, slipped silently out, and was soon over the hills and far away.

After the banquet His Serene Highness proceeded again with the other gentlemen into town amid trumpets, kettle-drums, and the music of his janissaries. Then the usual order of the day was followed; that is, a carousal was carried on the whole afternoon and evening, and then the party went to a pleasure-house at the entrance to the prince's zoological garden, where fire-works were set off at great expense, but usually with accidents. As every goblet was drained, cannons were fired; but the poor cannoneers, who knew better how to handle the plough than the cannon, were not seldom injured. "Vivat Kschondsie Radzivil," that is, "Long live Prince Radzivil," shouted the guests. The palm in this Bacchanalian sport was of course awarded to the prince; and those who awarded it were loaded by him with presents, not in perishable coin or golden snuff-boxes or anything of that sort, but in real estate with many hundred peasants. At the close a concert was given, during which His Serene Highness fell gently asleep, and was carried to the castle.

The expenses of such extravagance were of course extorted from the poor tenantry. If this was not sufficient, debts were contracted, and estates sold to wipe them out. Not even the twelve golden statues in life-size,—whether they represented the twelve apostles or the twelve giants, I do not know,—nor the golden table which had been made for himself, were spared on such emergencies. And thus the noble estates of this great prince were diminished, his treasures which had accumulated during many generations were exhausted, and his tenants——But I must break off.

The prince died not long ago without heirs of his body. His brother's son inherited the estates.

CHAPTER XIII.

Endeavour after mental Culture amid ceaseless Struggles with
Misery of every kind.

By means of the instruction received from my father, but
still more by my own industry, I had got on so well, that
in my eleventh year I was able to pass as a full rabbi.
Besides I possessed some disconnected knowledge in
history, astronomy, and other mathematical sciences. I
burned with desire to acquire more knowledge, but how
was this to be accomplished in the want of guidance, of
scientific books, and of all other means for the purpose ?
I was obliged therefore to content myself with making
use of any help that I could by chance obtain, without
plan or method.

In order to gratify my desire of scientific knowledge,
there were no means available but that of learning foreign
languages. But how was I to begin ? To learn Polish
or Latin with a Catholic teacher was for me impossible,
on the one hand because the prejudices of my own
people prohibited to me all languages but Hebrew, and
all sciences but the Talmud and the vast array of its
commentators, on the other hand because the prejudices

of Catholics would not allow them to give instruction in those matters to a Jew. Moreover I was in very low temporal circumstances. I was obliged to support a whole family by teaching, by correcting proofs of the Holy Scriptures, and by other work of a similar kind. For a long time therefore I had to sigh in vain for the satisfaction of my natural inclination.

At last a fortunate accident came to my help. I observed in some stout Hebrew volumes, that they contained several alphabets, and that the number of their sheets was indicated not merely by Hebrew letters, but that for this purpose the characters of a second and a third alphabet had also been employed, these being commonly Latin and German letters. Now, I had not the slightest idea of printing. I generally imagined that books were printed like linen, and that each page was an impression from a separate form. I presumed however that the characters, which stood in similar places, must represent one and the same letter, and as I had already heard something of the order of the alphabet in these languages, I supposed that, for example, *a*, standing in the same place as *aleph*, must likewise be an aleph in sound. In this way I gradually learnt the Latin and German characters.

By a kind of deciphering I began to combine various German letters into words ; but as the characters used along with the Hebrew letters might be something quite different from these, I remained always doubtful whether the whole of my labour in this operation would not be in vain, till fortunately some leaves of an old German book fell into my hand. I began to read. How great were my joy and surprise, when I saw from the connection, that the words completely corresponded with those which I had learned. 'Tis true, in my Jewish language many of the words were unintelligible ; but from the connection I was still able, with the omission of these words, to comprehend the whole pretty well.*

This mode of learning by deciphering constitutes still my peculiar method of comprehending and judging the thoughts of others ; and I maintain that no one can say he understands a book, as long as he finds himself compelled to deliver the thoughts of the author in the order and connection determined by him, and with the expressions which he has used. This is a mere work of memory, and no man can flatter himself with having comprehended an author till he is roused by his thoughts, which he apprehends at first but dimly, to reflect on the subject

---

* It was probably a reminiscence of this labour of deciphering, that led to the following outburst of sympathy :—" One day Maimon read in an English work, that the author had only commenced to learn the ABC when he was eighteen years of age, and that the first book which fell into his hands was one of Newton's works. His master (for he was a servant) came upon him at this task, and asked, ' What are you doing with that ? you can't read ?' ' O yes,' he replied, ' I have learnt to read, and I began with the most difficult subjects.' Maimon read this in my presence with tears in his eyes." (*Maimoniana*, pp. 230-1). —*Trans.*

himself, and to work it out for himself, though it may be under the impulse of another. This distinction between different kinds of understanding must be evident to any man of discernment.—For the same reason also I can understand a book only when the thoughts which it contains harmonise after filling up the gaps between them.

I still always felt a want which I was not able to fill. I could not completely satisfy my desire of scientific knowledge. Up to this time the study of the Talmud was still my chief occupation. With this however I found pleasure merely in view of its form, for this calls into action the higher powers of the mind; but I took no interest in its matter. It affords exercise in deducing the remotest consequences from their principles, in discovering the most hidden contradictions, in hunting out the finest distinctions, and so forth. But as the principles themselves have merely an imaginary reality, they cannot by any means satisfy a soul thirsting after knowledge.

I looked around therefore for something, by which I could supply this want. Now, I knew that there is a so-called science, which is somewhat in vogue among the Jewish scholars of this district, namely the Cabbalah, which professes to enable a man, not merely to satisfy his desire of knowledge, but also to reach an uncommon perfection and closeness of communion with God. Naturally therefore I burned with desire for this science. As however it cannot, on account of its sacredness, be

publicly taught, but must be taught in secret, I did not
know where to seek the initiated or their writings.

CHAPTER XIV.

I study the Cabbalah, and become at last a Physician.

CABBALAH,—to treat of this divine science somewhat
more in detail,—means, in the wider sense of the term,
tradition ; and it comprehends, not only the occult
sciences which may not be publicly taught, but also the
method of deducing new laws from the laws that are
given in the Holy Scriptures, as also some fundamental
laws which are said to have been delivered orally to
Moses on Mount Sinai.   In the narrower sense of the
term, however, Cabbalah means only the tradition of
occult sciences.   This is divided into *theoretical* and
practical Cabbalah.   The former comprehends the doctrines of God, of His attributes which are expressed by
means of His manifold names, of the origin of the world
through a gradual limitation of His infinite perfection,
and of the relation of all things to His supreme essence.
The latter is the doctrine which teaches how to work
upon nature at pleasure by means of those manifold
names of God, which represent various modes of working
upon, and relations to, natural objects.   These sacred
names are regarded, not as merely arbitrary, but as

natural signs, so that all that is done with these signs must have an influence on the object which they represent.

Originally the Cabbalah was nothing but psychology, physics, morals, politics, and such sciences, represented by means of symbols and hieroglyphs in fables and allegories, the occult meaning of which was disclosed only to those who were competent to understand it. By and by, however, perhaps as the result of many revolutions, this occult meaning was lost, and the signs were taken for the things signified. But as it was easy to perceive that these signs necessarily had meant something, it was left to the imagination to invent an occult meaning which had long been lost. The remotest analogies between signs and things were seized, till at last the Cabbalah degenerated into an art of *madness according to method*, or a systematic science resting on conceits. The big promise of its design, to work effects on nature at pleasure, the lofty strain and the pomp with which it announces itself, have naturally an extraordinary influence on minds of the visionary type, that are unenlightened by the sciences and especially by a thorough philosophy.

The principal work for the study of the Cabbalah is the *Zohar*, which is written in a very lofty style in the Syrian language. All other Cabbalistic writings are to be regarded as merely commentaries on this, or extracts from it.

There are two main systems of the Cabbalah,—the system of Rabbi Moses Kordovero, and that of Rabbi Isaac Luria.* The former is more *real*, that is, it approximates more closely to reason. The latter, on the other hand, is more *formal*, that is, it is completer in the structure of its system. The modern Cabbalists prefer the latter, because they hold that only to be genuine Cabbalah, in which there is no rational meaning. The principal work of Rabbi Moses Kordovero is the *Pardes* (Paradise). Of Rabbi Isaac Luria himself we have some disconnected writings; but his pupil, Rabbi Chajim Vitall, wrote a large work under the title, *Ez Chajim* (The Tree of Life), in which the whole system of his master is contained. This work is held by the Jews to be so sacred, that they do not allow it to be committed to print. Naturally, I had more taste for the Cabbalah of Rabbi Moses than for that of Rabbi Isaac, but durst not give utterance to my opinion on this point.

After this digression on the Cabbalah in general, I return to my story. I learned that the under-rabbi or preacher of the place was an adept in the Cabbalah; and therefore, to attain my object, I made his acquaintance. I took my seat beside him in the synagogue, and as I

---

* Both of these Cabbalists belonged to the sixteenth century. The former, as his name implies, belonged to Cordova in Spain; the latter, to the German community in Jerusalem (*Jost's Geschichte des Judenthums*, Vol. iii., pp. 137-140).—*Trans.*

observed once that after prayer he always read from a small book, and then put it past carefully in its place, I became very curious to know what sort of book this was. Accordingly, after the preacher had gone home, I went and took the book from the place where he had put it; and when I found that it was a Cabbalistic work, I went with it and hid myself in a corner of the synagogue, till all the people had gone out and the door was locked. I then crept from my hiding-place, and, without a thought about eating or drinking the whole day long, read the fascinating book till the doorkeeper came and opened the synagogue again in the evening.

Shaarei Kedushah, or *The Gates of Righteousness*, was the title of this book; and, leaving out of account what was visionary and exaggerated, it contained the principal doctrines of psychology. I did with it therefore as the Talmudists say Rabbi Meïr acted, who had a heretic for his teacher, "He found a pomegranate; he ate the fruit and threw the peel away." *

---

* Rabbi Meir's teacher was Elisha ben Abuyah, "the Faust of the Talmud," as he has been strikingly styled by Mr. Deutsch. The Talmud preserves a beautiful story illustrative of the devoted affection which Meïr continued to cherish for his apostate master. Four men, so runs the legend, entered *Paradise;* that is, according to Talmudic symbolism, they entered upon the study of that secret science with its bewildering labyrinth of speculative dreams, through which it is given only to a few rare spirits to find their way. Of these four, "one beheld and died, one beheld and lost his senses, one destroyed the young plants, one only entered in peace and

In two or three days I had in this way finished the book; but instead of satisfying my curiosity, it only excited it the more. I wished to read more books of the same sort. But as I was too bashful to confess this to the preacher, I resolved to write him a letter, in which I expressed my irresistible longing for this sacred science, and therefore entreated him earnestly to assist me with books. I received from him a very favourable answer. He praised my zeal for the sacred science, and assured me that this zeal, amid so little encouragement, was an obvious sign that my soul was derived from *Olam Aziloth* (the world of the immediate divine influence), while the souls of mere Talmudists take their origin from *Olam Jezirah* (the world of the creation). He promised, therefore, to assist me with books as far as lay in his power. But as he himself was occupied mainly with this science, and required to have such books constantly at hand, he

---

came out in peace." The destroyer of the young plants was Elisha ben Abuyah. Once he was passing the ruins of the temple on the great day of atonement, and heard a voice within "moaning like a dove,"—"All men shall be forgiven this day save Elisha ben Abuyah who, knowing me, has betrayed me." After his death flames hovered incessantly over his grave, until his loving disciple threw himself upon it and swore an oath of devout self-sacrifice, that he would not partake of the joys of heaven without his master, nor move from the spot until his master's soul had found forgiveness before the Throne of Grace. See Emanuel Deutsch's *Literary Remains*, p. 15; and Jost's *Geschichte des Judenthums*, Vol. ii., pp. 102-4.

could not lend them to me, but gave me permission to study them in his house at my pleasure.

Who was gladder than I! I accepted the offer of the preacher with gratitude, scarcely ever left his house, and sat day and night over the Cabbalistic books. Two representations especially gave me the greatest trouble. One was the *Tree*, or the representation of the divine emanations in their manifold and intricate complexities. The other was God's *Beard*, in which the hairs are divided into numerous classes with something peculiar to each, and every hair is a separate channel of divine grace. With all my efforts I could not find in these representations any rational meaning.

My prolonged visits however were extremely inconvenient to the preacher. He had, a short time before, married a pretty young wife ; and as his modest little house consisted of a single apartment, which was at once parlour, study, and bedroom, and as I sat in it at times reading the whole night, it happened not infrequently that my elevation above the sphere of sense came into collision with his sensibility. Consequently, he hit upon a good plan for getting rid of the incipient Cabbalist. He said to me one day, " I observe that it necessarily puts you to a great deal of inconvenience to spend your time constantly away from home for the sake of these books. You may take them home with you one by one if you please, and thus study them at your convenience."

To me nothing could be more welcome. I took home

one book after another, and studied them till I believed that I had mastered the whole of the Cabbalah. I contented myself not merely with the knowledge of its principles and manifold systems, but sought also to make a proper use of these. There was not a passage to be met with in the Holy Scriptures or in the Talmud, the occult meaning of which I could not have unfolded, according to Cabbalistic principles, with the greatest readiness.

The book entitled *Shaarei Orah* * came to be of very good service here. In this book are enumerated the manifold names of the ten *Sephiroth*, which form the principal subject of the Talmud, so that a hundred or more names are given to each. In every word of a verse in the Bible, or of a passage in the Talmud, I found therefore the name of some Sephirah. But as I knew the attribute of every Sephirah, and its relation to the rest, I could easily bring out of the combination of names their conjoint effect.

To illustrate this by a brief example, I found in the book just mentioned, that the name *Jehovah* represents the six highest Sephiroth (not including the first three), or the person of the Godhead *generis masculini*, while the word *Koh* means the *Shechinah* or the person of the Godhead *generis feminini*, and the word *amar* denotes sexual

---

* *The Gates of Light.—Trans.*

union. The words, " Koh amar Jehova,"* therefore,
I explained in the following way, " Jehovah unites with
the Shechinah," and this is high Cabbalism. Accordingly, when I read this passage in the Bible, I thought
nothing else, but that, when I uttered these words, and
thought their occult meaning, an actual union of these
divine spouses took place, from which the whole world
had to expect a blessing. Who can restrain the excesses
of imagination, when it is not guided by reason ?

With the *Cabbalah Maasith*, or the *practical Cabbalah*,
I did not succeed so well as with the theoretical. The
preacher boasted, not publicly indeed, but to everybody
in private, that he was master of this also. Especially he
professed *roeh veeno nireh* (to see everything, but not to
be seen by others), that is, to be able to make himself
invisible.

About this trick I was specially anxious, in order that
I might practise some wanton jokes on my comrades.
More particularly I formed a plan for keeping my ill-
tempered mother-in-law in check by this means. I
pretended that my object was merely to do good, and
guard against evil. The preacher consented, but said at
the same time, that on my part certain preparations were
required. Three days in succession I was to feast, and
every day to say some *Ichudim*. These are Cabbalistic
forms of prayer, whose occult meaning aims at produc-

---

* " Thus saith the Lord " in the English version. —*Trans.*

ing in the intellectual world sexual unions, through means of which certain results are to be brought about in the physical.

I did everything with pleasure, made the conjuration which he had taught me, and believed with all confidence that I was now invisible. At once I hurried to the *Beth Hamidrash*, the Jewish academy, went up to one of my comrades, and gave him a vigorous box on the ear. He however was no coward, and returned the blow with interest. I started back in astonishment; I could not understand how he had been able to discover me, as I had observed with the utmost accuracy the instructions of the preacher. Still I thought I might, perhaps, un-wittingly and unintentionally have neglected something. I resolved, therefore, to undertake the operation anew. This time, however, I was not going to venture on the test of a box on the ear; I went into the academy merely to watch my comrades as a spectator. As soon as I entered, however, one of them came up to me, and showed me a difficult passage in the Talmud, which he wished me to explain. I stood utterly confounded, and disconsolate over the failure of my hopes.

Thereupon I went to the preacher, and informed him of my unsuccessful attempt. Without blushing, he replied quite boldly, "If you have observed all my in-structions, I cannot explain this otherwise than by sup-posing that you are unfit for being thus divested of the visibility of your body." With great grief, therefore, I was obliged to give up entirely the hope of making myself invisible.

This disappointed hope was followed by a new delusion. In the preface to the *Book of Raphael*, which the angel of that name is said to have delivered to our first father Adam at his banishment from paradise, I found the promise, that whoever keeps the book in his house is thereby insured against fire. It was not long, however, before a conflagration broke out in the neighbourhood, when the fire seized my house too, and the angel Raphael himself had to go up into heaven in this chariot of fire.

Unsatisfied with the literary knowledge of this science, I sought to penetrate into its spirit ; and as I perceived that the whole science, if it is to deserve this name, can contain nothing but the secrets of nature concealed in fables and allegories, I laboured to find out these secrets, and thereby to raise my merely literary knowledge to a rational knowledge. This, however, I could accomplish only in a very imperfect manner at the time, because I had yet very few ideas of the sciences in general. Still, by independent reflection I hit upon many applications of this kind. Thus, for example, I explained at once the first instance with which the Cabbalists commonly begin their science.

It is this. Before the world was created, the divine being occupied the whole of infinite space alone. But God wished to create a world, in order that He might reveal those attributes of His nature which refer to other beings besides Himself. For this purpose He contracted Himself into the centre of His perfection, and issued into the space thereby left void ten concentric circles of light, out of which arose afterwards manifold figures (*Parzophim*) and gradations down to the present world of sense.

I could not in any way conceive that all this was to be taken in the common sense of the words, as nearly all Cabbalists represent it. As little could I conceive that, before the world had been created, a time had past, as I knew from my *Moreh Nebhochim*, that time is a modification of the world, and consequently cannot be thought without it. Moreover, I could not conceive that God occupies a space, even though it be infinite; or that He, an infinitely perfect being, should contract Himself, like a thing of circular form, into a centre.

Accordingly I sought to explain all this in the following way. God is prior to the world, not in time, but in His necessary being as the condition of the world. All things besides God must depend on Him as their cause, in regard to their essence as well as their existence. The creation of the world, therefore, could not be thought as a bringing forth *out of nothing*, nor as a formation of something independent on God, but only as a bringing forth *out of Himself*. And as beings are of different grades of perfection, we must assume for their explanation different grades of limitation of the divine being. But since this limitation must be thought as extending from the infinite being down to matter, we represent the beginning of the limitation in a figure as a centre (the lowest point) of the Infinite.

In fact, the Cabbalah is nothing but an expanded Spinozism, in which not only is the origin of the world explained by the limitation of the divine being, but also the origin of every kind of being, and its relation to the rest, are derived from a separate attribute of God. God, as the ultimate subject and the ultimate cause of all beings, is called Ensoph (the Infinite, of which, considered in itself, nothing can be predicated). But in relation to the infinite number of beings, positive attributes are ascribed to Him; these are reduced by the Cabbalists to ten, which are called the ten Sephiroth.

In the book, *Pardes*, by Rabbi Moses Kordovero, the question is discussed, whether the Sephiroth are to be taken for the Deity Himself or not. It is easy to be seen, however, that this question has no more difficulty in reference to the Deity, than in reference to any other being.

Under the ten circles I conceived the ten categories or predicaments of Aristotle, with which I had become acquainted in the *Moreh Nebhochim*,—the most universal predicates of things, without which nothing can be thought. The categories, in the strictest critical sense, are the logical forms, which relate not merely to a *logical* object, but to *real* objects in general, and without which these cannot be thought. They have their source, there-

H

fore, in the subject itself, but they become an object of consciousness only by reference to a real object. Consequently, they represent the ten Sephiroth, which belong, indeed, to the Ensoph in itself, but of which the reality is revealed only by their special relation to, and effect upon, objects in nature, and the number of which can be variously determined in various points of view.

But by this method of explanation I brought upon myself many an annoyance. For the Cabbalists maintain that the Cabbalah is not a human, but a divine, science; and that, consequently, it would be degradation of it, to explain its mysteries in accordance with nature and reason. The more reasonable, therefore, my explanations proved, the more were the Cabbalists irritated with me, inasmuch as they held that alone to be divine, which had no reasonable meaning. Accordingly I had to keep my explanations to myself. An entire work, that I wrote on the subject, I brought with me to Berlin, and preserve still as a monument of the struggle of the human mind after perfection, in spite of all the hindrances which are placed in its way.

Meanwhile this could not satisfy me. I wished to get an insight into the sciences, not as they are veiled in fables, but in their natural light. I had already, though very imperfectly, learned to read German; but where was I to obtain German books in Lithuania? Fortunately for me I learned that the chief rabbi of a neighbouring town, who in his youth had lived for a while in

Germany, and learned the German language there, and made himself in some measure acquainted with the sciences, continued still, though in secret, to work at the sciences, and had a fair library of German books.

I resolved therefore to make a pilgrimage to S——, in order to see the chief rabbi, and beg of him a few scientific books. I was tolerably accustomed to such journeys, and had gone once thirty miles* on foot to see a Hebrew work of the tenth century on the Peripatetic philosophy. Without therefore troubling myself in the least about travelling expenses or means of conveyance, and without saying a word to my family on the subject, I set out upon the journey to this town in the middle of winter. As soon as I arrived at the place, I went to the chief rabbi, told him my desire, and begged him earnestly for assistance. He was not a little astonished; for, during the thirty one years which had passed since his return from Germany, not a single individual had ever made such a request. He promised to lend me some old German books. The most important among these were an old work on Optics, and Sturm's *Physics.*

I could not sufficiently express my gratitude to this excellent chief rabbi; I pocketed the few books, and returned home in rapture. After I had studied these books thoroughly, my eyes were all at once opened. I believed that I had found a key to all the secrets of

---

* About 150 English miles.—*Trans.*

nature, as I now knew the origin of storms, of dew, of rain, and such phenomena. I looked down with pride on all others, who did not yet know these things, laughed at their prejudices and superstitions, and proposed to clear up their ideas on these subjects and to enlighten their understanding.

But this did not always succeed. I laboured once to teach a Talmudist, that the earth is round, and that we have antipodes. He however made the objection, that these antipodes would necessarily fall off. I endeavoured to show that the falling of a body is not directed towards any fixed point in empty space, but towards the centre of the earth, and that the ideas of Over and Under represent merely the removal from and approach to this centre. It was of no avail; the Talmudist stood to his ground, that such an assertion was absurd.

On another occasion I went to take a walk with some of my friends. It chanced that a goat lay in the way. I gave the goat some blows with my stick, and my friends blamed me for my cruelty. "What is the cruelty?" I replied. "Do you believe that the goat feels a pain, when I beat it? You are greatly mistaken; the goat is a mere machine." This was the doctrine of Sturm as a disciple of Descartes.

My friends laughed heartily at this, and said, "But don't you hear that the goat cries, when you beat it?" "Yes," I replied, "of course it cries; but if you beat a drum, it cries too." They were amazed at my answer, and in a short time it went abroad over the whole town, that I had become mad, as I held that *a goat is a drum.*

From my generous friend, the chief rabbi, I received afterwards two medical works, Kulm's *Anatomical Tables* and Voit's *Gaziopilatium.* The latter is a large medical dictionary, containing, in a brief form, not only explanations from all departments of medicine, but also their manifold applications. In connection with every disease is given an explanation of its cause, its symptoms, and the method of its cure, along with even the ordinary prescriptions. This was for me a real treasure. I studied the book thoroughly, and believed myself to be master of the science of medicine, and a complete physician.

But I was not going to content myself with mere theory in this matter ; I resolved to make regular application of it. I visited patients, determined all diseases according to their circumstances and symptoms, explained their causes, and gave also prescriptions for their cure. But in this practice things turned out very comically. If a patient told me some of the symptoms of his disease, I guessed from them the nature of the disease itself, and inferred the presence of the other symptoms. If the patient said that he could trace none of these, I stubbornly insisted on their being present all the same. The conversation therefore sometimes came to this :—

I. " You have headache also,"

Patient. "No."

I. "But you *must* have headache."

As many symptoms are common to several diseases, I took not infrequently *quid pro quo.* Prescriptions I could never keep in my head, so that, when I prescribed anything, I was obliged to go home first and turn up my *Gaziopilatium.* At length I began even to make up drugs myself according to Voit's prescriptions. How this succeeded, may be imagined. It had at least this good result, that I saw something more was surely required for a practical physician than I understood at the time.

CHAPTER XV.

A brief Exposition of the Jewish Religion, from its Origin down
to the most recent Times.

To render intelligible that part of the story of my life,
which refers to my sentiments regarding religion, I must
first give in advance a short practical *history of the Jewish
religion*, and at the outset say something of the idea of
religion in general, as well as of the difference between
natural and *positive* religion.

Religion in general is the expression of gratitude,
reverence and the other feelings, which arise from the
dependence of our weal and woe on one or more
powers to us unknown. If we look to the *expression of
these feelings in general*, without regard to the *particular
mode of the expression*, religion is certainly natural to man.
He observes many effects which are of interest to him,
but whose causes are to him unknown ; and he finds
himself compelled, by the universally recognised *Principle
of Sufficient Reason*, to suppose these causes, and to
express towards them the feelings mentioned.

This expression may be of two kinds, in conformity
either with the *imagination* or with *reason*. For either

man imagines the causes to be analogous to the effects, and ascribes to them in themselves such attributes as are revealed through the effects, or he thinks them merely as causes of certain effects, without seeking thereby to determine their attributes in themselves. These two modes are both natural to man, the former being in accordance with his earlier condition, the latter with that of his perfection.

The difference between these two modes of representation has as its consequence another difference of religions. The first mode of representation, in accordance with which the causes are supposed to be *similar* to the effects, is the mother of *polytheism* or *heathenism*. But the second is the basis of *true* religion. For as the kinds of effects are different, the causes also, if held to be like them, must be represented as different from one another. On the other hand, if, in accordance with truth, we conceive the idea of *cause in general* for these effects, without seeking to determine this cause, either *in itself* (since it is wholly unknown), or *analogically* by help of the imagination, then we have no ground for supposing several causes, but require to assume merely a single subject, wholly unknown, as cause of all these effects.

The different philosophical systems of theology are nothing but *detailed developments* of these different modes of representation. The *atheistic* system of theology, if so it may be called, rejects altogether this idea of a *first cause*, (as, according to the *critical* system at least, it is merely of *regulative use* as a necessary *idea of reason*). All effects are referred to particular known or unknown causes. In this there cannot be assumed even a *connection* between the various effects, else the *reason* of this connection would require to be sought beyond the connection itself.

The *Spinozistic* system, on the contrary, supposes one and the same substance as immediate cause of all various effects, which must be regarded as predicates of one and the same subject. *Matter* and *mind* are, with Spinoza, one and the same substance, which appears, now under the former, now under the latter attribute. This single substance is, according to him, not only the sole being that can be *self-dependent*, that is, independent of any external cause, but also the sole *self-subsistent* being, all so-called beings besides it being merely its *modes,* that is, particular limitations of its attributes. Every particular effect in nature is referred by him, not to its proximate cause (which is merely a *mode*), but immediately to this first cause, which is the common substance of all beings.

In this system *unity* is *real*, but *multiplicity* is merely *ideal.* In the atheistic system it is the opposite. *Multiplicity* is *real*, being founded on the *nature of things themselves.* On the other hand, the *unity*, which is observed in the order and regularity of nature, is merely an *accident*, by which we are accustomed to determine our *arbitrary* system *for the sake of knowledge.* It is inconceivable therefore how any one can make out the Spinozistic system to be atheistic, since the two systems are diametrically opposed to one another. In the latter the existence of *God* is denied, but in the former the existence of the *world*. Spinoza's ought therefore to be called rather the *acosmic* system.

The *Leibnitzian* system holds the mean between the two preceding. In it all *particular effects* are referred immediately to *particular causes ;* but these various effects are thought as *connected* in a single system, and the cause of this connection is sought in a being beyond itself.

Positive religion is distinguished from *natural* in the very same way as the positive laws of a state from natural laws. The latter are those which rest on a self-acquired, indistinct knowledge, and are not duly defined in regard to their application, while the former rest on a distinct knowledge received from others, and are completely defined in regard to their application.

A *positive* religion however must be carefully distinguished from a *political* religion. The former has for its end merely the correction and accurate definition of knowledge, that is, *instruction* regarding the first cause : and the knowledge is communicated to another, according to the measure of his capacity, just as it has been received. But the latter has for its end mainly the welfare of the state. Knowledge is therefore communicated, not just as it has been received, but only in so far as it is found serviceable to this end. Politics, merely as politics, requires to concern itself about *true religion* as little as about *true morality*. The injury, that might arise from this, can be prevented by other means which influence men at the same time, and thus all can be kept in equilibrium. Every political religion is therefore at the same time positive, but every positive religion is not also political.

Natural religion has no *mysteries* any more than merely positive religion. For there is no mystery implied in one man being unable to communicate his knowledge to another of defective capacity with the same degree of completeness which he himself has attained; otherwise mysteries might be attributed to all the sciences, and there would then be *mysteries of mathematics* as well as *mysteries of religion.* Only *political religion* can have mysteries, in order to lead men in an indirect way to the attainment of the *political end*, inasmuch as they are made to believe that thereby they can best attain their *private ends*, though this is not always in reality the case. There are *lesser* and *greater* mysteries in the political religions. The former consist in the *material* knowledge of all particular operations and their connection with one another. The latter, on the contrary, consist in the knowledge of the *form*, that is, of the end by which the former are determined. The former constitute the totality of the *laws of religion*, but the latter contains the *spirit of the laws.*

The *Jewish religion*, even at its earliest origin among the nomadic patriarchs, is already distinguished from the *heathen* as *natural religion*, inasmuch as, instead of the *many comprehensible* gods of heathenism, the *unity of an incomprehensible* God lies at its foundation. For as the particular causes of the effects, which in general give rise to a religion, are in themselves unknown, and we do not feel justified in transferring to the causes the attributes of the particular effects, in order thereby to characterise them, there remains nothing but the idea of cause in general, which must be related to all effects without distinction. This cause cannot even be *analogically* determined by the effects. For the effects are opposed to one another, and neutralise each other even in the same object. If therefore we ascribed them all to one and the same cause, the cause could not be analogically determined by any.

The *heathen* religion, on the other hand, refers every kind of effect to a special cause, which can of course be characterised by its effect. As a *positive* religion the Jewish is distinguished from the heathen by the fact, that it is not a merely political religion, that is, a religion which has for its end the social interest (in opposition to true knowledge and private interest); but in accordance with the spirit of its founder, it is adapted to the theocratic form of the national Government, which rests on the principle, that only the true religion, based on rational knowledge, can harmonise with the interest of the state as well as of the individual. Considered in its *purity*, therefore, it has no mysteries in the proper sense of the word ; that is to say, it has no doctrines which, in order to reach their end, men *will* not disclose, but merely such as *can* not be disclosed to all.

After the fall of the Jewish state the religion was separated from the state which no longer existed. The religious authorities were no longer, as they had been before, concerned about adapting the particular institutions of religion to the state ; but their care went merely to *preserve* the religion, on which the existence of the *nation* now depended. Moved by hatred towards those nations who had annihilated the state, and from anxiety lest with the fall of the state the religion also might fall, they hit upon the following means for the preservation and extension of their religion.

1. The fiction of a method, handed down from Moses, of expanding the laws, and applying them to particular cases. This method is not that which reason enjoins, of modifying laws according to their intention, in adaptation to time and circumstances, but that which rests upon certain rules concerning their literary expression.

2. The legislative force ascribed to the new decisions and opinions obtained by this method, giving to them an equal rank with the ancient laws. The subtle dialectic, with which this has been carried on down to our times, and the vast number of laws, customs and useless

ceremonies of all sorts, which it has occasioned, may be easily imagined.

The history of the Jewish religion can, in consequence of this, be appropriately divided into five great epochs. The first epoch embraces the *natural religion*, from the times of the patriarchs down to Moses at the exodus from Egypt. The second comprehends the *positive* or *revealed* religion, from Moses to the time of the *Great Synagogue* (*Keneseth Haggedolah*). This council must not be conceived as an assembly of theologians at a definite time ; the name applies to the theologians of a whole epoch from the destruction of the first temple to the composition of the Mishnah. Of these the first were the *minor prophets* (Haggai, Zachariah, Malachi, etc., of whom 120 are counted altogether), and the last was *Simon the Just.** These, as well as their forerunners from the time of Joshua, took as their basis the Mosaic laws, and added new laws according to time and circumstances, but in conformity with the traditional method, every dispute on the subject being decided by the *majority of voices.*

The third epoch extends from the composition of the Mishnah by Jehudah the Saint † to the composition of

---

* Highpriest about the time of Antiochus the Great, that is, the first half of the third century before Christ.—*Trans.*

† Also named below Jehudah Hanassi or Hakades, died probably in 219 or 220 A.D.—*Trans.*

the Talmud by Rabina and Rabassi. * Down to this epoch it was forbidden to commit the laws to writing, in order that they might not fall into the hands of those who could make no use of them. But as Rabbi Jehudah Hanassi, or, as he is otherwise called, Rabbenu Hakades observed, that, in consequence of their great multiplicity, the laws may easily fall into oblivion, he gave himself a licence to transgress a single one of the laws in order to preserve the whole. The law transgressed was that against committing the laws to writing; and in this licence he defended himself by a passage in the Psalms, "There are times, when a man shows himself well-pleasing to God by transgressing the laws." † He lived in the time of Antoninus Pius, was rich, and possessed all the faculties for such an undertaking. He therefore composed the Mishnah, in which he delivers the Mosaic laws in accordance either with a traditional or with a rational method of exposition. It contains also some laws which form the subject of dispute.

This work is divided into six parts. The first contains the laws relating to agriculture and horticulture; the

---

* *Rabbina* is a contraction for Rabbi Abina and *Rabassi* for Rabbi Ashe. Maimon puts Abina first, but he was the younger of the two. They both belonged to the fifth century.—*Trans.*

† This seems to be Psalm cxix., 126, rendered in our Authorised Version:—"It is time for thee, Lord, to work; for they have made void thy law." See Mendelssohn's *Jerusalem,* Vol. ii., p. iii., (Samuels' translation).—*Trans.*

second, those which refer to feasts and holidays. The third part comprehends the laws which define the mutual relations of the two sexes (marriage, divorce, and such subjects). The fourth part is devoted to the laws which deal with the teachers of the law; the fifth, to those which treat of the temple-service and sacrifices; and the sixth, to the laws of purification.

As the Mishnah is composed with the greatest precision, and cannot be understood without a commentary, it was natural, that in course of time doubts and disputes should arise, regarding the exposition of the Mishnah itself, as well as the mode of its application to cases which it does not sufficiently determine. All these doubts and their manifold solutions, controversies and decisions, were finally collected in the Talmud by the above-mentioned Rabina and Rabassi; and this forms the fourth epoch of Jewish legislation.

The fifth epoch begins with the conclusion of the Talmud, and extends down to our time, and so on for ever (*si diis placet*) till the advent of the Messiah. Since the conclusion of the Talmud the rabbis have been by no means idle. 'Tis true, they dare not alter anything in the Mishnah or the Talmud; but they still have plenty of work to do. Their business is to explain those two works, so that they shall harmonise; and this is no small matter, for one rabbi, with a superfine dialectic, is always finding contradictions in the explanations of another. They must also disentangle, from the labyrinth of various opinions, expositions, controversies and decisions, the laws which are applicable to every case ; and finally for new cases, by inferences from those already known, they must bring out new laws, hitherto left indeterminate in spite of all previous labours, and thus prepare a complete code of laws.

It is thus that a religion, in its origin *natural* and *conformable to reason*, has been abused. A Jew dare not eat or drink, lie with his wife or attend to the wants of nature, without observing an enormous number of laws. With the books on the *slaughter* of animals alone (the condition of the knife and the examination of the entrails) a whole library could be filled, which certainly would come near to the Alexandrian in extent. And what shall I say of the enormous number of books treating of those laws which are no longer in use, such as the laws of sacrifice, of purification, etc. ? The pen falls from my hand, when I remember that I and others like me were obliged to spend in this soul-killing business the best days of our lives when the powers are in their full vigour, and to sit up many a night, to try and bring out some sense where there was none, to exercise our wits in the discovery of contradictions where none were to be found, to display acuteness in removing them where they were obviously to be met, to hunt after a shadow through a long series of arguments, and to build castles in the air.

The abuse of Rabbinism has, as will be seen, a twofold source.

I

1. The first is an *artificial method* of expounding the Holy Scriptures, which distinguishes itself from the *natural* method by the fact, that, while the latter rests on a thorough *knowledge of the language* and the true *spirit of the legislator* in view of the circumstances of the time, as these are known from history, the former has been devised rather for the sake of the laws passed to meet existing emergencies. The rabbis look upon the Holy Scriptures, not only as the source of the fundamental laws of Moses, and of those which are deducible from these by a rational method, but also as a vehicle of the laws to be drawn up by themselves according to the wants of the time. The artificial method here, like every other of the same kind, is merely a means of bringing the new laws at least into an *external connection* with the old, in order that they may thereby find a better introduction among the people, be reduced to principles, divided into classes, and therefore more easily impressed on the memory. No reasonable rabbi will hold, that the laws, which are referred in this way to passages of the Holy Scriptures, render the true sense of these passages; but if questioned on this point, he will reply, "These laws are necessities of the time, and are referred to those passages merely for this reason."

2. The second source of the abuse of Rabbinism is to be found in the manners and customs of other nations, in whose neighbourhood the Jews have lived, or among whom they have been gradually scattered since the fall

of the Jewish state. These manners and customs they were obliged to adopt in order to avoid becoming objects of abhorrence. Of this sort are the laws, *not to uncover the head* (at least in holy places and at holy ceremonies), *to wash the hands* (before meals and prayers), to fast the whole day till sunset, to say a number of daily prayers, to make pilgrimages, to walk round the altar, etc.,—all manifestly of *Arabian* origin.

From hatred also towards those nations that destroyed the Jewish state, and afterwards made the Jews undergo manifold oppressions, they have adopted various customs, and among others many religious usages which are opposite to those of the *Greeks* and *Romans*.

In all this the rabbis had the Mosaic laws themselves for a model, these being sometimes in agreement, sometimes in hostility, with the Egyptian laws which lie at their root, as has been shown in the most thorough manner by the celebrated Maimonides in his work, *Moreh Nebhochim*.

It is remarkable, that, with all rabbinical extravagancies in the *practical* department, namely the laws and customs, the *theoretical* department of the Jewish theology has still always preserved itself in its purity. Eisenmenger may say what he will, it may be shown by unanswerable arguments, that all the limited figurative representations of God and His attributes have their source merely in an endeavour to adapt the ideas of theology to the common understanding. The rabbis followed in this the principle

which they had established in reference to the Holy
Scriptures themselves, namely, that *the Holy Scriptures
use the language of the common people*, inasmuch as
religious and moral sentiments and actions, which form
the immediate aim of theology may in this manner be
most easily extended.   They therefore represent God to
the common understanding as an earthly King, who
with His ministers and the advisers of His cabinet, the
angels, takes counsel concerning the government of the
world.   But for the educated mind they seek to take
away all anthropomorphic representations of God, when
they say, "It was an act of high daring on the part of
the prophets, to represent the Creator as like His creature,
as when, for example, it is said in Ezekiel (i., 26), 'And
upon the throne was an appearance like man.'"

I have disclosed the abuses of the rabbis in regard to
religion without any partiality.   At the same time however
I must not be silent about their good qualities, but do
them justice as impartially.   Compare then Mahomed's
description of the reward of the pious with the rabbinical
representation.   The former runs: —"Here (in paradise)
there are as many dishes as there are stars in heaven.
Maidens and boys fill the cups, and wait on the table.
The beauty of the maidens surpasses all imagination.   If
one of these maidens were to appear in the sky or in the
air by night, the world would become as bright as when
the sun is shining ; and if she were to spit into the sea,
its salt water would be turned into honey, and its bitter

into sweet. Milk, honey, white wine will be the rivers which water this delicious abode. The slime of these rivers will be made of sweet-smelling nutmegs, and their pebbles of pearls and hyacinths. The angel Gabriel will open the gates of paradise to faithful Musselmans. The first thing to meet their eyes will be a table of diamonds of such enormous length, that it would require 70,000 days to run round it. The chairs, which stand around the table, will be of gold and silver, the tablecloths of silk and gold. When the guests have sat down, they will eat the choicest dishes of paradise, and drink its water. When they are satisfied, beautiful boys will bring them *green* garments of costly stuff, and necklaces and earrings of gold. To every one will then be given a citron; and when he has brought it to his nose to feel its odour, a maiden of enchanting beauty will come out. Every one will embrace his own with rapture, and this intoxication of love will last fifty years without interruption. Each couple will obtain an enchanting palace for a dwelling, where they will eat and drink and enjoy all sorts of pleasure for ever and ever.*" This description is beautiful; but how sensuous! The rabbis, on the other hand, say, " Above (in the blessed abode of the pious) there is neither eating nor drinking, but the pious sit crowned, and delight themselves with the vision of the Godhead."

---

* *Charakteristik der Asiatischen Nationen*, Theil ii., pp. 159-160.

Eisenmenger seeks, in his *Entdecktes Judenthum* (Theil I., Kap. 8), by a crass exposition to throw ridicule on the Platonic doctrine of reminiscence, which the rabbis maintain; but what may not be made ridiculous in the same way? He also makes sport, with equal injustice, of other rabbinical teachings. With the Stoics, for example, the rabbis call wise men *Kings*; they say, that God does nothing without previously taking counsel with his angels, that is, Omnipotence works upon nature not immediately, but by means of the natural forces; they teach, that everything is predestined by God, except the practice of virtue. These are the subjects of Eisenmenger's mockery; but does any reasonable theologian find in these anything ridiculous or impious? I should be obliged to write a whole book, if I were to answer all the unjust charges and jeers which have been brought against the Talmudists, not by Christian writers alone, but even by Jews who wished to pass for *illuminati*.

To be just to the rabbis it is necessary to penetrate into the true spirit of the Talmud, to become thoroughly familiar with the manner in which the ancients generally, but especially the Orientals, deliver theological, moral, and even physical truths in fables and allegories, to become familiar also with the style of Oriental hyperbole in reference to everything that can be of interest to man. Moreover, the rabbis should be treated in the spirit in which they themselves excused Rabbi Meir who had a heretic for his teacher,—the spirit expressed in a passage already quoted. If justice is thus dealt to the rabbis, the Talmud will certainly not show all the absurdities which its opponents are disposed too readily to find.

The rabbinical method of referring theoretical or practical truths, even by the oddest exegesis, to passages in the Holy Scriptures or any other book in general esteem, as if they were truths brought out of such passages by a rational exegesis,—this method, besides procuring an introduction for the truths among common men, who are not capable of grasping them on their own merits, and accept them merely on authority, is also to be regarded as an excellent aid to the memory ; for since, as presumed, these passages are in everybody's mouth, the truths drawn from them are also retained by their means. Consequently it very often occurs in the Talmud, when the question concerns the deduction of a new law from the Holy Scriptures, that one rabbi derives the law from this or that passage, while another brings the objection, that this cannot be the true meaning of the passage, inasmuch as the true meaning is this or that. To such an objection every one is wont to reply, that it is a new law of the rabbis, who merely refer it to the passage mentioned.

As it is therefore universally presupposed that this method is familiar, the Talmudists regard it as unnecessary to inculcate it anew on every occasion. A single example will suffice to illustrate this. One Talmudist asked another the meaning of the following passage in the Book of Joshua (xv., 22), *Kinah Vedimonah Vead-adah.** The latter replied, " Here are enumerated the then familiar places of the Holy Land." " Of course !" rejoined the other. " I know very well that these are names of places. But, Rabbi —— knows how to bring out of these, besides the proper meaning, something *use-ful,* namely this :—' (Kinah) He to whom his neighbour gives occasion for revenge, (Vedimonah) and who yet, out of generosity, keeps silence, taking no revenge, (Veadadah) to him will the Eternal execute justice.'" What a fine opportunity this would be for laughing at the poor Talmudist, who derives a moral sentence from particular names of places, and besides makes in an extraordinary manner a compound out of the last name, *Sansannah,*† if he had not himself explained that he is seeking to know, not the *true meaning* of the passage, but merely a *doctrine* which may be referred to it.

Again, the Talmudists have referred to a passage in Isaiah the important doctrine, that in morals the princi-pal object is, not theory, but practice, by which theory receives its true value. The passage runs as follows :—
" The expectation of thy happiness "—that is, the happi-

---

* " And Kinah and Dimonah and Adadah " in the English Authorised Version.—*Trans.*

† Here apparently Maimon makes a slip. He seems to forget the passage he had selected for illustration ; and his eye, if not his memory, glances at the last word in verse 30, instead of verse 22. —*Trans.*

ness promised by the prophet—" will have for its consequence strength, help, wisdom, knowledge, and the fear
of God." * Here they refer the first six subjects to the
six *Sedarim* or divisions of the Mishnah, which are the
foundation of all Jewish learning. *Emunath* (Expectation) is Seder Seraim ; *Etecho* (Happiness) is Seder
Moad, and so on. That is to say, you may be ever so
well versed in all these six *sedarim ;* yet the main point
is the last, the fear of God.

As far as rabbinical morals in other respects are concerned, I know in truth nothing that can be urged
against them, except perhaps their excessive strictness in
many cases. They form in fact genuine Stoicism, but
without excluding other serviceable principles, such as
perfection, universal benevolence, and the like. Holi-
ness with them extends even to the thoughts. This
principle is, in the usual fashion, referred to the following passage in the Psalms, "Thou shalt have no strange
God in thee " ; † for in the human heart, it is argued, no
strange God can dwell, except evil desires. It is not
allowed to deceive even a heathen either by deeds or by
words—not even in cases where he could lose nothing
by the deceit. For example, the common form of courtesy, "I am glad to see you well," is not to be used, if it
does not express the real sentiments of the heart. The

---

* Probably Isaiah xxxiii., 6.—*Trans.*

† Psalm, lxxxi., 9.—*Trans.*

examples of Jews who cheat Christians and heathens, which are commonly adduced against this statement, prove nothing, inasmuch as these Jews do not act in accordance with the principles of their own morals.

The commandment, "Thou shalt not covet anything that is thy neighbour's," is so expounded by the Talmudists, that we must guard against even the wish to possess any such thing. In short, I should require to write a whole book, if I were to adduce all the excellent doctrines of rabbinical morals.

The influence of these doctrines in practical life also is unmistakable. The Polish Jews, who have always been allowed to adopt any means of gain, and have not, like the Jews of other countries, been restricted to the pitiful occupation of *Schacher* or usurer, seldom hear the reproach of cheating. They remain loyal to the country in which they live, and support themselves in an honourable way.

Their charity and care for the poor, their institutions for nursing the sick, their special societies for burial of the dead, are well enough known. It is not nurses and grave-diggers *hired for money*, but the *elders of the people*, who are eager to perform these acts. The Polish Jews are indeed for the most part not yet enlightened by science, their manners and way of life are still rude ; but they are loyal to the religion of their fathers and the laws of their country. They do not come before you with courtesies, but their promise is sacred. They are not gallants, but your women are safe from any snares with them. Woman, indeed, after the manner of the Orientals in general, is by them not particularly esteemed; but all the more on that account are they resolved on fulfilling their duties towards her. Their children do not learn by heart any *forms* for expressing love and respect for their parents—for they do not keep French *demoiselles;*—but they show that love and respect all the more heartily.

The sacredness of their marriages, and the ever fresh tenderness which arises from this, deserve especially to be mentioned. Every month the husband is wholly separated from his wife for a fortnight (the period of monthly purification in accordance with the rabbinical laws); they may not so much as touch one another, or eat out of the same dish or drink out of the same cup. By this means satiety is avoided; the wife continues to be in the eyes of her husband all that she was as maiden in the eyes of her lover.

Finally, what innocence rules among unmarried persons! It often happens that a young man or woman of sixteen or eighteen years is married without knowing the least about the object of marriage. Among other nations this is certainly very seldom the case.

CHAPTER XVI.

Jewish Piety and Penances.

IN my youth I was of a somewhat strong religious disposition; and as I observed in most of the rabbis a good deal of pride, quarrelsomeness, and other evil qualities, they became objects of dislike to me on that account. I sought therefore as my model only those among them, who are commonly known by the name of *Chasidim*, or *the Pious*. These are they who devote the whole of their lives to the strictest observances of the laws and moral virtues. I had afterwards occasion to remark that these on their part do harm, less indeed to *others*, but all the more to *themselves*, inasmuch as they root out the wheat with the tares;* while they seek to suppress their desires and passions, they suppress also their powers and cramp their activity, so much so as in most cases by their exercises to bring upon themselves an untimely death.

Two or three instances, of which I was myself an eye-witness, will be sufficient to establish what has been said.

---

* In the original, "Das Kind mit dem Bade ausschütten."—*Trans.*

A Jewish scholar, at that time well known on account of his piety, Simon of Lubtsch, had undergone the severest exercises of penance. He had already carried out the *T'shubath Hakana*—the penance of Kana—which consists in fasting daily for six years, and avoiding for supper anything that comes from a living being (flesh, milk, honey, etc.). He had also practised *Golath*, that is, a continuous wandering, in which the penitent is not allowed to remain two days in the same place ; and, in addition, he had worn a hair-shirt next his skin. But he felt that he would not be doing enough for the satisfaction of his conscience unless he further observed the *T'shubath Hamishkal*—the penance of weighing—which requires a particular form of penance proportioned to every sin. But as he found by calculation, that the number of his sins was too great to be atoned in this way, he took it into his head to starve himself to death. After he had spent some time in this process, he came in his wanderings to the place where my father lived, and, without anybody in the house knowing, went into the barn, where he fell upon the ground in utter faintness. My father came by chance into the barn, and found the man, whom he had long known, lying half-dead on the ground, with a *Zohar* (the principal book of the Cabbalists) in his hand. As he knew well what sort of man this was, he brought him at once all sorts of refreshments ; but the man would make no use of them in any way. My father came several times, and repeated his urgent request, that Simon would take something ; but it was of no avail. My father had to attend to something in the house, whereupon Simon, to escape from his importunity, exerted all his strength, raised himself up, went out of the barn, and at last out of the village. When my father came back into the barn again, and found the man no longer there, he ran after him, and found him lying dead not far from the village. The affair was generally made known among the Jews, and Simon became a saint.

Jossel of Klezk proposed nothing less than to hasten the advent of the Messiah. To this end he performed strict penance, fasted, rolled himself in snow, undertook night-watches and similar severities. By all sorts of such operations he believed that he was able to accomplish the overthrow of a legion of evil spirits, who kept guard on the Messiah, and threw obstacles in the way of his coming.* To these exercises he added at last many Cabbalistic fooleries—fumigations, conjurations, and similar practices—till at length he lost his wits on the subject, believed that he really saw spirits with his eyes open, calling each of them by name. He would then

---

* In the same way a fool, called Chosek, was going to starve the city of Lemberg, against which he was enraged ; and for this purpose he placed himself behind the wall, in order to blockade the city with his body. The result of the blockade, however, was that he nearly died of hunger, while the city knew nothing whatever of a famine.

beat about him, smash windows and stoves under the idea that these were his foes, the evil spirits, somewhat after the manner of his forerunner Don Quixote. At last he lay down in complete exhaustion, from which he was with great difficulty restored, by the physician of Prince Radzivil.

Unfortunately I could never get further in pious exercises of this sort, than to abstain for a considerable while from everything that comes from a living being ; and during the Days of Atonement I have sometimes fasted three days together. I once resolved indeed on undertaking the *T'shubath Hakana ;* but this project, like others of the same sort, remained unfulfilled, after I had adopted the opinions of Maimonides, who was no friend of fanaticism or pietism. It is remarkable, that at the time when I still observed the rabbinical regulations with the utmost strictness, I yet would not observe certain ceremonies which have something comical about them. Of this kind, for example, was the *Malketh* (Beating) before the Great Day of Atonement, in which every Jew lays himself on his face in the synagogue, while another with a narrow strip of leather gives him thirty-nine lashes. Of the same sort is *Haphorath Nedarim*, or the act of setting free from vows on New Year's Eve. In this three men are seated, while another appears before them, and addresses to them a certain form, the general drift of which is as follows :—" Sirs, I know what a heinous sin it is, not to fulfil vows ; and in-

asmuch as I have doubtless this year made some vows
which I have not fulfilled, and which I can no longer re-
collect, I beg of you that you will set me free from the
same. I do not indeed repent of the good resolutions
to which I have bound myself by these vows ; I repent
merely of the fact, that in making such resolutions I did
not add, that they were not to have the force of a vow,"
etc., etc. Thereupon he withdraws from the judgment-
seat, pulls off his shoes, and sits down on the bare
ground, by which he is supposed to banish himself till
his vows are dissolved. After he has sat for some time,
and said a prayer by himself, the judges begin to call
aloud, " Thou art our brother ! thou art our brother !
thou art our brother ! There is no vow, no oath, no
banishment any longer, after thou hast submitted thyself
to the judgment. Rise from the ground and come to
us ! " This they repeat three times, and with that the
man is at once set free from all his vows.

At serio-comic scenes of this sort I could only with
the greatest difficulty refrain from laughing. A blush of
shame came over me, when I was to undertake such performances. I sought therefore, if I was pressed on the
subject, to free myself by the pretext, that I had either
already attended to it, or was going to attend to it, in
another synagogue. A very remarkable psychological
phenomenon ! It might be thought impossible for any
one to be ashamed of actions which he saw others per-
forming without the slightest blush of shame. Yet this

was the case here. This phenomenon can be explained only by the fact, that in all my actions I had regard first to the nature of the action in itself (whether it was right or wrong, proper or improper), then to its nature in relation to some end, and that I justified it as a means, only when it was not in itself incapable of being justified. This principle was developed afterwards in my whole system of religion and morals. On the other hand, the most of men act on the principle, that the end justifies the means.

K

CHAPTER XVII.

Friendship and Enthusiasm.

IN the place where I resided I had a bosom friend, Moses Lapidoth by name. We were of the same age, the same studies, and nearly the same external circumstances, the only difference being, that at an early period I already showed an inclination to the sciences, while Lapidoth had indeed a love of speculation, and also great acuteness and power of judgment, but had no wish to proceed further than he could reach by a mere sound common sense. With this friend I used to hold many a conversation on subjects of mutual interest, especially the questions of religion and morals.

We were the only persons in the place, who ventured to be not mere imitators, but to think independently about everything. It was a natural result of this, that, as we differed from all the rest of the community in our opinions and conduct, we separated ourselves from them by degrees ; but, as we had still to live by the community, our circumstances on this account became every day worse and worse. 'Tis true, we noted this fact, but nevertheless we were unwilling to sacrifice our favourite inclinations for any interest in the world. We consoled ourselves therefore, as best we might, over our loss, spoke constantly of the vanity of all things, of the religious and moral faults of the common herd, upon whom we looked down with a sort of noble pride and contempt.

We used especially to open our minds, *à la Mande-ville*, on the hollowness of human virtue. For example, smallpox had been very prevalent in the place, and thereby many children had been carried off. The elders held a meeting to find out the secret sins, on account of which they were suffering this punishment, as they viewed it. After instituting an inquiry it was found, that a young widow of the Jewish people was holding too free intercourse with some servants of the manor. She was sent for, but no sort of inquisition could elicit from her anything beyond the fact, that these people were in the habit of drinking mead at her house, and that, as was reasonable, she received them in a pleasant and polite manner, but that in other respects she was unconscious of any sin in the matter. As no other evidence was forthcoming, she was about to be acquitted, when an elderly matron came flying like a fury and screamed, " Scourge her ! scourge her ! till she has confessed her sin ! If you do not do it, then may the guilt of the death of so many innocent souls fall upon you ! " Lapidoth was present with me at this scene, and said, "Friend, do you suppose that Madam is making so fierce a complaint against this woman, merely because she is seized with a holy zeal and feeling for the general welfare? Oh no! She is enraged, merely because the widow still possesses attractions, while she herself can no longer make claim to any." I assured him that his opinion was thoroughly in accordance with my own.

Lapidoth had poor parents-in-law. His father-in-law was Jewish sexton, and by his slender pay could support his family only in a very sorry style. Every Friday the poor man was therefore compelled to listen to all sorts of reproach and abuse from his wife, because he could not provide her with what was indispensable for the holy Sabbath. Lapidoth told me about this with the addition:—" My mother-in-law wants to make me to believe that she is zealous merely for the honour of the holy Sabbath. Nay, verily; she is zealous merely for the honour of her own holy paunch, which she cannot fill as she would like; the holy Sabbath serves her merely as a pretext."

Once when we were taking a walk on the wall round the town, and conversing about the tendency of men, which is evinced in such expressions, to deceive themselves and others, I said to Lapidoth, " Friend, let us be fair, and pass our censure on ourselves, as well as on others. Is not the contemplative life which we lead, and which is by no means adapted to our circumstances, to be regarded as a result of our indolence and inclination to idleness, which we seek to defend by reflections on the vanity of all things? We are content with our present circumstances; why? Because we cannot alter them without first fighting against our inclination to idleness. With all our pretence of contempt for everything outside of us, we cannot avoid the secret wish to be able to enjoy better food and clothing than at present. We reproach our friends as vain men addicted to the pleasures of sense, because they have abandoned our mode of life, and undertaken occupations adapted to their powers. But wherein consists our superiority over them, when we merely follow our inclination as they follow theirs? Let us seek to find this superiority merely in the fact, that we at least confess this truth to ourselves, while they profess as the motive of their actions, not the satisfaction of their own particular desires, but the impulse to general utility." Lapidoth, on whom my words produced a powerful impression, answered with some warmth, "Friend, you are perfectly right. If we cannot now mend our faults, we will not deceive ourselves about them, but at least keep the way open for amendment."

In conversations of this kind we two cynics spent our pleasantest hours, while we made ourselves merry sometimes at the expense of the world, sometimes at our own. Lapidoth, for example, whose old dirty clothes had all fallen into rags, and one of whose sleeves was wholly parted from the rest of his coat, while he was not in a position even to have it mended, used to fix the sleeve on his back with a pin, and to ask me, " Don't I look like a *Schlachziz* (a Polish noble)?" I, again, could not sufficiently commend my rent shoes, which were quite open at the toes, because, as I said, "They do not squeeze the foot."

The harmony of our inclinations and manner of life, along with some difference in our talents, made our conversation all the more agreeable. I had more talent for the sciences, made more earnest endeavours after thoroughness and accuracy of knowledge than Lapidoth. He, on the other hand, had the advantage of a lively imagination, and consequently more talent for eloquence and poetry than I. If I produced a new thought, my friend knew how to illustrate it, and, as it were, to give it embodiment in a multitude of examples. Our affection for one another went so far, that, whenever it was practicable, we spent day and night in each other's company, and the first thing we did, on returning home from the places where we severally acted as family-tutors, was to visit each other, even before seeing our own families. At last we began to neglect on this account the usual hours of prayer. Lapidoth first undertook to prove, that the Talmudists themselves offered up their prayers, not exclusively in the synagogue, but sometimes in their study-chambers. Afterwards he pointed out also, that the prayers held to be necessary are not all equally so, but that some may be dispensed with altogether: even those, which are recognised as necessary, we curtailed by degrees, till at last they were totally neglected.

Once, when we went for a walk on the wall during the

hour of prayer, Lapidoth said to me, " Friend, what is going to become of us? We do not pray now at all."

" What do you mean by that?" I inquired.

" I throw myself," said Lapidoth, " on the mercy of God, who certainly will not punish his children severely for a slight neglect."

" God is not merely *merciful*," I replied ; " He is also *just*. Consequently this reason cannot help us much."

" What do you mean by that?" asked Lapidoth.

I had by this time obtained from Maimonides more accurate ideas of God and of our duties towards Him. Accordingly I replied, " Our destination is merely the *attainment of perfection through the knowledge of God and the imitation of His actions*. Prayer is simply the expression of our knowledge of the divine perfections, and, as a result of this knowledge, is intended merely for the common man who cannot of himself attain to this knowledge ; and therefore it is adapted to his mode of conception. But as we see into the end of prayer, and can attain to this end directly, we can dispense altogether with prayer as something superfluous."

This reasoning appeared to us both to be sound. We resolved therefore, for the purpose of avoiding offence, to go out of the house every morning with our *Taleth* and *Tephilim* (Jewish instruments of prayer), not, however, to the synagogue, but to our favourite retreat, the wall, and by this means we fortunately escaped the Jewish Inquisition.

But this enthusiastic companionship, like everything else in the world, had to come to an end. As we were both married, and our marriages were tolerably fruitful, we were obliged, for the purpose of supporting our families, to accept situations as family-tutors. By this means we were not infrequently separated, and afterwards were able to spend merely a few weeks in the year together.

CHAPTER XVIII.

The Life of a Family-Tutor.

THE place, where I first occupied the position of family-tutor, was at the distance of a league from my residence. The family was that of a miserable farmer in a still more miserable village ; and my salary was five thalers in Polish money. The poverty, ignorance, and rudeness in the manner of life, which prevailed in this house, were indescribable. The farmer himself was a man of about fifty years, the whole of whose face was overgrown with hair, ending in a dirty, thick beard as black as pitch. His language was a sort of muttering, intelligible only to the boors, with whom he held intercourse daily. Not only was he ignorant of Hebrew, but he could not speak a word of Jewish ; his only language was Russian, the common patois of the peasantry. His wife and children were of the same stamp. Moreover, the apartment, in which they lived, was a hovel of smoke, black as coal inside and out, without a chimney, but with merely a small opening in the roof for the exit of the smoke,—an opening which was carefully closed as soon as the fire was allowed to go out, so that the heat might not escape.

The windows were narrow strips of pine laid crosswise over each other, and covered with paper. This apartment served at once for sitting, drinking, eating, study and sleep. Think of this room intensely heated, and the smoke, as is generally the case in winter, driven back by wind and rain till the whole place is filled with it to suffocation. Here hang a foul washing and other dirty bits of clothing on poles laid across the room in order to kill the vermin with the smoke. There hang sausages to dry, while their fat keeps constantly trickling down on the heads of people below. Yonder stand tubs with sour cabbage and red beets, which form the principal food of the Lithuanians. In a corner the water is kept for daily use, with the dirty water alongside. In this room the bread is kneaded, cooking and baking are done, the cow is milked, and all sorts of operations are carried on.

In this magnificent dwelling the peasants sit on the bare ground; you dare not sit higher if you do not wish to be suffocated with the smoke. Here they guzzle their whiskey and make an uproar, while the people of the house sit in a corner. I usually took my place behind the stove with my dirty half-naked pupils, and expounded to them out of an old tattered Bible, from Hebrew into Russian Jewish. All this together made such a splendid group as deserved to be sketched only by a Hogarth, and to be sung only by a Butler.

It may be easily imagined, how pitiable my condition here must have been. Whiskey had to form my sole comfort ; it made me forget all my misery. This was increased by the fact, that a regiment of Russians, who were rioting at that time with every conceivable cruelty on the estates of Prince Radzivil, was stationed in the village and its neighbourhood. The house was constantly full of drunken Russians, who committed all sorts of excesses, hewed to pieces tables and benches, threw glasses and bottles into the faces of the people of the house, and so on. To give merely one example, a Russian, who was stationed in this house as guard, and whose charge it was to secure the house against all violence, came home once drunk, and demanded something to eat. A dish of millet with butter was placed before him cooked. He shoved the dish away, and shouted an order for more butter. A whole small tub of butter was brought, when he shouted again an order for another dish. This was brought immediately, whereupon he threw all the butter into it, and called for spirits. A whole bottle was brought, and he poured it likewise into the dish. Thereafter milk, pepper, salt, and tobacco, in large quantities had to be brought to him, the whole being put in, and the mixture devoured. After he had taken some spoonfuls, he began to strike about him, pulled the host by the beard, struck him in the face with his fist, so that the blood flowed out of his mouth, poured some of his glorious broth down his throat, and went on in this riotous manner till he became so drunk that he could no longer support himself, and fell to the ground.

Such scenes were at that time very common everywhere in Poland. If a Russian army passed a place, they took with them a *prowodnik*, or guide, to the next place. But instead of seeking to be supplied by the mayor or the village magistrate, they used to seize the first person whom they met on the road. He might be young or old, male or female, healthy or sick, it mattered nothing to them ; for they knew the road well enough from special charts, and only sought an opportunity for outrage. If it happened that the person seized did not know the way at all, and did not show them the right road, they did not allow themselves to be sent astray on this account ; they selected the road all right, but they cudgelled the poor prowodnik till he was half-dead, *for not knowing the way !*

I was once seized as a prowodnik myself. I did not indeed know the way, but luckily I hit upon it by chance. Fortunately, therefore, I reached the proper place, and the only violence I suffered, besides a good many blows and kicks from the Russian soldiers, was the threat, that, if ever I led them astray, I should certainly be flayed alive—a threat which they might be trusted with carrying into execution.

The other places which I filled as tutor were more or less similar to this. In one of these a remarkable psychological incident occurred in which I took the principal part and which is to be described in the sequel. An incident of the same kind, however, which happened to another person and of which I was simply eye-witness, must be mentioned here.

A tutor in the next village, who was a somnambulist, rose one night from his bed and went to the village churchyard with a volume of the Jewish ceremonial laws in his hand. After remaining some time there he returned to his bed. In the morning he rose up, without remembering the least of what had happened during the night, and went to the chest where his copy of the ceremonial laws was usually kept, in order to take out the first part, *Orach Chajim* or the Way of Life, which he was accustomed to read every morning. The code consists of four parts, each of which was bound separately, and all the four had certainly been locked up in the chest. He was therefore astonished to find only three of the parts, *Joreh Deah* or the Teacher of Wisdom, being awanting. As he knew about his disease he searched everywhere, till at last he came to the churchyard where he found the *Joreh Deah* lying open at the chapter, *Hilchoth Abheloth* or the Laws of Mourning. He took this for a bad omen and came home much disquieted. On being asked the cause of his disquietude he related the incident which had occurred, with the addition, "Ah! God knows how my poor mother is !" He begged of his master the loan of a horse and permission to ride to the nearest town, where his mother lived, in order to enquire after her welfare. As he had to pass the place where I was tutor, and I saw him riding in great excitement without being willing to dismount even for a little while, I asked him the cause of his excitement when he related to me the above-mentioned incident.

I was astonished, not so much about the particular circumstances of this incident, as about somnambulism in general, of which till then I had known nothing. My friend, on the other hand, assured me that somnambulism was a common occurrence with him, and that it meant nothing, but that the circumstance of the *Hilchoth Abheloth* made him forebode some misfortune. Thereupon he rode off, arrived at his mother's house, and found her seated at her frame for needlework. She asked him the reason of his coming, when he replied that he had come merely to pay her a visit, as he had not seen her for a long time. After he had rested for a good while, he rode back ; but his disquietude was by no means wholly removed, and the thought of the *Hilchoth Abheloth* he could not get out of his head. The third day after, a fire broke out in the town where his mother lived, and the poor woman perished in the flames. Scarcely had the son heard of the conflagration, when he began to lament that his mother had so miserably perished. He rode off in all haste to the town, and found what he had foreboded.

CHAPTER XIX.

Also on a Secret Society, and therefore a Long Chapter.

ABOUT this time I became acquainted with a sect of my nation, called the *New Chasidim*, which was then coming into prominence. *Chasidim* is the name generally given by the Hebrews to the *pious*, that is, to those who distinguish themselves by exercising the strictest piety. These were, from time immemorial, men who had freed themselves from worldly occupations and pleasures, and devoted their lives to the strictest exercise of the laws of religion and penance for their sins. As already mentioned, they sought to accomplish this object by prayers and other exercises of devotion, by chastisement of the body and similar means.

But about this time some among them set themselves up for founders of a new sect. They maintained that true piety does not by any means consist in chastisement of the body, by which the spiritual quiet and cheerfulness, necessary to the knowledge and love of God, are disturbed. On the contrary, they maintained that man must satisfy all his bodily wants, and seek to enjoy the pleasures of sense, so far as may be necessary for the development of our feelings, inasmuch as God has created all for his glory. The true service of God, according to them, consists in exercises of devotion with exertion of all our powers, and annihilation of self before God ; for they maintain that man, in accordance with his destination, can reach the highest perfection only when he regards himself, not as a being that exists and works for himself, but merely as an organ of the Godhead. Instead therefore of spending their lives in separation from the world, in suppression of their natural feelings, and in deadening their powers, they believed that they acted much more to the purpose, when they sought to develop their natural feelings as much as possible, to bring their powers into exercise, and constantly to widen their sphere of work.

It must be acknowledged, that both of these opposite methods have something true for a foundation. Of the former the foundation is obviously Stoicism, that is, an endeavour to determine actions by free will in accordance with a higher principle than passion ; the latter is founded on the system of perfection. Only both, like everything else in the world, may be abused, and are abused in actual life. Those of the first sect drive their penitential disposition to extravagance; instead of merely regulating their desires and passions by rules of moderation, they seek to annihilate them ; and, instead of endeavouring, like the Stoics, to find the principle of their actions in pure reason, they seek it rather in religion. This is a pure source, it is true; but as these people have false ideas of religion itself, and their virtue has for its foundation merely the future rewards and punishments of an arbitrary tyrannical being who governs by mere caprice, in point of fact their actions flow from an impure source, namely the principle of interest. Moreover, in their case this interest rests merely on fancies, so that, in this respect, they are far below the grossest Epicureans, who have, it is true, a low, but still a real interest as the end of their actions. Only then can religion yield a principle of virtue, when it is itself founded on the idea of virtue.

The adherents of the second sect have indeed more correct ideas of religion and morals; but since in this respect they regulate themselves for the most part in accordance with obscure feelings, and not in accordance with distinct knowledge, they likewise necessarily fall into all sorts of extravagances. Self-annihilation of necessity cramps their activity, or gives it a false direction. They have no natural science, no acquaintance with psychology; and they are vain enough to consider themselves organs of the Godhead,—which of course they are, to an extent limited by the degree of perfection they attain. The result is, that on the credit of the Godhead they perpetrate the greatest excesses; every extraordinary suggestion is to them a divine inspiration, and every lively impulse a divine call.

These sects were not in fact different sects of religion; their difference consisted merely in the mode of their religious exercises. But still their animosity went so far, that they decried each other as heretics, and indulged in mutual persecution. At first the new sect held the upper hand, and extended itself nearly over the whole of Poland, and even beyond. The heads of the sect ordinarily sent emissaries everywhere, whose duty it was to preach the new doctrine and procure adherents. Now, the majority of the Polish Jews consist of scholars, that is, men devoted to an inactive and contemplative life ; for every Polish Jew is destined from his birth to be a rabbi, and only the greatest incapacity can exclude him from the office. Moreover, this new doctrine was to make the way to blessedness easier, inasmuch as it declared that fasts and vigils and the constant study of the Talmud are not only useless, but even prejudicial to that cheer-fulness of spirit which is essential to genuine piety. It was therefore natural that the adherents of the doctrine spread far and wide in a short time.

Pilgrimages were made to K. M. and other holy places, where the enlightened superiors of this sect abode. Young people forsook parents, wives and children, and went in troops to visit these superiors, and hear from their lips the new doctrine. The occasion, which led to the rise of this sect was the following.*

---

* In our times, when so much is said both *pro* and *contra* about secret societies, I believe that the history of a particular secret society, in which I was entangled, though but a short time, should not be passed over in this sketch of my life.

I have already remarked that, since the time when the Jews lost their national position and were dispersed among other nations where they are more or less tolerated, they have had no internal form of government but their religious constitution, by which they are held together and still form, in spite of their political dispersion, an organic whole. Their leaders, therefore, have allowed themselves to be occupied with nothing so much as with imparting additional strength to this, the only bond of union by which the Jews still constitute a nation. But the doctrines of their faith and the laws of their religion take their origin in the Holy Scriptures, while these leave much that is indefinite in regard to their exposition and application to particular cases. Consequently the aid of tradition is of necessity called in, and by this means the method of expounding the Holy Scriptures, as well as the deduction of cases left undetermined by them, is made to appear as if specified in determinate laws. This tradition could not of course be entrusted to the whole nation, but merely to a particular body—a sort of legislative commission.

By this means, however, the evil was not avoided. Tradition itself left much that was still indeterminate. The deduction of particular cases from the general, and the new laws demanded by the circumstances of different times, gave occasion for many controversies ; but through these very controversies and the mode of their settlement, this body became always more numerous, and its influence on the nation more powerful. The Jewish constitution is therefore in its form aristocratic, and is accordingly exposed to all the abuses of an aristocracy. The unlearned classes of the people, being burdened with the care of supporting not only themselves but also the indispensable learned class, were unable to give their attention to abuses of the kind. But from time to time men have arisen out of the legislative body itself, who have not only denounced its abuses, but have even called in question its authority.

Of this sort was the founder of the Christian religion, who at the very outset placed himself in opposition to the tyranny of this aristocracy, and brought back the whole ceremonial law to its origin, namely, a pure moral system, to which the ceremonial law stands related as means to end. In this way the reformation at least of a part of the nation was accomplished. Of the same sort also was the notorious Shabbethai Zebi, who, at the close of last century * set himself up as Messiah, and was going to abolish the whole ceremonial law, especially the rabbinical institutions. A moral system founded upon reason would, owing to the deeply rooted prejudices of the nation at that time, have been powerless to work out a wholesome reformation. To their prejudices and fanaticism therefore it was necessary to

---

* That is, of course, the 17th century.—*Trans.*

oppose prejudices and fanaticism. This was done in the following way.

A secret society, whose founders belonged to the dis-affected spirits of the nation, had already taken root in it for a long time. A certain French rabbi, named Moses de Leon, is said, according to Rabbi Joseph Candia, to have composed the *Zohar*, and to have foisted it upon the nation as an old book having for its author the cele-brated Talmudist, Rabbi ben Jochai. This book con-tains, as stated above, an exposition of the Holy Scrip-tures in accordance with the principles of the Cabbalah ; or rather, it contains these principles themselves delivered in the form of an exposition of the Holy Scriptures, and drawn, as it were, from these. It has, like Janus, a double face, and admits, therefore, of a double interpre-tation.

The one is that which is given with great diffuseness in Cabbalistic writings, and has been brought into a sys-tem. Here is a wide field for the imagination, where it can revel at will without being in the end better instructed on the matter than before. Here are delivered, in figu-rative language, many moral and physical truths, which lose themselves at last in the labyrinth of the hyperphysi-cal. This method of treating the Cabbalah is peculiar to Cabbalistic scholars, and constitutes the lesser mys-teries of this secret society.

The second method, on the other hand, concerns the secret political meaning of the Cabbalah, and is known

only to the superiors of the secret society.   These superiors themselves, as well as their operations, remain ever
unknown ; the rest of the society you may become
acquainted with, if you choose.   But the latter *cannot*
betray political secrets which are unknown to themselves.
while the former *will not* do it, because it is against their
interest.   Only the lesser (purely literary) mysteries are
entrusted to the people, and urged upon them as matters
of the highest importance.   The greater (political) mysteries are not taught, but, as a matter of course, are
brought into practice.

A certain Cabbalist, Rabbi Joel Baalshem * by name,
became very celebrated at this time on account of some
lucky cures which he effected by means of his medical
acquirements and his conjuring tricks, as he gave out
that all this was done, not by natural means, but solely
by help of the *Cabbalah Maasith* (the practical Cabbalah),
and the use of sacred names.   In this way he played a
very successful game in Poland.   He also took care to
have followers in his art.   Among his disciples were
some, who took hold of his profession, and made themselves a name by successful cures and the detection of
robberies.   With their cures the process was quite natu-

---

* *Baalshem* is one who occupies himself with the practical Cabbalah, that is, with the conjuration of spirits and the writing of
amulets, in which the names of God and of many sorts of spirits are
employed.

ral. They employed the common means of medicine, but after the usual method of the conjurer they sought to turn the attention of the spectator from these, and direct it to their Cabbalistic hocus-pocus. The robberies they either brought about themselves, or they discovered them by means of their detectives, who were spread all over the country.

Others of greater genius and a nobler mode of thinking, formed far grander plans. They saw that their private interest, as well as the general interest, could be best promoted by gaining the people's confidence, and this they sought to command by enlightenment. Their plan was therefore moral and political at the same time.* At first it appeared as if they would merely do away with the abuses which had crept into the Jewish system of religion and morals ; but this drew after it of necessity a complete abrogation of the whole system. The principal points which they attacked were these :—

1. The abuse of rabbinical learning. Instead of simplifying the laws and rendering them capable of being known by all, the learning of the rabbis leaves them still more confused and indefinite. Moreover, being occupied only with the study of the laws, it gives as much

---

* As I never attained the rank of a superior in this society, the exposition of their plan cannot be regarded as a fact verified by experience, but merely as an inference arrived at by reflection. How far this inference is well founded, can be determined merely by analogy according to the rules of probability.

attention to those which are no longer of any application, such as the laws of sacrifice, of purification, etc., as to those which are still in use. Besides, it is not the study, but the observance of the laws, that forms the chief concern, since the study of them is not an end in itself, but merely a means to their observance. And, finally, in the observance of the laws the rabbis have regard merely to the external ceremony, not to the moral end.

2. The abuse of piety on the part of the so-called penitents. These become very zealous, it is true, about the practice of virtue. Their motive to virtue, however, is not that knowledge of God and His perfection, which is based on reason ; it consists rather in false representations of God and His attributes. They failed therefore of necessity to find true virtue, and hit upon a spurious imitation. Instead of aspiring after likeness to God, and striving to escape from the bondage of sensual passions into the dominion of a free will that finds its motive in reason, they sought to annihilate their passions by annihilating their powers of activity, as I have already shown by some deplorable examples.

On the other hand, those who sought to enlighten the people required, as an indispensable condition of true virtue, a cheerful state of mind disposed to every form of active exertion ; and they not only allowed, but even recommended, a moderate enjoyment of all kinds of pleasure as necessary for the attainment of this cheerful disposition. Their worship consisted in a voluntary elevation above the body, that is, in an abstraction of the thoughts from all created things, even from the individual self, and in union with God. By this means a kind of self-denial arose among them, which led them to ascribe, not to themselves, but to God alone, all the actions undertaken in this state. Their worship therefore consisted in a sort of speculative adoration, for which they held no special time or formula to be necessary, but they left each one to determine it according to the degree of his knowledge. Still they chose for it most commonly the hours set apart for the public worship of God. In their public worship they endeavoured mainly to attain that elevation above the body, which has been described ; they became so absorbed in the idea of the divine perfection, that they lost the idea of everything else, even of their own body, and, as they gave out, the body became in this state wholly devoid of feeling.

Such abstraction, however, was a very difficult matter ; and accordingly, whenever they came out of this state by new suggestions taking possession of their minds, they laboured, by all sorts of *mechanical operations*, such as movements and cries, to bring themselves back into the state once more, and to keep themselves in it without interruption during the whole time of their worship. It was amusing to observe how they often interrupted their prayers by all sorts of extraordinary tones and comical gestures, which were meant as threats and reproaches against their adversary, the Evil Spirit, who tried to dis-

turb their devotion; and how by this means they wore
themselves out to such an extent, that, on finishing their
prayers, they commonly fell down in complete exhaustion.

It is not to be denied that, however sound may be the
basis of such a worship, it is subject to abuse just as
much as the other. The internal activity following upon
cheerfulness of mind, must depend on the degree of
knowledge acquired. Self-annihilation before God is
only then well-founded, when a man's faculty of knowledge, owing to the grandeur of its object, is so entirely
occupied with that object, that he exists, as it were, out
of himself, in the object alone. If, on the contrary, the
faculty of knowledge is limited in respect of its object, so
that it is incapable of any steady progress, then the
activity mentioned, by being concentrated on this single
object, is repressed rather than stimulated. Some simple
men of this sect, who sauntered about idly the whole day
with pipe in mouth, when asked, what they were thinking
about all the time, replied, "We are thinking about
God." This answer would have been satisfactory, if they
had constantly sought, by an adequate knowledge of
nature, to extend their knowledge of the divine perfections.
But this was impossible in their case, as their knowledge
of nature was extremely limited; and consequently the
condition, in which they concentrated their activity upon
an object which, in respect of their capacity, was unfruitful, became of necessity unnatural. Moreover, their

actions could be ascribed to God, only when they were the results of an accurate knowledge of God ; but when they resulted from a very limited degree of this knowledge, it was inevitable that all sorts of excesses should be committed on the credit of God, as unfortunately the issue has shown.

But the fact, that this sect spread so rapidly, and that the new doctrine met with so much applause among the majority of the nation, may be very easily explained. The natural inclination to idleness and a life of speculation on the part of the majority, who from birth are destined to study, the dryness and unfruitfulness of rabbinical studies, and the great burden of the ceremonial law, which the new doctrine promised to lighten, finally the tendency to fanaticism and the love of the marvellous, which are nourished by this doctrine,—these are sufficient to make this phenomenon intelligible.

At first the rabbis and the pietists opposed the spread of this sect in the old fashion ; but in spite of this, for the reasons just mentioned, it maintained the upper hand. Hostilities were practised on both sides. Each party sought to gain adherents. A ferment arose in the nation, and opinions were divided.

I could not form any accurate idea of the new sect, and did not know what to think of it, till I met with a young man, who had already been initiated into the society, and had enjoyed the good fortune of conversing with its superiors. This man happened to be travelling

through the place of my abode, and I seized the opportunity of asking for some information about the internal
constitution of the society, the mode of admission, and
so forth. The stranger was still in the lowest grade of
membership, and consequently knew nothing about the
internal constitution of the society. He was therefore
unable to give me any information on the subject ; but,
as far as the mode of admission was concerned, he
assured me that that was the simplest thing in the world.
Any man, who felt a desire of perfection, but did not
know how to satisfy it, or wished to remove the hindrances to its satisfaction, had nothing to do but apply
to the superiors of the society, and *eo ipso* he became a
member. He did not even require, as you must do on
applying to a medical doctor, to say anything to these
superiors about his moral weakness, his previous life, and
matters of that sort, inasmuch as nothing was unknown
to the superiors, they could see into the human heart,
and discern everything that is concealed in its secret
recesses, they could foretell the future, and bring near at
hand things that are remote. Their sermons and moral
teachings were not, as these things commonly are, thought
over and arranged in an orderly manner beforehand.
This method is proper only to the man, who regards
himself as a being existing and working for himself apart
from God. But the superiors of this sect hold that their
teachings are divine and therefore infallible, only when
they are the result of self-annihilation before God, that

is, when they are suggested to them *ex tempore*, by the exigence of circumstances, without their contributing anything themselves.

As I was quite captivated by this description I begged the stranger to communicate to me some of these divine teachings. He clapped his hand on his brow as if he were waiting for inspiration from the Holy Ghost, and turned to me with a solemn mien and his arms half-bared, which he brought into action somewhat like Corporal Trim, when he was reading the sermon. Then he began as follows :—

" 'Sing unto God a new song ; His praise is in the congregation of saints ' (Psalm cxlix., 1). Our superiors explain this verse in the following way. The attributes of God as the most perfect being must surpass by far the attributes of every finite being ; and consequently His praise, as the expression of His attributes, must likewise surpass the praise of any such being. Till the present time the praise of God consisted in ascribing to Him supernatural operations, such as the discovery of what is concealed, the foreseeing of the future, and the production of effects immediately by His mere will. Now, however, the saints, that is, the superiors, are able to perform such supernatural actions themselves. Accordingly in this respect God has no longer pre-eminence over them ; and it is therefore necessary to find some new praise, which is proper to God alone."

Quite charmed with this ingenious method of inter-

preting the Holy Scriptures, I begged the stranger for
some more expositions of the same kind. He proceeded
therefore in his inspired manner:—" 'When the minstrel
played, the spirit of God came upon him' (2 Kings iii.
15). This is explained in the following way. As long as
a man is self-active, he is incapable of receiving the influence of the Holy Ghost; for this purpose he must
hold himself like an instrument in a purely passive state.
The meaning of the passage is therefore this. When the
minstrel (הַמְנַגֵּן, the servant of God), becomes like his
instrument (כְּנַגֵּן), then the spirit of God comes upon
him."*

"Now," said the stranger again, "hear the interpretation of a passage from the Mishnah, where it is said,
'The honour of thy neighbour shall be as dear to thee
as thine own.' Our teachers explain this in the following
way. It is certain that no man will find pleasure in doing
honour to himself: this would be altogether ridiculous.
But it would be just as ridiculous to make too much of
the marks of honour received from another, as these
confer on us no more intrinsic worth than we have al-

---

* The ingenuity of this interpretation consists in the fact, that in
Hebrew נגן may stand for the infinitive of *play*, as well as for a
musical instrument, and that the prefix כ may be translated either
as, in the sense of *when*, or *as*, in the sense of *like*. The superiors
of this sect, who *wrenched passages of the Holy Scriptures from their
context*, regarding themselves as merely vehicles of their teachings,
selected accordingly that interpretation of this passage, which fitted
best their principle of *self-annihilation* before God.

ready. This passage therefore means merely, that the honour of thy neighbour (the honour which thy neighbour shows to thee) must be of as little value in thine eyes, as thine own (the honour which thou showest to thyself)."

I could not help being astonished at the exquisite refinement of these thoughts ; and charmed with the ingenious exegesis, by which they were supported.* My imagination was strained to the highest pitch by these descriptions, and consequently I wished nothing so much as the pleasure of becoming a member of this honourable society. I resolved therefore to undertake a journey to M——, where the superior B—— resided. I waited with the greatest impatience for the close of my period of service, which lasted still for some weeks. As soon as this came to an end, instead of going home (though I was only two miles away), I started at once on my pilgrimage. The journey extended over some weeks.

At last I arrived at M——, and after having rested from my journey I went to the house of the superior under the idea that I could be introduced to him at once. I was told, however, that he could not speak to me at the time, but that I was invited to his table on

---

* Maimon in a footnote here refers, by way of a parallel, to the interpretation by a Catholic theologian of a passage in Ezekiel (xliv., 1-2) as an allegorical prophecy of the Virgin Mary ; but most readers will probably prefer to leave the exposition of the allegory to the imagination of those who choose to follow it out. — *Trans.*

Sabbath along with the other strangers who had come to visit him ; that I should then have the happiness of seeing the saintly man face to face, and of hearing the sublimest teachings out of his own mouth ; that although this was a public audience, yet, on account of the individual references which I should find made to myself, I might regard it as a special interview.

Accordingly on Sabbath I went to this solemn meal, and found there a large number of respectable men who had met here from various quarters. At length the great man appeared in his awe-inspiring form, clothed in white satin. Even his shoes and snuffbox were white, this being among the Cabbalists the colour of grace. He gave to every new comer his salaam, that is, his greeting. We sat down to table and during the meal a solemn silence reigned. After the meal was over, the superior struck up a solemn inspiriting melody, held his hand for some time upon his brow, and then began to call out, "Z—— of H——, M—— of R——," and so on. Every new comer was thus called by his own name and the name of his residence, which excited no little astonishment. Each recited, as he was called, some verse of the Holy Scriptures. Thereupon the superior began to deliver a sermon for which the verses recited served as a text, so that although they were disconnected verses taken from different parts of the Holy Scriptures they were combined with as much skill as if they had formed a single whole. What was still more extraordinary, every one of the new comers believed that he discovered, in that part of the sermon which was founded on his verse, something that had special reference to the facts of his own spiritual life. At this we were of course greatly astonished.

It was not long, however, before I began to qualify the high opinion I had formed of this superior and the whole society. I observed that their ingenious exegesis was at bottom false, and, in addition to that, was limited strictly to their own extravagant principles, such as the doctrine of self-annihilation. When a man had once learned these, there was nothing new for him to hear. The so-called miracles could be very naturally explained. By means of correspondence and spies and a certain knowledge of men, by physiognomy and skilful questions, the superiors were able to elicit indirectly the secrets of the heart, so that they succeeded with these simple men in obtaining the reputation of being inspired prophets.

The whole society also displeased me not a little by their cynical spirit and the excess of their merriment. A single example of this may suffice. We had met once at the hour of prayer in the house of the superior. One of the company arrived somewhat late, when the others asked him the reason. He replied that he had been detained by his wife having been that evening confined with a daughter. As soon as they heard this, they began to congratulate him in a somewhat uproarious fashion. The superior thereupon came out of his study and asked

M

the cause of the noise. He was told that we were congratulating our friend, because his wife had brought a girl into the world. " A girl !" he answered with the greatest indignation, " he ought to be whipped."* The poor fellow protested. He could not comprehend why he should be made to suffer for his wife having brought a girl into the world. But this was of no avail : he was seized, thrown down on the floor, and whipped unmercifully. All except the victim fell into an hilarious mood over the affair, upon which the superior called them to prayer in the following words, " Now, brethren, *serve the Lord with gladness !* "

I would not stay in the place any longer. I sought the superior's blessing, took my departure from the society with the resolution to abandon it for ever, and returned home.

Now I shall say something of the internal constitution of the society. The superiors may, according to my experience, be brought under four heads : (1) the prudent, (2) the crafty, (3) the powerful,† (4) the good.

---

* A trait of these, as of all uncultivated men, is their contempt of the other sex.

† Of this class I became acquainted with one. He was a young man of twenty-two, of very weak bodily constitution, lean and pale. He travelled in Poland as a missionary. In his look there was something so terrible, so commanding, that he ruled men by means of it quite despotically. Wherever he came he inquired about the constitution of the congregation, rejected whatever displeased him, and made new regulations which were punctually followed. The

The highest class, which rules all the others, is of course the first. These are men of enlightenment, who have attained a deep knowledge of the weaknesses of men and the motives of their actions, and have early learned the truth that prudence is better than power, inasmuch as power is in part dependent on prudence, while prudence is independent of power. A man may have as many powers and in as high a degree as he will, still his influence is always limited. By prudence, however, and a sort of psychological mechanics, that is, an insight into the best possible use of these powers and their direction, they may be infinitely strengthened. These prudent leaders, therefore, have devoted themselves to the art of ruling free men, that is, of using the will and powers of other men, so that while these believe themselves to be advancing merely their own ends, they are in reality advancing the ends of their leaders. This can be maintained by a judicious combination and regulation of the powers, so that by the slightest touch upon this instrument it may produce the greatest effect. There is here no deceit, for, as presupposed, the others themselves reach their own ends by this means best.

---

elders of the congregation, for the most part old respectable men, who far excelled him in learning, trembled before his face. A great scholar, who would not believe the infallibility of this superior, was seized with such terror by his threatening look, that he fell into a violent fever of which he died. Such extraordinary courage and determination had this man attained merely through early exercises in Stoicism.

The second class, the crafty, also use the will and the powers of others for the attainment of their ends; but in regard to these ends they are more short-sighted or more impetuous than the former class. It often happens, therefore, that they seek to attain their ends at the expense of others; and their skill consists not merely in attaining their own ends, like the first class, but in carefully concealing from others the fact that they have not reached theirs.

The powerful are men who, by their inborn or acquired moral force, rule over the weakness of others, especially when their force is such as is seldom found in others, as, for example, the control of all the passions but one, which is made the end of their actions.

The good are weak men who are merely passive in respect of their knowledge and power of will, and whose ends are reached, not by controlling, but by allowing themselves to be controlled.

The highest class, that of the prudent, supervising all the others without being under their supervision, as a matter of course rules them all. It makes use of the crafty on their good side, and seeks to make them harmless on their other side by outwitting them, so that when they believe they are deceiving, they themselves are deceived. It makes use, moreover, of the powerful for the attainment of more important ends, but seeks, when necessary, to keep them in check by the opposition of several, it may be weaker, powers. Finally it makes use of the good for the attainment of its ends, not merely with them but also with others, inasmuch as it commends these weak brethren to the others as an example of submission that is worthy of imitation, and by this means clears out of the way those hindrances that arise from the independent activity of the others.

This highest class begins usually with Stoicism, and ends with Epicureanism. Its members consist of pious men of the first sort, that is, such as have for a considerable time devoted themselves to the strictest exercise of religious and moral laws, to the control of their desires and passions. But they do not, like the Stoic, look upon Stoicism as an end in itself; they regard it merely as a means to the highest end of man, namely, happiness. They do not therefore remain at the Stoical stage, but, after having obtained from it all that is necessary to the highest end, they hasten to that end itself, the enjoyment of happiness. By their exercise in the strictest Stoicism their sensibility for all sorts of pleasure is heightened and ennobled, instead of becoming duller, as it is with gross Epicureans. By means of this exercise also they are placed in a position to defer every pleasure that presents itself till they have determined its real worth, which a gross Epicurean will not do.

The first impulse to Stoicism, however, must lie in the temperament, and it is only by a kind of self-deception that it is shifted to the account of voluntary activity. But this vanity imparts courage for actual undertakings of a voluntary nature, and this courage is continually fired by their successful issue. As the superiors of this sect are not men of science, it is not to be supposed that they have hit upon their system by the guidance of reason alone. Rather, as already said, the motive was, in the first instance, temperament, in the second, religious ideas ; and it was only after that, that they could attain to a clear knowledge and practice of their system in its purity.

This sect was therefore, in regard to its end and its means, a sort of secret society, which had nearly acquired dominion over the whole nation ; and consequently one of the greatest revolutions was to have been expected, if the excesses of some of its members had not laid bare many weak spots, and thus put weapons into the hands of its enemies. Some among them, who wished to pass for genuine Cynics, violated all the laws of decency, wandered about naked in the public streets, attended to the wants of nature in the presence of others, and so on. By their practice of extemporising, as a consequence of their principle of self-annihilation, they introduced into their sermons all sorts of foolish, unintelligible, confused stuff. By this means some of them became insane, and believed that in fact they were no longer in existence. To all this must be added their pride and contempt of others who did not belong to their sect, especially of the rabbis, who, though they had their faults, were still far more active and useful than these ignorant idlers. Men began to find out their weaknesses, to disturb their meetings, and to persecute them everywhere. This was brought about especially by the authority of a celebrated rabbi, Elias of Wilna,* who stood in great esteem among the Jews, so that now scarcely any traces of the society can be found scattered here and there.

---

* Born 1720 ; died 1797. See Jost's *Geschichte des Judenthums*, Vol. iii., pp. 248-250.—*Trans.*

CHAPTER XX.

Continuation of the Former, and also something about Religious
Mysteries.

AFTER the account of the secret society in the last chapter, this seems the most appropriate place to state, for the
examination of the thoughtful reader, my opinion about
mysteries in general, and about the *mysteries of religion*
in particular.

Mysteries in general are modes of the causal relation
between objects in nature,—modes which are real or held
to be real, but which cannot be disclosed to every man
by the natural use of his powers of knowledge. *Eternal
truths,* that is, those necessary relations of objects which
are founded on the nature of our powers of knowledge,
however few may be familiar with them, are not, according to this definition, mysteries, because any one can
discover them by the use of his powers of knowledge.

On the other hand, the results of *sympathy* and *anti-
pathy,* the medical *specifics,* and similar effects, which
some men fall upon by mere accident, and which they
afterwards find confirmed by means of observations and
experiments, are genuine *mysteries of nature,* which can
be made known to another person, not by the use of his

powers of knowledge, but only either by an accident of the same kind, or by communication from the first discoverer. If mysteries of this sort are not confirmed by observation and experiment, the belief in their reality is called *superstition*.

Religion is a covenant formed between man and another moral being of a higher genus. It presupposes a natural relation between man and this higher moral being, so that, by the mutual fulfilment of their covenant, they advance the interest of each other. If this natural relation (not being merely arbitrary and conventional) is real, and the mutual obligation of the contracting persons is founded on this relation, then it forms a *true*, but otherwise a *false*, natural religion. If the mutual obligation between man and the higher being or his representatives is drawn up in a formal code, there arises a *positive* or *revealed religion*.

The true religion, natural as well as revealed, which, as already observed, constitutes Judaism, consists in a contract, at first merely understood, but afterwards expressed, between man and the Supreme Being, who revealed Himself to the patriarchs in person (in dreams and prophetic appearances), and made known by them His will, the reward of obeying it and the punishment of disobedience, regarding which a covenant was then with mutual consent concluded. Subsequently, through his representative Moses, He renewed His covenant with the Israelites in Egypt, determining more precisely their mutual obligations; and this was afterwards on both sides formally confirmed on Mount Sinai.

To the thoughtful reader I do not need to say, that the representation of a covenant between God and man is to be taken merely *analogically*, and not in its strict sense. The absolutely Perfect Being can reveal Himself merely *as idea to the reason.* What revealed itself to the patriarchs and prophets, suitably to their power of comprehension, in figure, in an anthropomorphic manner, was not the absolutely Perfect Being Himself, but a representative of Him, His sensible image. The covenant, which this Being concludes with man, has not for its end the mutual satisfaction of wants; for the Supreme Being has no wants, and the wants of man are satisfied, not by means of this covenant, but only by observation of those relations between himself and other natural objects, which are founded on the laws of nature. This covenant, therefore, can have its foundation nowhere but in the nature of reason, without reference to any end.

Heathenism, in my opinion, is distinguished from Judaism mainly by the fact, that the latter rests upon the *formal*, absolutely necessary laws of reason, while the former (even if it be founded on the nature of things and therefore real) rests upon the *material* laws of nature which are merely hypothetically necessary. From this the inevitable result is polytheism; every particular cause is personified by imagination, that is, represented as a moral being, and made a particular deity. At first this result was a matter of mere *Empiricism* ; but by and by men had occasion to observe that these causes, which were represented as particular deities, were dependent on each other in their effects, and in a certain aspect subordinate to each other. There thus arose gradually a whole system of heathen theology, in which every deity maintains his rank, and his relation to the rest is determined.

Judaism, on the other hand, in its very origin contemplated a *system*, that is, a unity among the forces of nature ; and thereby it received at last this *pure formal* unity. This unity is merely of *regulative* use, that is, for the complete systematic connection of all the phenomena of nature ; and it presupposes a knowledge of the *multiplicity* of the various forces in nature. But owing to their excessive love of system, and their anxiety for the preservation of the *principle* in its purity, the Israelites seem to have wholly neglected its application. The result was that they preserved a religion which was pure indeed, but at the same time very unfruitful, both for the extension of knowledge and for its application in practical life. By this cause may be explained their constant murmuring against the leaders of their religion, and their repeated relapse into idolatry. They could not, like enlightened nations at the present day, direct their attention to purity of principle and useful application of their religion at the same time, and therefore of necessity they failed either in the one or in the other. Finally the Talmudists introduced a merely *formal* application of religion which aimed at no real end ; and by this means they made matters worse and worse.

This religion, therefore, which, by the intention of its founder, should have formed the Jews into the wisest and most intelligent of nations, made them by its injudicious application the most ignorant and unreasonable of all. Instead of the knowledge of nature being combined with the knowledge of religion, and the former subordinated to the latter merely as the material to the formal, the former was altogether neglected ; and the principle, maintained in its mere abstractness, continued without any application.

Mysteries of religion are objects and acts, which are adapted to ideas and principles, and the inner meaning of which is of great importance, but which have in their outward form something unseemly or ridiculous or otherwise objectionable. They must therefore, even in regard to their outward form, be kept concealed from the vulgar eye, which cannot penetrate into the inner meaning of anything ; and accordingly for it they must be a double mystery. That is to say, the objects or acts themselves constitute the lesser mysteries, and their inner meaning the greater mysteries.

Of this sort, for example, among the Jews, in the tabernacle, and afterwards in the Holy of Holies in the temple, was the ark of the covenant, which, according to the testimony of renowned authors, showed much resemblance to the sacred chest in the innermost shrine of some heathen temples. Thus we find among the Egyptians the casket of Apis, that concealed from the vulgar eye this dead animal, which as a symbol indeed had an important meaning, but in itself presented a repulsive aspect. The ark of the covenant in the first temple contained, it is true, according to the testimony of Holy Scripture, nothing besides the two tables of the law ; but of the ark in the second temple, built after the Babylonian captivity, I find in the Talmud a passage which is too remarkable not to be adduced. According to this passage the enemies, who seized the temple, found in the Holy of Holies the likeness of two persons of different sex embracing, and profaned the sacred object by a crass exposition of its inner meaning. This likeness was said to be a vivid sensible representation of the union between the nation and God, and, in order to guard against abuse, had to be withdrawn from the eye of the common people, who cling to the symbol, but do not penetrate to its inner meaning. For the same reason the *cherubim* also were concealed behind the veil.

Of the same sort were the mysteries of the ancients in general. But the greatest of all mysteries in the Jewish religion consists in the name, Jehovah, expressing *bare existence*, in abstraction from all *particular kinds of existence*, which cannot of course be conceived without *existence in general*. The doctrine of the unity of God, and the dependence of all beings on Him, in regard to their possibility as well as their actuality, can be perfectly comprehended only in conformity with a *single system*. When Josephus, in his apology against Apion, says, "The first instruction of our religion relates to the Godhead, and teaches that God comprehends all things, is an absolutely Perfect and Blessed Being, and is the *sole cause of all existence*," I believe that these words contain the best explanation of the otherwise difficult passage, where Moses says to God, "Behold, when I come unto the children of Israel, and shall say unto them, The God of your fathers hath sent me unto you, and they shall ask, What is his name? what shall I answer unto them?" and God replies, "Thus shalt thou say unto the children of Israel, Jehovah, the God of your fathers, the God of Abraham, Isaac, and Jacob hath sent me unto you, for this is my name for ever, and this is my memorial unto all generations."* For, in my opinion, this passage means nothing more than that the Jewish religion lays at its foundation the unity of God as the *immediate* cause of all existence; and it says therefore precisely the same as the remarkable inscription on the pyramid at Sais, "I am all that is and was and shall be; my veil has no mortal removed," and that other inscription under the column of Isis, "I am that which is." The name, Jehovah, is called by the Talmudists *Shem haezam (nomen proprium)*,

---

* *Exodus*, iii., 13, 14.

the name of the essence, which belongs to God in Himself, without reference to His operations. The other names of God, however, are *appellative*, and express attributes which he has in common with all His creatures, only that they belong to Him in the most eminent degree. For example, *Elohim* is a lord, a judge. *El* is a mighty one, *Adonai*, a lord ; and the same is the case with all the rest. The Talmudists drive this point so far as to maintain, that the Holy Scriptures consist merely of the manifold names of God.

The Cabbalists made use of this principle. Having enumerated the chief attributes of God, arranged them in order and brought them into a system which they call *Olam Eziloth* or *Sephiroth*, they not only picked out an appropriate name for each in the Holy Scriptures, but they made in addition all sorts of combinations of these attributes in various relations, which they expressed by similar combinations of the corresponding names. They could therefore easily expound the Holy Scriptures according to their method, inasmuch as they found therein nothing but what they had before put in themselves.

Besides these there may also be mysteries in a religion which consist in the knowledge that the religion, as understood by enlightened people, has no mysteries at all. This knowledge may be connected either with an endeavour to destroy gradually among the people the belief in mysteries, and to banish the so-called lesser mysteries by publishing the greater, or, on the contrary, with an endeavour to preserve among the people the belief in mysteries, and to make the preservation of the lesser mysteries part of the subject of the greater.

The Jewish religion, according to the spirit of its founder, is of the first kind. Moses, as well as the prophets who followed him, sought constantly to inculcate that the end of religion is not *external ceremonies*, but the knowledge of the true God as the sole incomprehensible cause of all things, and the practice of virtue in accordance with the prescriptions of reason.

The heathen religions, on the other hand, show evident traces of the second kind. Still I am not, like some, inclined to believe that everything in these was planned for *intentional deception*, but I believe that the founders of these religions were for the most part deceived deceivers; and this mode of representing the matter is far more in accordance with human nature. I am also unable to imagine that such secret designs could be propagated, by means of a formal tradition, from generation to generation. And, moreover, what would have been the use of this? Have not later generations the same faculty as the earlier of contriving schemes to reach their ends? There are princes who have never read Macchiavelli, and yet have admirably carried his principles into practice.

With regard to the society of pietists described above I am persuaded that it had as little connection with the free-masons as with any other secret society. But conjectures are allowed, and here we have to do merely with the *degree of probability.* In my opinion there are in every state societies which are essentially secret, but which externally have no appearance of being such. Every body of men with a common interest is to me a secret society. Its aim and principal operations may be ever so well known, still the *most important* of these remain concealed to the uninitiated. Of such a secret society, as of others, much good as well as evil may therefore be said ; and so long as they do not carry their mischief too far, they are always tolerated.

The Society of Pietists had a similar end in view to that of the Order of Illuminati in Bavaria, and employed nearly the same means. Its aim was to spread itself among people wandering in the dark ; and it made use of superstition in a remarkable manner, as means to this end. It sought chiefly to attract the youth to itself, and by a sort of empirical knowledge of men, to educate every member to that, for which he seemed to be destined by nature, and to assign him his proper place. Every member of the society was allowed to acquire as much knowledge of its aim and internal constitution, as enabled him to look merely backwards on his subordinates, but not forwards on his superiors. These superiors understood the art of communicating truths of reason by means of sublime figures, and of translating these figurative representations into truths of reason. It

N

might almost be said of them, that *they understood the language of animals*—a very important art, which is indispensable to every teacher of the people. By doing away with a gloomy piety, their doctrines met with acceptance among the lively youth. The principle of self-annihilation, taught by them, is, when well understood, nothing else than the foundation of self-activity. By its means all the modes of thought and action, which have become rooted by education, habit and communication with others, and by which human activity is wont to receive a wrong direction, are to be destroyed, and one's own free mode of action introduced. Moral and æsthetic feeling can in fact be preserved and perfected by this principle alone. It is only when ill understood, that it can be injurious, as I have shown by the example of this society itself.

CHAPTER XXI.

Journeys to Königsberg, Stettin and Berlin, for the purpose of extending my knowledge of men.

MY external circumstances were becoming worse and worse. I was unwilling any longer to adapt myself to my ordinary occupations, and found myself therefore everywhere out of my sphere. On the other hand, I was also unable in the place of my abode to satisfy sufficiently my favourite inclination to the study of the sciences. So I determined to betake myself to Germany, there to study medicine and, as opportunity offered, other sciences also. But the question was, how such a long journey was to be made. I knew indeed, that some merchants in the place of my abode were soon to make a journey to Königsberg in Prussia; but I had only a slight acquaintance with them, and could not therefore expect that they would take me with them for nothing. After much deliberation I fell at last upon a capital expedient.

I had among my friends a very learned and pious man, who stood in great esteem among all the Jews of the town. To him I revealed my purpose, and took him into counsel on the subject. I laid before him my miserable circumstances, pointed out to him, that, as my inclinations had been once directed to the knowledge of God and His works, I was no longer fit for any ordinary occupation ; and I represented to him especially, that I was now obliged to support myself by my scholarship alone, as an instructor in the Bible and the Talmud, which, according to the judgment of some rabbis, was not altogether allowable. I explained to him, that on this account I wished to study medicine as a profane art, by which means I might be of service, not only to myself, but to the whole of the Jews in this neighbour-hood, as there was no regular physician here, and those, who gave themselves out for such, were the most ignorant shavers, who packed men out of the world by their cures.

These reasons produced an extraordinary effect on so devout a man. He went to a merchant of his acquaintance, represented to him the importance of my under-taking, and persuaded him to take me with him to Königsberg on his own vessel. The merchant could refuse nothing to so godly a man, and therefore gave his consent.

Accordingly I set out with this Jewish merchant for Königsberg in Prussia. When I arrived there, I went to the Jewish medical doctor of the place, opened to him my proposal to study medicine, and begged him for advice and support. As his professional occupations prevented him from conveniently speaking with me on the subject, and as he could not understand me well at any rate, he referred me to some students who lodged in his house. As soon as I showed myself to these young gentlemen, and opened to them my proposal, they burst into loud laughter. And certainly for this they were not to be blamed. Imagine a man from Polish Lithuania of about five and twenty years, with a tolerably stiff beard, in tattered dirty clothes, whose language is a mixture of Hebrew, Jewish German, Polish and Russian, with their several grammatical inaccuracies, who gives out that he understands the German language, and that he has attained some knowledge of the sciences. What were the young gentlemen to think?

They began to poke fun at me, and gave me to read Mendelssohn's *Phaedo*, which by chance lay on the table. I read in the most pitiful style, both on account of the peculiar manner in which I had learned the German language, and on account of my bad pronunciation. Again they burst into loud laughter; but they said, I must explain to them what I had read. This I did in my own fashion; but as they did not understand me, they demanded that I should translate what I had read into Hebrew. This I did on the spot. The students, who understood Hebrew well, fell into no slight astonishment, when they saw that I had not only grasped correctly the meaning of this celebrated author, but also expressed it happily in Hebrew. They began therefore to interest themselves on my account, procured for me some cast-off clothing, and board during my stay in Königsberg. At the same time they advised me to go to Berlin, where I should best attain my object. To make the journey suit my circumstances, however, they advised me to go by ship from Königsberg to Stettin, and thence to Frankfurt on the Oder, from which place I should easily find means of getting to Berlin.

I went therefore by ship, and had nothing for food but some toast, some herring, and a flask of spirits. I was told in Königsberg, that the journey might take ten or, at the most, fourteen days. This prophecy, however, was not fulfilled. In consequence of contrary winds, the voyage lasted five weeks. In what circumstances, therefore, I found myself, may be easily imagined. There were in the vessel besides me no other passengers, but an old woman, who sang hymns all the time for her comfort. The Pomeranian German of the crew I could understand as little as they could my medley of Jewish, Polish and Lithuanian. I got nothing warm to eat the whole time, and was obliged to sleep on hard stuffed bags. The vessel came also sometimes into danger. Of course the most of the time I was seasick.

At last I arrived at Stettin, where I was told that I could make the journey to Frankfurt quite pleasantly on foot. But how was a Polish Jew in the most wretched circumstances, without a pfennig to buy food, and without knowing the language of the country, to make a journey even of a few miles? Yet it had to be done.

Accordingly I set out from Stettin, and as I thought over my miserable situation, I sat down under a lime-tree, and began to weep bitterly. I soon became somewhat lighter in heart; I took courage, and went on. After I had gone two or three miles, towards evening I arrived at an inn thoroughly worn out. It was the eve of the Jewish fast, which falls in August. Already I was nearly starving with hunger and thirst, and I was to fast still the whole of the next day. I had not a pfennig to spend and nothing of any value to sell.

After long reflection it occurred to me, that I must still have in my coat-pocket an iron spoon, which I had taken with me on board ship. I brought it, and begged the landlady of the inn to give me a little bread and beer for it. She refused at first to take the spoon, but after much importunity she was at last induced to grant a glass of sour beer in exchange. I was obliged therefore to content myself with this, drank my glass of beer, and went off to the stable to sleep on straw.

In the morning I proceeded on my journey, having previously inquired for a place, where there were Jews, in order that I might be able to go into the synagogue, and sing with my brethren the lamentations over the destruction of Jerusalem. This was done, and after the prayers and singing,—about midday,—I went to the Jewish schoolmaster of the place, and held some conversation with him. He soon discovered that I was a full rabbi, began to interest himself about me, and procured me a supper at the house of a Jew. He also gave me a letter of introduction to another schoolmaster in the neighbouring town, recommending me as a great Talmudist and an honourable rabbi. Here also I met with a fair reception. I was invited to the Sabbath dinner by the most respectable and richest Jew of the place, and went into the synagogue, where I was shown to the highest seat, and received every mark of honour usually bestowed on a rabbi.

After the close of the service the rich Jew referred to took me to his house, and put me in the place of honour at his table, that is between himself and his daughter. She was a young girl of about twelve years, dressed in the most beautiful style. I began, as rabbi, to hold a very learned and edifying discourse; and the less the gentleman and lady understood it, the more divine it seemed to them. All at once I observed, to my chagrin, that the young lady began to put on a sour look, and to make wry faces. At first I did not know how to explain this; but, after a while, when I turned my eyes upon myself and my miserable dirty suit of rags, the whole mystery was at once unriddled. The uneasiness of the young lady had a very good cause. And how could it be otherwise? Since I left Königsberg, about seven weeks before, I had never had a clean shirt to put on; and I had been obliged to lie in the stables of inns on bare straw, on which who knows how many poor travellers had lain before? Now all at once my eyes were opened to see my misery in its appalling magnitude. But what was I to do? How was I to help myself out of this unfortunate situation? Gloomy and sad I soon bade farewell to these good people, and proceeded on my journey to Berlin under a continued struggle with want and misery of every kind.

At last I reached this city. Here I believed that I should put an end to my misery, and accomplish all my wishes. But alas I was sadly deceived. In this capital, as is well known, no Jewish beggars were allowed. Accordingly the Jewish community of the place, in order to make provision for their poor, have built at the Rosenthaler gate a house, in which the poor are received, and questioned by the Jewish elders about what they want in Berlin. According to the results of such inquiry, they are either taken into the city, if they are sick or want employment, or they are sent forward on their journey. I was therefore conducted to this house, which was filled partly with sick people, partly with a lewd rabble. For a long while I looked round in vain for a man, with whom I might talk about my affairs.

At last I observed a man, who, to judge by his dress, was surely a rabbi. I went to him, and how great was my joy to learn from him, that he was really a rabbi, and pretty well known in Berlin! I conversed with him on all sorts of subjects connected with rabbinical learning; and as I was very open-hearted, I related to him the course of my life in Poland, revealed to him my purpose of studying medicine in Berlin, showed him my commentary on the *Moreh Nebhochim*, and so forth. He listened to all, and seemed to interest himself very much in my behalf. But all at once he disappeared out of sight.

At length towards evening came the Jewish elders. Each of the persons in the house was called, and questioned about his wants. When my turn came, I said quite frankly, that I wished to remain in Berlin, in order to study medicine. The elders refused my request point-blank, gave me a pittance in charity, and went away. The reason of this conduct towards me in particular was nothing else than the following.

The rabbi, of whom I spoke, was a zealot in his orthodoxy. Accordingly when he had discovered my sentiments and purposes, he went into town, and informed the elders about my heretical mode of thinking. He told them, that I was going to issue a new edition of the *Moreh Nebhochim* with a commentary, and that my intention was not so much to study medicine, but mainly to devote myself to the sciences in general, and to extend my knowledge. This the orthodox Jews look upon as something dangerous to religion and good morals. They believe this to be specially true of the Polish rabbis, who, having by some lucky accident been delivered from the bondage of superstition, suddenly catch a gleam of the light of reason, and set themselves free from their chains.

And this belief is to some extent well-founded. Persons in such a position may be compared to a man, who, after being famished for a long time, suddenly comes upon a well-spread table, who will attack the food with violent greed, and fill himself even to surfeiting.

The refusal of permission to stay in Berlin came upon me like a thunderclap. The ultimate object of all my hopes and wishes was all at once removed beyond my reach, just when I had seen it so near. I found myself in the situation of Tantalus, and did not know where to turn for help. I was especially pained by the treatment I received from the overseer of this poorhouse, who, by command of his superiors, urged my speedy departure, and never left off till he saw me outside of the gate. There I threw myself on the ground and began to weep bitterly. It was a Sunday, and many people went, as usual, to walk outside of the city. Most of them never turned aside to a whining worm like me, but some compassionate souls were very much struck with the sight, and asked the cause of my wailing. I answered them ; but, partly on account of my unintelligible language, partly because my speech was broken by frequent weeping and sobbing, they could not understand what I said.

I was so deeply affected by this vexation, that I fell into a violent fever. The soldiers, who kept guard at the gate, reported this at the poorhouse. The overseer came, and carried me in. I stayed there over the day, and made myself glad with the hope of becoming thoroughly sick, so as to enforce a longer sojourn in the place, during which I thought I might form some acquaintances, by whose influence I hoped to receive protection and permission to remain in Berlin. But alas! in this hope I was deceived. The following day I rose quite lively again without a trace of fever. I was therefore obliged to go. But whither? That I did not know myself. Accordingly I took the first road that I came upon, and surrendered myself to fate.

CHAPTER XXII.

Deepest Stage of Misery, and Deliverance.

IN the evening I came to an inn, where I met a poor tramp who was a Jewish beggar by profession. I was uncommonly pleased to meet one of my brethren, with whom I could talk, and to whom this neighbourhood was pretty well known. I resolved therefore to wander about the country with this companion, and to preserve my life in this way, though two such heterogeneous persons were nowhere to be met with in the world. I was an educated rabbi; he was an idiot. I had hitherto maintained myself in an honourable way; he was a beggar by profession. I had ideas of morality, propriety, and decency; he knew nothing of these. Finally, I was in sound health, it is true, but still of weakly constitution; he, on the other hand, was a sturdy, able-bodied fellow, who would have made the best of soldiers.

Notwithstanding these differences, I stuck close to the man, as, in order to prolong life, I was compelled to become a vagrant in a strange land. In our wanderings I laboured to communicate to my companion ideas of religion and of true morality, while he in return instructed

me in the art of begging. He taught me the usual formulas of the art, and recommended me especially to
curse and swear, whenever I was sent away without anything. But with all the trouble, which he gave himself
in the matter, his teachings would not take any hold on
me. The formulas of begging appeared to me absurd
I thought, if a man was once compelled to beg help of
others, he should express his feelings in the most simple
form. As far as cursing was concerned, I could not understand why a man, who refused another's request,
should draw a curse upon himself; and then it seemed
to me, that the man thus treated would be thereby em-
bittered, and the beggar be all the less likely to attain
his object. When therefore I went to beg with my comrade, I conducted myself always as if I were begging and
cursing at the same time, but in fact I never spoke a
single intelligible word. If, on the other hand, I went
alone, I had absolutely nothing to say; but from my
appearance and conduct could easily be seen what was
wanted. My comrade sometimes scolded me on account
of my slowness in learning his art, and this I bore with
the greatest patience.

In this way we wandered about in a district of a few
miles for nearly half a year. At last we resolved to turn
our steps towards Poland. When we arrived at Posen
we took up our quarters in the Jewish poorhouse, the
master of which was a poor jobbing tailor. Here I
formed the resolve, at whatever cost, to bring my

wandering to a close. It was harvest-time, and already began to be pretty cold. I was almost naked and barefoot. By this vagrant life, in which I never got any regular meals, for the most part had to content myself with bits of mouldy bread and water, and at night was obliged to lie on old straw, sometimes even on the bare earth, my health had seriously suffered. Besides, the sacred seasons and fast-days in the Jewish calendar were coming on; and as at that time I was of a somewhat strong religious disposition, I could not endure the thought of passing in complete idleness this period which others employed for the welfare of their souls.

I resolved, therefore, for the present at least, to go no farther, and, at all events if it should come to the worst, to throw myself before the synagogue, and either die there or excite the compassion of my brethren, and by that means bring my sufferings to an end. Consequently as soon as my comrade awoke in the morning, began to make arrangements for a begging tour, and summoned me to the same, I told him that I would not go with him at present; and when he asked how I intended to sustain life in any other way, I was able to answer nothing but " God will surely help."

I then went off to the Jewish school. Here I found a number of scholars, some of whom were reading, while others took advantage of the master's absence to pass the time in play. I also took a book to read. The scholars, who were struck by my strange dress,

approached and asked me whence I came and what I
wanted. Their questions I answered in my Lithuanian
dialect, at which they began to laugh, and make merry
at my expense. For this I cared little. But I
recollected that, some years before, a chief rabbi from
my neighbourhood had been appointed to the same
office in Posen, and that he had taken with him an
acquaintance and a good friend of mine as his secretary.
Accordingly I asked the boys about this friend. To my
extreme grief I learned that he was no longer in Posen,
as the chief rabbi had been afterwards promoted to the
same office in Hamburg, and his secretary had gone
with him to that place. They told me, however, that his
son, a boy about twelve years old, had been left behind
in Posen with the present chief rabbi, who was a son-in-
law of his predecessor.

This information saddened me not a little. Still the
last circumstance gave me some hope. I inquired after
the dwelling of the new chief rabbi, and went to it ; but,
as I was almost naked, I shrank from entering, and
waited until I saw some one going into the house, whom
I begged to be so good as to call my friend's son out.
The boy recognised me at once, and manifested his
astonishment at seeing me here in such a pitiable plight.
I replied, that this was not the time to relate all the misfortunes which had brought me into this state, and that
at present he should consider merely how he might somewhat relieve my distress.

This he promised to do. He went to the chief rabbi, and announced me as a great scholar and a pious man, who by extraordinary accidents had fallen into a very miserable condition. The chief rabbi, who was an excellent man, an acute Talmudist, and of very gentle character, was touched by my distress, and sent for me to come in. He conversed with me a while, discussing some of the most important subjects in the Talmud, and found me well versed in all branches of Jewish learning. Then he inquired about my intentions, and I told him that I wished to be introduced as a tutor into some family, but that meanwhile my only desire was to be able to celebrate the sacred season here, and for this short period at least to interrupt my travels.

The good-hearted rabbi bade me, so far as this was concerned, to lay aside all anxiety, spoke of my desire as a small matter, which it was nothing more than reasonable to want. He then gave me what money he had by him, invited me to dine with him every Sabbath, as long as I remained here, and bade his boy procure a respectable lodging for me. The boy came back soon, and conducted me to my lodging. I expected this to be only a small chamber in the house of some poor man. I was therefore not a little astonished, when I found myself in the house of one of the oldest Jews of the town, and that here had been prepared for me a neat little room, which was the study of the master, he and his son being both scholars.

o

As soon as I had looked round a little, I went to the housewife, and, thrusting some coppers into her hand, I asked her to get me some gruel for supper. She began to smile at my simplicity, and said, " No, no, sir, that is not our agreement. The chief rabbi has not given you such a recommendation, that you are obliged to have us making you gruel for money." She then went on to explain, that I was not only to lodge in her house, but also to eat and drink with them, as long as I stayed in the town. I was astonished at this unexpected good fortune; but my delight was still greater, when after supper I was shown to a clean bed. I could not believe my eyes, and asked several times, " Is this really for me ? " I can say with truth, that never, before or since this incident, have I felt such a degree of happiness, as when I lay down that night, and felt my limbs, which for half a year had been overwearied and almost broken, recovering their former strength in a soft bed.

I slept till late in the day. I had scarcely risen when the chief rabbi sent for me to come and see him. When I made my appearance he asked me how I was pleased with my lodging. I could not find words to express my feelings on the subject, and exclaimed in ecstasy, " I have slept in a bed ! " At this the chief rabbi was uncommonly pleased. He then sent for the school precentor, and as soon as this man appeared he said to him, " Go to the shop of ——, and get cloth for a suit to this gentleman." Thereupon he turned to me and asked what sort of stuff I liked. Overpowered by the feeling of gratitude and esteem for this excellent man I could answer nothing. The tears streaming down my cheeks served for my only answer.

The chief rabbi also ordered for me some new linen. In two days everything was ready. Dressed in my new linen and new suit I went to the chief rabbi. I was going to express my gratitude to him, but could scarcely get out a few broken words. For the chief rabbi this was a charming sight. He waived my thanks, and said that I was not to think too highly of him for this, inasmuch as what he had done for me was a mere trifle not worth mentioning.

Now the reader may perhaps suppose that this chief rabbi was a wealthy man, for whom the expense to which he put himself on my account was really a trifle ; but I can give the assurance that this was far from being the case. He had merely a moderate income ; and as he occupied himself wholly with study, his wife had the management of his affairs, and especially the charge of housekeeping. Actions of this sort, therefore, had to be done without the knowledge of his wife, and under the pretext that he received from other people the money for the purpose. Moreover, he lived a very temperate life, fasted every day except Sabbath, and never ate flesh the whole week through. Nevertheless, to satisfy his benevolent inclinations he could not avoid making debts. His severe manner of life, his many studies and vigils, weakened his strength to such a degree that he died about the thirty-sixth year of his life. His death took place after he had been appointed chief rabbi in Fördet, to which place he was followed by a large number of disciples. I can never think of this godly man without being deeply affected.

In my former lodging at the poor tailor's I had left some trifles which I now went to fetch. The tailor, his wife, and my former comrade in beggary, who had already heard of the happy change in my affairs, expected me with the greatest impatience. It was a touching scene. The man, who three days before arrived in this poor hut, quite debilitated, half naked, and barefoot, whom the poor inmates of the house regarded as an outcast of nature, and whose comrade in linen blouse had looked down upon him with mockery and contempt, —this man (his fame before him) now comes into the same hut with a cheerful face, and in reverend garb dressed as a chief rabbi.

They all testified their joy and surprise at the transformation. The poor woman took her babe in her arms and, with tears in her eyes, begged a blessing for him. My comrade begged me very affectingly for forgiveness on account of his rough treatment. He said that he deemed himself fortunate in having had such a fellow-traveller, but would hold himself unfortunate if I would not forgive the faults he had committed in ignorance. I spoke to them all very kindly, gave the little one my blessing, handed to my old comrade all the cash I had in my pocket, and went back deeply affected.

Meanwhile my fame was spread through the whole town by the conduct towards me of the chief rabbi, as well as that of my new host, who was himself a scholar, and had formed a high opinion of my talents and learning from frequent conversations and discussions which we had held together. All the scholars of the town, therefore, came to see me and discuss with me as a famous travelling rabbi; and the more intimately they came to know me, so much the higher rose their esteem.

This period was undoubtedly the happiest and most honourable in my life. The young scholars of the town passed a resolution at their meeting to make up for me a salary, for which I was to deliver lectures to them on the celebrated and profound work of Maimonides, *Moreh Nebhochim.* This proposal, however, was never carried out, because the parents of these young people were anxious lest their children should be thereby led astray, and by independent thinking on religion be made to waver in their faith. They acknowledged indeed that, with all my fondness for religious speculation, I was still a pious man and an orthodox rabbi. But they could not rely upon their children having sufficient judgment, to be able to enter upon this course without passing from one extreme to the other, from superstition to unbelief; and therein perhaps they were right.

After I had spent about four weeks in this way, the

man, with whom I lodged, came to me, and said, "Herr Solomon, allow me to make a proposal to you. If you are inclined merely to solitary study, you may remain here as long as you like. If, however, you do not wish to withdraw into such complete retirement, but are inclined to be of service to the world with your talents, there is a wealthy man here—one of the most prominent people of the town—who has an only son, and wishes nothing so much as to have you for his tutor. This man is my brother-in-law. If you will not do it for his sake, please do it for mine, and to gratify the chief rabbi, as he has deeply at heart the education of my nephew, who is connected by marriage with his family." This offer I accepted with delight. I came therefore into this family under advantageous conditions as tutor, and remained with them two years in the greatest honour. Nothing was done in the house without my knowledge. I was always met with the greatest respect. I was held in fact to be almost something more than human.

Thus the two years flowed on imperceptibly and happily for me. But during the time some little incidents took place, which I believe should not be altogether omitted in this history.

In the first place the esteem entertained for me in this house went so far, that *malgré moi* they were going to make me a prophet. My pupil was betrothed to the daughter of a chief rabbi, who was a brother-in-law of the chief rabbi in Posen. The bride, a girl of about twelve years, was brought to Posen by her parents-in-law at the feast of Pentecost. On the occasion of this visit I observed that the girl was of a very phlegmatic temperament and somewhat consumptive. I mentioned this to the brother of my host, and added with a significant look, that I was very anxious for the girl, as I did not believe that her health would last long. After the feast was over the girl was sent home, and a fortnight afterwards a letter was received announcing her death. On this account, not only in the house where I lived, but in the whole town, I was taken for a prophet, who had been able to foretell the death of this girl. As I wished nothing less than to deceive, I endeavoured to bring these superstitious people to a different train of thought. I told them that anybody, who had made observations in the world, would have been able to foretell the same thing. But it was of no use. Once for all I was a prophet, and had to remain one.

Another incident occurred in a Jewish house one Friday when they were preparing fish for the Sabbath. The fish was a carp, and it seemed to the cook who was cutting it up as if it uttered a sound. This threw everybody into a panic. The rabbi was asked what should be done with this dumb fish that had ventured to speak. Under the superstitious idea that the carp was possessed with a spirit, the rabbi enjoined that it should be wrapped in a linen cloth, and buried with pomp.

Now, in the house where I lived, this awe-inspiring

event became the subject of conversation. Having by this time emancipated myself pretty thoroughly from superstitions of this sort by diligent study of the *Moreh Nebhochim*, I laughed heartily over the story, and said, that, if instead of burying the carp, they had sent it to me, I should have tried how such an inspired carp would taste.

This *bon mot* became known. The learned men fell into a passion about it, denounced me as a heretic, and sought to persecute me in every way. But the respect, entertained for me in the house where I was tutor, made all their efforts fruitless. As I found myself in this way safe, and the spirit of fanaticism, instead of deterring me, rather spurred me on to further reflection, I began to push matters a little farther, frequently slept through the time of prayer, went seldom to the synagogue, and so on. At last the measure of my sins became so full, that nothing could secure me any longer from persecution.

At the entrance to the Common Hall in Posen there has been, no one knows for how long, a stag-horn fixed into the wall. The Jews are unanimously of the conviction, that any one who touches this horn is sure to die on the spot; and they relate a multitude of instances in proof. This would not go down with me at all, and I made fun of it. So one day when I was passing the stag-horn with some other Jews, I said to them, "You Posen fools, do you think that any one who touches this horn must die on the spot? See, I dare to touch it!"

Horror-struck, they expected my death on the spot; but as nothing happened, their anxiety for me was converted into hatred. They looked on me as one who had profaned the sanctuary.

This fanaticism stirred up in me the desire to go to Berlin, and destroy by enlightenment the remnant of superstition which still clung to me. I therefore begged leave of my employer. He expressed the wish indeed, that I should remain longer in his house, and assured me of his protection against all persecution. But as I had once for all taken my resolution, I was determined not to alter it. I therefore bade goodbye to my employer and his whole family, took a seat on the Frankfurt post, and set out for Berlin.

CHAPTER XXIII.

Arrival in Berlin—Acquaintances—Mendelssohn—Desperate Study
of Metaphysics—Doubts—Lectures on Locke and Adelung.

As I came to Berlin this time by post, I did not require
to remain outside the Rosenthaler Gate to be examined
by the Jewish elders; I proceeded without any difficulty
into the city, and was allowed to take up my quarters
where I chose.   To *remain* in the city, however, was a
different thing.   The Jewish police-officers—L. M. of
those days was a terrible fellow,—went every day round
all the hotels and other houses designed for the reception
of strangers, made inquiry into the quality and occupation of newcomers, as well as the probable length of their
stay, and allowed them no rest till they had either found
some occupation in the city, or were out of it again, or
—the alternative goes without saying.   I had taken a
lodging on the New Market with a Jew, who was accustomed to receive in his house poor travellers that had
not much to spend, and who the following day received
a visit of this sort.

The Jewish police-officer, L. M., came and examined
me in the strictest manner.   I told him that I wished to

enter into service as a family-tutor in Berlin, and that
therefore the length of my stay could not be exactly
determined. I appeared to him suspicious; he believed
he had seen me here before, and evidently looked on me
as a comet, which comes nearer to the earth the second
time than the first, and so makes the danger more threat-
ing. But when he saw by me a *Milloth Higgayon* or
Hebrew Logic, drawn up by Maimonides, and annotated
by Mendelssohn, he went into a perfect rage. "Yes! yes!"
he exclaimed, "that's the sort of books for me!" and as
he turned to me with a threatening look, "Pack," he said,
"out of Berlin as quick as you can, if you don't wish to
be led out with all the honours!" I trembled, and knew
not what to do; but as I had learnt that there was a
Polish Jew, a man of talent, residing in Berlin for the
sake of study, and received with esteem in the best
families, I paid him a visit.

He received me as a countryman in a very friendly
manner, asked about my home in Poland, and what had
brought me to Berlin. When I told him in reply, that
from my childhood I had discovered an inclination to
the sciences, had already made myself acquainted with
this and that Hebrew work which touches upon these,
and now had come to Berlin in order to be *Maamik
Bechochmah* (to become absorbed in the sciences), he
smiled at this quaint rabbinical phrase, but gave me his
full approval; and after conversing with me for some
time, he begged me to visit him often, which I very

willingly promised to do, and went away rejoicing in spirit.

The very next day I visited my Polish friend again, and found with him some young people belonging to a prominent Jewish family, who visited him often, and conversed with him on scientific subjects. They entered into conversation with me, found much amusement in my jargon, as well as in my simplicity and open-heartedness; in particular they laughed heartily at the phrase, *Maamik Bechochmah*, of which they had heard already. All this gave me courage, and they assured me that I should not find myself mistaken in the expectation of being able to be *Maamik Bechochmah* in Berlin. And when I made known my fear about the above-mentioned police-officer, they made me pluck up courage by promising to obtain protection for me from their family, so that I might remain in Berlin as long as I chose.

They kept their word, and Herr D—— P——, a well-to-do man of excellent character, of many attainments and fine taste, who was an uncle of these young men, not only paid me much attention, but also procured for me a respectable lodging, and invited me to the Sabbath dinner. Others of the family also sent me meals at my room on fixed days. Among these was a brother of these young men, in other respects an honourable man, who was not without attainments. But as he was a zealous Talmudist, he inquired earnestly whether with my inclination towards the sciences I had not quite neglected the Talmud ; and as soon as he learnt, that I was so *Maamik Bechochmah* as to neglect the study of the Talmud, he gave up sending me my meals.

As I now had permission to remain in Berlin, I thought of nothing but how to carry my purpose into effect. Accidentally one day I went into a butter-shop, and found the dealer in the act of anatomising a somewhat old book for use in his trade. I looked at it, and found, to my no small astonishment, that it was Wolff's *Metaphysics, or the Doctrine of God, of the World, and of Man's Soul.* I could not understand, how in a city so enlightened as Berlin such important works could be treated in this barbarous fashion. I turned therefore to the dealer, and asked him, if he would not sell the book. He was ready to part with it for two groschen. Without thinking long about it I gave the price at once, and went home delighted with my treasure.

At the very first reading I was in raptures with the book. Not only this sublime science in itself, but also the order and mathematical method of the celebrated author,—the precision of his explanations, the exactness of his reasoning, and the scientific arrangement of his exposition,—all this struck a new light in my mind.

With the Ontology, the Cosmology, and the Psychology all went well ; but the Theology created many diffi-culties, inasmuch as I found its dogmas, not only not in harmony, but even in contradiction, with the preceding propositions. At the very beginning I could not assent to Wolff's argument *a posteriori* for the existence of God in accordance with the Principle of Sufficient Reason ; and I raised the objection to it, that, inasmuch as, according to Wolff's own confession, the Principle of Sufficient Reason is abstracted from particular cases of experience, the only point which can be proved by it is, that every object of experience must have its sufficient reason in some other object of experience, but not in an object beyond all experience. I also compared these new metaphysical doctrines with those of Maimonides, or rather of Aristotle, which were already known to me ; and I could not bring them into harmony at all.

I resolved therefore to set forth these doubts in the Hebrew language, and to send what I wrote to Herr Mendelssohn, of whom I had already heard so much. When he received my communication, he was not a little astonished at it, and replied to me at once, that in fact my doubts were well founded, that I should not however allow myself to be discouraged on their account, but should continue to study with the zeal with which I had begun.

Encouraged by this, I wrote in Hebrew a dissertation in which I brought into doubt the foundations of Revealed as well as of Natural Theology. All the thirteen articles of faith, laid down by Maimonides, I attacked with philosophical arguments, with the exception of one, namely the article on reward and punishment, which I conceded merely in its philosophical interpretation, as referring to the natural consequences of voluntary actions. I sent this dissertation to Mendelssohn, who was not a little amazed, that a Polish Jew, who had scarcely got the length of seeing the Metaphysics of Wolff, was already able to penetrate into their depths so far, that he was in a position to shake their results by means of a correct Ontology. He invited me to visit him, and I accepted his invitation. But I was so shy, the manners and customs of the Berliners were so new to me, it was not without fear and embarrassment, that I ventured to enter a fashionable house. When therefore I opened Mendelssohn's door, and saw him and other gentlefolks who were there, as well as the beautiful rooms and elegant furniture, I shrank back, closed the door again, and had a mind not to go in. Mendelssohn however had observed me. He came out and spoke to me very kindly, led me into his room, placed himself beside me at the window, and paid me many compliments about my writing. He assured me, that, if I went on in this way, I should in a short time make great progress in Metaphysics ; and he promised also to resolve my doubts. Not satisfied with this, the worthy man looked after my maintenance also, recommended me to the most eminent, enlightened and wealthy Jews, who made provision for my board and other wants. Their tables I was at liberty to enjoy when I chose, and their libraries were open to my use.

Especially worthy of mention among these gentlemen was H——, a man of many attainments and excellent disposition, who was a particular friend and disciple of Mendelssohn. He took great pleasure in my conversation, often discussed with me the most important subjects in Natural Theology and Morals, on which I expressed my thoughts to him quite frankly and without disguise. I went over with him in a conversational way all the systems known to me that are generally denounced, and defended them with the greatest pertinacity. He met me with objections; I answered them, and brought in my turn objections against the opposite systems. At first this friend regarded me as a speaking animal, and entertained himself with me, as one is apt to do with a dog or a starling that has been taught to speak a few words. The odd mixture of the animal in my manners, my expressions, and my whole outward behaviour, with the rational in my thoughts, excited his imagination more than the subject of our conversation roused his understanding. By degrees the fun was turned to earnest. He began to give his attention to the subjects themselves; and as, notwithstanding his other capabilities and attainments, he had no philosophical head, and the liveliness of his imagination generally interfered with the ripeness of his judgment, the results of our conversations may be readily imagined.

A few examples will be sufficient to give an idea of the manner in which I conducted a discussion at the time, of the ellipses in my diction arising from my deficiency in expressions, and of the way in which I illustrated everything by examples. I endeavoured once to make Spinoza's system intelligible,—to show that all things are merely accidents of a single substance. My friend interrupted me and said, "But, good heavens ! are not you and I different men, and do we not each possess an existence of our own?" "Close the shutters," I called in reply to his objection. This strange expression threw him into astonishment ; he did not know what I meant. At last I explained myself. "See," said I, "the sun shines through the windows. This square window gives you a square reflection, and the round window a round reflection. Are they on that account different things, and not rather one and the same sunshine?"

On another occasion I defended Helvetius' system of self-love. He brought against it the objection, that we surely love other persons as well as ourselves. "For instance," said he, "I love my wife;" and to confirm this he gave her a kiss. "That proves nothing against me," I replied. "For, why do you kiss your wife? Because you find pleasure in doing it."

Herr A—— M—— also, a good honest fellow, and at that time a wealthy man, allowed me free access to his house. Here I found Locke in the German translation, and I was pleased with him at the first hasty glance, for I recognised him as the best of the modern philosophers, as a man who had no interest but the truth. Accordingly I proposed to the tutor of Herr A—— M——, that he should take lessons from me on this admirable work. At

P

first he smiled at my simplicity in proposing, that I, who had scarcely got the length of seeing Locke, should give lessons to him whose native tongue was German, and who had been brought up in the sciences. He acted, however, as if he found nothing offensive in the matter, accepted my proposal, and fixed an hour for the lessons. I presented myself at the time appointed, and began the lessons; but as I could not read a word of German correctly, I told my pupil to read aloud paragraph by paragraph in the text, and that then I should give him an exposition of each. My pupil, who pretended to be in earnest, consented to this also, to carry on the joke; but how great was his astonishment when he found, that no joke was to be played in the matter, that in fact my expositions and remarks, though delivered in my own peculiar language, evinced a genuine philosophical spirit.

It was still more amusing, when I became acquainted with the family of Widow Levi, and made the proposal to her son, the young Herr Samuel Levi,* who is still my Maecenas, that he should take lessons from me in the German language. The studious youth, incited by my reputation, was resolved to make a trial, and wished me to explain Adelung's *German Grammar.* I, who had never seen Adelung's Grammar, did not allow myself to be at all disconcerted on this account.† My pupil was

---

* These names are taken from *Maimoniana,* p. 108.—*Trans.*

† The method, in which, as before explained, I had learnt to

obliged to read Adelung bit by bit, while I not only expounded it, but added glosses of my own. In particular I found a good deal to take exception to in Adelung's philosophical explanation of the parts of speech; and I drew up an explanation of my own, which I communicated to my intelligent pupil, by whom it is still preserved.

As a man altogether without experience I carried my frankness at times a little too far, and brought upon myself many vexations in consequence. I was reading Spinoza. His profound thought and his love of truth pleased me uncommonly; and as his system had already been suggested to me by the Cabbalistic writings, I began to reflect upon it anew, and became so convinced of its truth, that all the efforts of Mendelssohn to change my opinion were unavailing. I answered all the objections brought against it by the Wolfians, brought objections against their system myself, and showed, that, if the *nominal definitions* of the Wolfian Ontology are converted into *real definitions*, conclusions the very opposite of theirs are the result. Moreover, I could not explain the persistency of Mendelssohn and the Wolfians generally in adhering to their system, except as a political dodge

read and to understand books without any preparatory studies, and to which I had been driven in Poland by the want of books, grew to such an expertness, that I felt certain beforehand of being able to understand anything.

and a piece of hypocrisy, by which they studiously endeavoured to descend to the mode of thinking common in the popular mind; and this conviction I expressed openly and without reserve. My friends and well-wishers, who for the most part had never themselves speculated on philosophical subjects, but blindly adopted the results of the systems prevailing at the time as if they were established truths, did not understand me, and therefore also were unable to follow me in my opinions.

Mendelssohn, whose usual course was to tack, did not wish to oppose my love of inquiry, secretly even took pleasure in it, and said, that at present indeed I was not on the right road, but that the course of my thoughts must not be checked, because, as Descartes rightly remarked, doubt is the beginning of thorough philosophical speculation.

CHAPTER XXIV.

Mendelssohn—A chapter devoted to the memory of a worthy friend.

Quis desiderio sit pudor aut modus tam cari capitis ?

THE name of Mendelssohn is too well known to the
world, to make it necessary for me here to dwell long on
the portraiture of the great intellectual and moral qualities
of this celebrated man of our nation.   I shall sketch
merely those prominent features of his portrait, which
have made the strongest impression upon me.   He was
a good Talmudist, and a pupil of the celebrated Rabbi
Israel, or, as he is otherwise named after the title of a
Talmudic work which he wrote, Nezach Israel (the
strength of Israel),—a Polish rabbi who was denounced
for heresy by his countrymen.   This rabbi had, besides
his great Talmudic capabilities and acquirements, a good
deal of scientific talent, especially in mathematics, with
which he had attained a thorough acquaintance, even in
Poland, from the few Hebrew writings on this science,
as may be seen in the above-mentioned work.   In this
work there are introduced solutions of many important
mathematical problems, which are applied either to the

explanation of some obscure passages in the Talmud, or to the determination of a law. Rabbi Israel of course was more interested in the extension of useful knowledge among his countrymen than in the determination of a law, which he used merely as a vehicle for the other. He showed, for example, that it is not right for the Jews in our part of the world to turn exactly to the East at prayer ; for the Talmudic law requires them to turn to Jerusalem, and, as our part of the world lies north-west from Jerusalem, they ought to turn to the south-east. He shows also how, by means of spherical trigonometry, the required direction may be determined with the utmost exactness in all parts of the world, and many other truths of a similar kind. Along with the celebrated Chief Rabbi Fränkel, he contributed much to develop the great abilities of Mendelssohn.

Mendelssohn possessed a thorough acquaintance with mathematics ; and this science he valued, not only for its self-evidence, but also as the best exercise in profound reasoning. That he was a great philosopher, is well enough known. He was not indeed an originator of new systems ; he had however amended the old systems, especially the Leibnitio-Wolfian, and had applied it with success to many subjects in philosophy.

It is hard to say whether Mendelssohn was endowed with more acuteness or with depth of intellect. Both faculties were found united in him in a very high degree. His exactness in definition and classification, and his fine distinctions, are evidences of the former talent, while his profound philosophical treatises afford proofs of the latter.

In his character, as he himself confessed, he was by nature a man of strong passions, but by long exercise in Stoical morality he had learnt to keep them under control. A young man, under the impression that Mendelssohn had done him a wrong, came one day to upbraid him, and indulged in one impertinence after another. Mendelssohn stood leaning on a chair, never turned his eye from his visitor, and listened to all his impertinences with the utmost Stoical patience. After the young man had vented all his passion, Mendelssohn went to him and said, "Go! You see that you fail to reach your object here; you can't make me angry." Still on such occasions Mendelssohn could not conceal his sorrow at the weakness of human nature. Not infrequently I was myself overheated in my disputes with him, and violated the respect due to such a man,—a fact on which I still reflect with remorse.

Mendelssohn possessed deep knowledge of human nature,—a knowledge which consists not so much in seizing some unconnected features of a character, and representing them in theatrical fashion, as in discovering those essential features of a character, from which all the others may be explained, and in some measure predicted. He was able to describe accurately all the springs of action and the entire moral wheelwork of a man, and understood thoroughly the mechanism of the soul. This gave a character, not only to his intercourse and other dealings with men, but also to his literary labours.

Mendelssohn understood the useful and agreeable art of throwing himself into another person's mode of thought. He could thus supply whatever was deficient, and fill up the gaps in the thoughts of another. Jews newly arrived from Poland, whose thoughts are for the most part confused, and whose language is an unintelligible jargon, Mendelssohn could understand perfectly. In his conversations with them he adopted their expressions and forms of speech, sought to bring down his mode of thinking to theirs, and thus to raise theirs to his own.

He understood also the art of finding out the good side of every man and of every event. Not infrequently, therefore, he found entertainment in people whose intercourse, owing to the eccentric use of their powers, is by others avoided ; and only downright stupidity and dullness were offensive to him, though they were so in the highest degree. I was once an eye-witness of the manner in which he entertained himself with a man of the most eccentric style of thinking and the most extravagant behaviour. I lost all patience on the occasion, and after the man was gone I asked Mendelssohn in wonder, " How could you have anything to do with this fellow ? " " We examine attentively," he said, " a machine whose construction is unknown to us, and we seek to make intelligible its mode of working. Should not this man claim a like attention? should we not seek in the same way to render intelligible his odd utterances, since he certainly has his springs of action and his wheel-work as well as any machine?"

In discussion with a reasoner who held stubbornly to a system once adopted Mendelssohn was stubborn himself, and took advantage of the slightest inaccuracy in his opponent's way of thinking. On the other hand, with a more accommodating thinker he was accommodating also, and used commonly to close the discussion with the words, "We must hold fast, not to mere words, but to the things they signify."

Nothing was so offensive to him as an *esprit de bagatelle* or affectation; with anything of this sort he could not conceal his displeasure. H—— once invited a party, in which Mendelssohn was the principal guest, and he entertained them the whole time with talk about some hobby of his, which was not exactly of the choicest kind. Mendelssohn showed his displeasure by never deigning to give the slightest attention to the worthless creature. Madam —— was a lady who affected an excess of sensibility, and as is customary with such characters, used to reproach herself in order to extort praise from others. Mendelssohn sought to bring her to reason by showing her impressively how exceptionable her conduct was and how she ought to think seriously about improvement.

In a disconnected conversation he took little part himself; he acted rather as observer then, and took pleasure in watching the conduct of the rest of the company. If, on the other hand, the conversation was coherent, he took the warmest interest in it himself, and, by a skilful turn, he could, without interrupting the conversation, give it a useful direction.

Mendelssohn could never take up his mind with trifles; matters of the greatest moment kept him in restless activity, such as the principles of Morals and of Natural Theology, the immortality of the soul, etc. In all these branches of inquiry, in which humanity is so deeply interested, he has also, as I hold, done as much as can be done on the principles of the Leibnitio-Wolfian philosophy. Perfection was the compass which he had constantly before his eyes, and which directed his course, in all these investigations. His God is the Ideal of the highest perfection, and the idea of the highest perfection lies at the basis of his Ethics. The principle of his Æsthetics is sensuous perfection.

My discussion with him on our first acquaintance referred mainly to the following points. I was a faithful adherent of Maimonides before I became acquainted with modern philosophy ; and, as such, I insisted on the negation * of all positive attributes to God, inasmuch as these can be represented by us only as finite. Accord-

---

* Here there seems in the original an evident misprint of *Vereinigung* for *Verneinung.—Trans.*

ingly I proposed the following dilemma : Either God is *not* the absolutely perfect being, in which case his attributes may by us be not only *conceived*, but also *known*, that is, represented as realities belonging to an object ; or He *is* the absolutely perfect being, and then the idea of God is conceived by us, but its reality is merely *assumed* as problematic.   Mendelssohn, on the other hand, insisted on the affirmation, with regard to God, of all realities,—a position which goes very well with the Leibnitio-Wolfian philosophy, because it requires, in order to prove the reality of an idea, nothing more than that it is thinkable, that is, fulfils the law of Non-Contradiction.

My moral theory was then genuine Stoicism. It aimed at the attainment of free will and the ascendency of reason over the feelings and passions.   It made the highest destination of man to be the maintenance of his *differentia specifica*, the knowledge of the truth ; and all other impulses, common to us with the irrational animals, were to be put in operation merely as means to this chief end.   The knowledge of the good was not distinguished by me from the knowledge of the true ; for, following Maimonides, I held the knowledge of the truth to be the highest good of man.   Mendelssohn, on the other hand, maintained that the idea of perfection, which lies at the basis of Ethics, is of much wider extent than the mere knowledge of the truth.   All natural impulses, capacities and powers, as something good in themselves (not merely as means to something good), were to be brought into exercise as realities. The highest perfection was the idea of the maximum, or the greatest sum, of these realities.

The immortality of the soul, for me, following Maimonides, consisted in the union with the Universal Spirit of that part of the faculty of knowledge which has been brought into exercise, in proportion to the degree of that exercise ; and in accordance with this doctrine I held those only to be partakers of this immortality, who occupy themselves with the knowledge of eternal truths, and in the degree in which they do so. The soul, therefore, must, with the attainment of this high immortality, lose its individuality. That Mendelssohn, in accordance with modern philosophy, thought differently on this subject, every one will readily believe.

His sentiments in reference to revealed or positive religion I can give here, not as something made known to me by himself, but merely in so far as I have been able to infer them from his utterances on the subject in his writings with the assistance of my own reflections. For at that time, as an incipient freethinker, I explained all revealed religion as in itself false, and its use, so far as the writings of Mendelssohn had enabled me to understand it, as merely temporary. Moreover, being a man without experience, I thought it an easy matter to convince others in opposition to their firmly rooted habits and long-cherished prejudices, while I assumed the usefulness of such a reformation to be undoubted.

Mendelssohn therefore was unable to hold any conversation with me on the subject, since he could not but fear lest, as has happened, and happens still, in the case of several others, I should pronounce his arguments in reply to be mere pieces of sophistry, and should attribute motives to him on that account. From his utterances, however, in the preface to his *Manasseh ben Israel* as well as in his *Jerusalem*, it is clear that, though he did not consider any revealed *doctrines* to be eternal truths, yet he accepted revealed laws of religion as such, and that he held the laws of the Jewish religion, as the fundamental laws of a theocratic constitution, to be immutable as far as circumstances allow.

So far as I am concerned, I am led to assent entirely to Mendelssohn's reasoning by my own reflections on the fundamental laws of the religion of my fathers. The fundamental laws of the Jewish religion are at the same time the fundamental laws of the Jewish state. They must therefore be obeyed by all who acknowledge themselves to be members of this state, and who wish to enjoy the rights granted to them under condition of their obedience. But, on the other hand, any man who separates himself from this state, who desires to be considered no longer a member of it, and to renounce all his rights as such, whether he enters another state or betakes himself to solitude, is also in his conscience no longer bound to obey those laws. I assent moreover to Mendelssohn's remark, that a Jew cannot, by simply passing over to the Christian religion, free himself from the laws of his own religion, because Jesus of Nazareth observed these laws himself and commanded his followers to observe them. But how, if a Jew wishes to be no longer a member of this theocratic state, and goes over to the heathen religion, or to the philosophical, which is nothing more than pure natural religion ? How, if, merely as a member of a political state, he submits to its laws, and demands from it his rights in return, without making any declaration whatever about his religion, since the state is reasonable enough not to require from him a declaration with which it has nothing to do ? I do not believe Mendelssohn would maintain that even in this case a Jew is bound in conscience to observe the laws of his fathers' religion merely because it is the religion of his fathers. As far as is known, Mendelssohn lived in accordance with the laws of his religion. Presumably, therefore, he always regarded himself as still a member of the theocratic state of his fathers, and consequently acted up to his duty in this respect. But any man who abandons this state is acting just as little in violation of his duty.

On the other hand I consider it wrong in Jews, who from family attachments and interests profess the Jewish religion, to transgress its laws, where, according to their own opinion, these do not stand in the way of those motives. I cannot therefore understand the conduct of Mendelssohn in reference to a Jew of Hamburg who openly transgressed the laws of his religion, and who was on that account excommunicated by the chief rabbi. Mendelssohn wanted to cancel the excommunication on the ground that the church has no rights in civil matters. But how can he then maintain the perpetuity of the Jewish ecclesiastical state? For what is a state without rights, and wherein consists, according to Mendelssohn, the rights of this ecclesiastical state? "How," says Mendelssohn, (in the preface to *Manasseh ben Israel*, p. 48), "can a state allow one of its useful and respected citizens to suffer misfortune through its laws?" Surely not, I reply; but the Hamburg Jew suffers no misfortune by virtue of the excommunication. He required only to say or do nothing which legally leads to this result, and he would then have avoided the sentence. For excommunication is merely tantamount to saying :— "So long as you put yourself in opposition to the laws of our communion, you are excluded from it ; and you must therefore make up your mind whether this open disobedience or the privileges of our communion can most advance your blessedness." This surely cannot have escaped a mind like Mendelssohn's, and I leave it to others to decide how far a man may be inconsistent for the sake of human welfare.

Mendelssohn had to endure many an injustice at the hands of otherwise estimable men, from whom such treatment might least have been expected. Lavater's officiousness is well enough known, and disapproved by all right-thinking men.* The profound Jacobi had a predilection for Spinozism, with which surely no independent thinker can find fault, and wanted to make out Mendelssohn, as well as his friend Lessing, to be Spinozists, in spite of themselves. With this view he published a correspondence on the subject, which was never intended to appear in print, and be subjected to public inspection. What was the use of this? If Spinozism is true, it is so without Mendelssohn's assent. Eternal truths have nothing to do with the majority of votes, and least of all where, as I hold, the truth is of such a nature, that it leaves all expression behind.

Such an injustice must have given Mendelssohn much annoyance. A celebrated physician maintained even,

---

* The incident referred to was the following. Lavater had translated into German a work, which had a great reputation in its day, by the eminent Swiss scientific writer, Bonnet, on the evidences of Christianity. Out of respect for Mendelssohn, Lavater dedicated the translation to him, requiring him, however, either to refute the work, or to do " what policy, love of truth, and probity demand,— what Socrates would doubtless have done, had *he* read the work, and found it unanswerable." Mendelssohn was thus placed in an awkward dilemma. He could not well let the challenge pass unacknowledged ; and yet, owing to the disabilities under which the Jews laboured all over the world, he would have seriously imperilled their interests by appearing even to impugn the evidences of Christianity. He had, moreover, resolved never to enter into religious controversy. Under the circumstances his reply was masterly as it was dignified and candid. Lavater saw his mistake ; and it is but due to him to say, that he publicly apologised for it in the fullest and frankest manner.— *Trans.*

that it caused his death; but, though I am not a physician, I venture to gainsay the assertion. Mendelssohn's conduct in relation to Jacobi, as well as to Lavater, was that of a hero. No, no! this hero died in the fifth act.

The acute preacher, Jacob, in Halle published, after Mendelssohn's death, a book entitled, *Examination of Mendelssohn's Morgenstunden*, in which he shows that, according to the *Critique of Pure Reason*, all metaphysical doctrines are to be rejected as baseless. But why does this concern Mendelssohn more than any other metaphysician? Mendelssohn did nothing but develop to greater completeness the Leibnitio-Wolfian philosophy, apply it to many important subjects of human inquiry, and clothe it in an attractive garb. It is just as if any one were to attack Maimonides, who has written an excellent astronomical treatise on Ptolemaic principles, by writing a book with the title, *Examination of the Hilchoth Kidush Hakodesh of Maimonides*, in which he should seek to refute his author on Newtonian principles! But enough of this.

CHAPTER XXV.

My aversion at first for belles lettres, and my subsequent conversion —Departure from Berlin—Sojourn in Hamburg—I drown myself in the same way as a bad actor shoots himself—An old fool of a woman falls in love with me, but her addresses are rejected.

FOR *belles lettres* I discovered not the slightest inclination; I could not even conceive how any man was to form a science of what pleases or displeases—a matter which, according to my opinion at the time, could have merely a subjective ground. One day when I was taking a walk with Mendelssohn, our conversation fell upon the subject of the poets, whom he recommended me to read. " No," I replied, " I am going to read none of the poets. What is a poet but a liar ?" Mendelssohn smiled at this and said, " You agree in this with Plato, who banished all poets from his Republic. But I hope that with time you will think differently on the subject. And so it happened soon.

Longinus' *On the Sublime* fell into my hand. The examples of the sublime which he adduces from Homer, and particularly the celebrated passage of Sappho, made a deep impression on my mind. I thought to myself, these are but foolish trifles, it is true, but the imagery and descriptions are really very beautiful. After that I read Homer himself, and was forced to laugh heartily at the foolish fellow. What a serious air, I said to myself, over such childless stories! By and by, however, I found a great deal of pleasure in the reading. Ossian, on the other hand, whom I got to read afterwards (of course only in German translations) produced on me a peculiarly awe-inspiring effect. The pomp of his style, the impressive brevity of his descriptions, the purity of his sentiments, the simplicity of the objects described by him, and lastly, the similarity of his poetry to that of the Hebrews, charmed me uncommonly. Thus I found also a great deal of gratification in Gessner's Idylls.

My friend, the Pole of whom I spoke in the preceding chapter, who occupied himself mainly with *belles lettres*, was greatly delighted at my conversion. I used to dispute with him the utility of these studies; and once, when he was reading to me as a model of vigour in expression a passage of the Psalms, in which King David shows himself a master in cursing, I interrupted him with the words, "What sort of an art is this? Why, my mother-in-law—God bless her!—when she was squabbling with a neighbour woman, used to curse much more wildly than that!"

Now, however, he had his triumph over me. Mendelssohn also and my other friends were uncommonly pleased at this change. They wished me to devote myself regularly to the *humaniora*, as without these a man can scarcely make his own intellectual productions useful to the world. It was very difficult, however, to convince me of this. I was always in haste to enjoy the present, without thinking that, by due preparation, I could make this enjoyment greater and more lasting.

I now found gratification, not only in the study of the sciences, but generally in everything good and beautiful, with which I became acquainted; and I carried this out with an enthusiasm which passed all limits. The hitherto suppressed inclination to the pleasures of sense also asserted its claims. The first occasion of this was the following. For many years some men, who were occupied in various kinds of teaching, had insinuated themselves into the most prominent and wealthy families of the Jewish nation. They devoted themselves especially to the French language (which was then regarded as the highest point of enlightenment), to geography, arithmetic, bookkeeping, and similar studies. They had also made themselves familiar with some phrases and imperfectly understood results of the more profound sciences and philosophical systems, while their intercourse with the fair sex was marked by studious gallantry. As a result of all this, they were great favourites in the families where they visited, and were regarded as clever fellows. Now, they began to observe that my reputation was always on the increase, and that the respect for my attainments and talents went so far, that they were being thrown wholly into the shade. Accordingly they thought of a stratagem, by which they might be able to ward off the threatened evil.

They resolved to draw me into their company, to show me every demonstration of friendship, and to render me every possible service. By this means they hoped, in the first place, as a result of our intercourse, to win for themselves some of the respect which was shown to me, and, in the second place, to obtain, from my frank and communicative spirit, some additional knowledge of those sciences which as yet they knew only in name. But, in the third place, as they knew my enthusiasm for everything which I once recognised as good, they expected to intoxicate me with the allurements of sensual pleasure, and to cool in some measure my ardour in the study of science, which would at the same time alienate my friends, my intimacy with whom made them so jealous.

Accordingly they invited me into their society, testified their friendship and esteem for me, and begged the honour of my company. Suspecting no harm, I received their advances with pleasure, especially as I reflected that Mendelssohn and my other friends were too grand for everyday intercourse with me. It became therefore a very desirable object with me, to find some friends of a middle class, with whom I could associate *sans façon*, and enjoy the charms of familiarity. My new friends took me into gay society, to taverns, on pleasure excursions, at last also to ——;* and all this at their own

---

* This " hiatus *haud* valde deflendus " is in the original.—*Trans.*

expense. I, on my side, in my happy humour, opened up to them in return all the mysteries of philosophy, explained to them in detail all the peculiar systems, and corrected their ideas on various subjects of human knowledge. But as things of this sort cannot be poured into a man's head, and as these gentlemen had no special capacity for them, of course they were not able to make any great progress by this kind of instruction. When I observed this, I began to express some sort of contempt for them, and made no attempt to conceal the fact, that it was mainly the roast and the wine that gave me pleasure in their company. This did not please them particularly ; and as they were unable to reach their object with me completely, they tried to reach it at least in part. They told tales to my grand friends behind my back about the most trifling incidents and expressions. For instance, they asserted that I charged Mendelssohn with being a philosophical hypocrite, that I declared others to be endowed with but shallow pates, that I was seeking to spread dangerous systems, and that I was wholly abandoned to Epicureanism. (As if they were genuine Stoics !) They even began at last openly to manifest their enmity.

All this of course had its effect ; and to add to the impression, my friends observed that in my studies I followed no fixed plan, but merely my inclination. Accordingly they proposed to me that I should study medicine, but could not induce me to do it. I observed that the theory of medicine contains many departments as auxiliary sciences, each of which requires a specialist for its thorough mastery, while the practice of medicine implies a peculiar genius and faculty of judgment, that are seldom to be met with. I observed at the same time, that the most of physicians take advantage of the ignorance of the public. In accordance with established usage they spend some years at the universities, where they have an opportunity indeed of attending all the lectures, but in point of fact attend very few. At the close of their course, by means of money and fair words, they get a dissertation written for them ; and thus, after a very simple fashion, become medical practitioners.

As already mentioned, I had a great liking for painting ; but I was advised against this, because I was already well advanced in years, and consequently might not have sufficient patience for the minute exercises required for this art. At last the proposal was made to me, to learn pharmacy ; and as I had already obtained some acquaintance with physics as well as chemistry, I consented. My object in this, however, was not to make any practical use of my attainments, but merely to acquire theoretical knowledge. Accordingly, instead of setting to with my own hands, and thereby acquiring expertness in this art, at important chemical processes I played the part of a mere spectator. In this way I learnt pharmacy, yet without being in the position of becoming an apothecary. After the lapse of a three years' apprenticeship,

Madame Rosen, in whose shop I was apprenticed, was duly paid by H. J. D. the promised fee of sixty thalers. I received a certificate, that I had perfectly mastered the art of pharmacy ; and this ended the whole matter.

This, however, contributed not a little to alienate my friends. At last Mendelssohn asked me to come and see him, when he informed me of this alienation, and pointed out to me its causes. They complained, (1) that I had not made up my mind to any plan of life, and had thereby rendered fruitless all their exertions in my behalf ; (2) that I was trying to spread dangerous opinions and systems; and (3) that, according to general rumour, I was leading a rather loose life, and was very much addicted to sensual pleasures.

The first of these complaints I endeavoured to answer by referring to the fact, which I had mentioned to my friends at the very first, that, in consequence of my peculiar training, I was indisposed for any kind of business, and adapted merely for a quiet speculative life, by which I could not only satisfy my natural inclination, but also, by teaching and similar means, provide for my support in a certain fashion. " As to the second point," I proceeded, "the opinions and systems referred to are either true or false. If the former, then I do not see how the knowledge of the truth can do any harm. If the latter, then let them be refuted. Moreover, I have explained these opinions and systems only to gentlemen who desire to be enlightened, and to rise above all prejudices. But the truth is, that it is not the mischievous nature of the opinions, it is the incapacity of those gentlemen to comprehend them, coupled with their reluctance to make such a humiliating confession, that sets them in arms against me. In reference to the third reproach, however, I must say with downright honesty, Herr Mendelssohn, we are all Epicureans. The moralists can prescribe to us merely rules of prudence; that is to say, they can prescribe the use of means for the attainment of given ends, but not the ends themselves. But," I added, "I see clearly that I must quit Berlin; whither, is a matter of indifference." With this I bade Mendelssohn farewell. He gave me a very favourable testimonial of my capabilities and talents, and wished me a prosperous journey.

To my other friends also I bade farewell, and in brief but emphatic terms thanked them for the favours they had shown. One of my friends was taken aback, when I bade him goodbye, at my using the brief form, "I hope you will enjoy good health, my dear friend; and I thank you for all the favours you have bestowed upon me." It seemed to this excellent, but prosaically poetical man, as if the form were too curt and dry for all his friendliness towards me. So he replied with evident displeasure, "Is this all that you have learnt in Berlin?" I made no answer, however, but went away, booked by the Hamburg post, and departed from Berlin.

On leaving I received from Samuel Levi* a letter of introduction to one of his correspondents. When I arrived in Hamburg, I went to the merchant to whom this letter was addressed, and delivered it. He received me well, and invited me to his table during my stay in the city. But as he knew nothing except how to make money, and took no particular interest in scholarship or science, he evidently entertained me merely on account of my letter of introduction, because he had to do something to gratify his correspondent. As I knew nothing of trade, however, and besides made no very presentable figure, he endeavoured to get rid of me as soon as possible, and with a view to that asked me where I meant to go when I left Hamburg. When I replied that I was going to Holland, he gave me the well-meant advice to hasten my departure, as this was the best season of the year for travelling.

Accordingly I took out a passage on a Hamburg vessel that was to sail for Holland in two or three weeks. For travelling companions I had two barbers, a tailor, and a shoemaker. These fellows made themselves merry, caroused bravely, and sang all sorts of songs. In this joviality I could not take a part ; in fact they scarcely understood my language, and teased me on that account in a thousand ways, though I bore it all with patience. The vessel glided pleasantly down the Elbe to a village

---

* This name is taken from *Maimoniana. —Trans.*

at the mouth of the river some miles below Hamburg. Here we were obliged to lie about six weeks, prevented by contrary winds from putting out to sea. The ship's crew, along with the other passengers, went to the village tavern, where they drank and played. For me, however, the time became very dreary, and I was besides so sick, that I nearly despaired of my recovery.

At last we got a favourable wind, the vessel stood out to sea, and on the third day after our departure we arrived before Amsterdam. A boat came out to the ship to take the passengers into the city. At first I would not trust myself to the Dutch boatman, because I was afraid of falling into the hands of the crimps, against whom I had been warned in Hamburg ; but the captain of our ship assured me that he knew the boatman well, and that I might trust myself to him without any anxiety. Accordingly I came into the city ; but as I had no acquaintances here, and as I knew that at the Hague there was a gentleman belonging to a prominent Berlin family, and that he had obtained from Berlin a tutor with whom I was acquainted, I set out for that place in a drag-boat.

Here I took lodgings at the house of a poor Jewish woman , but before I had time to rest from my journey, a man of tall, spare figure, in untidy clothing, and with a pipe in his mouth, came in, and, without observing me, commenced to speak with my landlady. At last she said to him, " Herr H———, here is a stranger from Berlin ; pray, speak to him." The man thereupon turned to me, and asked me who I was. With my usual instinctive frankness and love of truth, I told him that I was born in Poland, that my love of the sciences had induced me to spend some years in Berlin, and that now I had come to Holland with the intention of entering some situation, if an opportunity offered itself. When he heard that I was a man of learning, he began to speak with me on various subjects in philosophy, and especially in mathematics, in which he had done a good deal. He found in me a man after his own heart, and we formed at once a bond of friendship with one another.

I now went to seek the tutor from Berlin, to whom I referred before. He introduced me to his employer as a man of high talent, who had made a great figure in Berlin, and had brought letters of introduction from that city. This gentleman, who made much of his tutor, as well as of everything that came from Berlin, invited me to dinner. As my external appearance did not appear to promise much, and I was besides thoroughly exhausted and depressed by my sea-voyage, I made a comical figure at table, and our host evidently did not know what to think of me. But as he put great confidence in the written recommendation of Mendelssohn and the oral recommendation of his tutor, he suppressed his astonishment, and invited me to his table as long as I chose to remain here. In the evening he invited his brothers-in-law to meet me. They were children of B——, celebrated for his wealth as well as his beneficence ; and as they were men of learning themselves, they were expected to sound me. They conversed with me on various subjects in the Talmud, and even in the Cabbalah. As I showed myself thoroughly initiated into the mysteries of this sort of learning, even explained to them passages which they regarded as inexplicable, and untied the most complicated knots of argument, their admiration was excited, and they believed they had come upon a great man.

It was not long, however, before their admiration turned to hatred. The occasion of this was the following. In connection with the Cabbalah they told me of a godly man, who had now for many years been a resident of London, and who was able to perform miracles by means of the Cabbalah. I expressed some doubts on the subject, but they assured me they had been present at performances of the kind during this man's residence at the Hague. To this I replied as a philosopher, that I did not indeed question the truth of their statement, but that perhaps they had not duly investigated the matter themselves, and gave out their pre-conceived opinions as facts. Moreover, I declared that I must regard with scepticism the effect of the Cabbalah in general, until it is shown that that effect is of such a kind as cannot be explained in accordance with the known laws of Nature. This declaration they held to be heresy.

At the end of the meal the wine-cup was passed to me, that I might, in accordance with the usual custom, pronounce the blessing over it. This however I declined with the explanation, that I did so not from any false shame of speaking before a number of men, because in Poland I had been a rabbi, and had very often held disputations and delivered sermons before large assemblies, and, in order to prove this, was now willing to deliver public lectures every day. It was merely, I explained further, the love of truth and the reluctance to do anything inconsistent, that made it impossible for me, without manifest aversion, to say prayers which I regarded as a result of an anthropomorphic system of theology.

At this their patience was completely exhausted ; they reviled me as a damnable heretic, and declared it would be a deadly sin to tolerate me in a Jewish house. Our host, who was no philosopher indeed, but a reasonable and enlightened man, did not mind much what they said ; my humble talents were of more value in his eyes than my piety. Accordingly they broke up immediately after dinner, and left the house in deep displeasure ; but all their subsequent efforts to drive me from their brother-in-law's house were fruitless. I remained in it about nine months, lived at perfect freedom, but very retired, without any occupation or any rational society.

Here I cannot pass over in silence an event which was remarkable both in a psychological and in a moral point of view. In Holland I wanted nothing but an occupation suited to my powers, and naturally, therefore, I became hypochondriac. From feelings of satiety, not infrequently I fell upon the idea of making away with myself, and of thus putting an end to an existence which had become a burden to me. But no sooner did I come to action, than the love of life always assumed the upper hand again. Once, at the Feast of Haman, in accordance with the custom of the Jews, I had banquetted very heartily in the house where I took my meals. After the feast, about midnight I returned to my lodging; and as I had to pass along one of the canals that are laid out everywhere in Holland, it occurred to me that this was a very convenient opportunity for carrying out the design which I had often formed. I thought to myself, "My life is a burden. At present, indeed, I have no wants; but how will it be with me in the future, and by what means shall I preserve my life, since I am of no use for anything in the world? I have already resolved, on cool reflection at different times, to put an end to my life, and nothing but my cowardice has restrained me hitherto. Now, when I am pretty drunk, on the brink of a deep canal, the thing may be done in a moment without any difficulty." Already I had bent my body over the canal, in order to plunge in; but only the upper part of the body obeyed the command of the mind, trusting that the lower part would certainly refuse its services for such a purpose. So I stood for a good while with half the body bent over the water, and propped myself carefully with my legs firmly planted on the ground, so that a spectator might have fancied I was merely making my bow to the water. This hesitation destroyed my whole plan. I felt like a man who is going to take medicine, but, wanting the resolution required, raises the cup time after time to his mouth, and sets it down again. I began at last to laugh at myself, as I reflected that my sole motive for suicide was a real superfluity for the present and an imaginary want for the future.* I therefore let the project drop for the time being, went home, and thus brought the serio-comic scene to an end.

Still another comical scene must be mentioned here. At the Hague there lived at that time a woman of about forty-five, who was said to have been very pretty in youth, and supported herself by giving lessons in French. One day she called upon me at my lodging, introduced herself, and expressed an irresistible desire for scientific conversation. She declared therefore that she would

---

* The love of life, that is, the instinct of self-preservation, seems rather to increase than to decrease with the diminution or uncertainty of the means of living, inasmuch as man is thereby spurred to greater *activity*, which developes a stronger *consciousness of life.* Only this want must not have reached its maximum ; for the necessary result of that is *despair*, that is a conviction of the impossibility of preserving life, and consequently a desire to put an end to it. Thus every passion, and therefore also the love of life, is increased by the obstacles which come in the way of its gratification : only these obstacles must not make the gratification of the passions *impossible*, else despair is the result.

visit me frequently in my lodging, and requested the honour of a visit from me in return.

This advance I met with great pleasure, returned her visits several times ; and thus our intercourse became more and more intimate. We conversed usually on subjects in philosophy and *belles lettres*. As I was still at that time a married man, and, except for her enthusiasm in learning, Madam had little attraction for me, I thought of nothing beyond mere entertainment. The lady, however, who had been a widow now for a pretty long while, and had, according to her own story, conceived an affection for me, began to express this by looks and words in a romantic manner, which struck me as very comical. I could never believe, that a lady could fall in love with me in earnest. Her expressions of affection therefore I took for mere airs of affectation. She, on the other hand, showed herself more and more in earnest, became at times thoughtful in the midst of our conversation, and burst into tears.

It was during a conversation of this sort, that we fell upon the subject of love. I told her frankly, that I could not love a woman except for the sake of womanly excellences, such as beauty, grace, agreeableness, etc., and that any other excellences she might possess, such as talents or learning, could excite in me only esteem, but by no means love. The lady adduced against me arguments *a priori* as well as instances from experience, especially from French novels, and tried to correct my

R

notions of love. I could not, however, be so easily convinced; and as the lady was carrying her airs to an absurd length, I rose and took my leave. She accompanied me to the very door, grasped me by the hand, and would not let me go. I asked her somewhat sharply, " What's the matter with you, madam?" With trembling voice and tearful eyes she replied, " I love you."

When I heard this laconic declaration of love, I began to laugh immoderately, tore myself from her grasp, and rushed away. Some time afterwards she sent me the following *billet doux :—*

" Sir,

      I have been greatly mistaken in your character. I took you for a man of noble thoughts and exalted feelings; but I see now that you are a genuine Epicurean. You seek nothing but pleasure. A woman can please you only on account of her beauty. A Madame Dacier, for example, who has studied thoroughly all the Greek and Latin authors, translated them into her native language, and enriched them with learned annotations, could not please you. Why? Because she is not pretty. Sir, you, who are otherwise so enlightened, ought to be ashamed to cherish such pernicious principles; and if you will not repent, then tremble before the revenge of the injured love of

Yours, etc."

To this I returned the following reply :—

" Madam,

    That you have been mistaken, is shown by the result. You say that I am a genuine Epicurean. In this you do me a great honour. Much as I abhor the title of an *epicure*, on the other hand I feel proud of the title of *genuine Epicurean.* Certainly it is beauty alone that pleases me in a woman ; but as this can be heightened by other qualities, these must also be pleasing as means towards the chief end. On the other hand, I can merely *esteem* such a woman on account of her talents ; *love* her I cannot, as I have already explained in conversation. For the learning of Madame Dacier I have all respect : she could at all events fall in love with the Greek heroes who were at the siege of Troy, and expect in return the love of their *manes* that were constantly hovering around her ; but nothing more. For the rest, Madam, as far as your revenge is concerned, I do not fear it, since Time, which destroys all things, has shattered your weapons, that is, your teeth and nails.

       Yours, etc."

Thus ended this strange love-affair.

I discovered that in Holland there was nothing for me to do, inasmuch as the main desire of the Dutch Jews is to make money, and they manifest no particular liking for the sciences. Besides, in consequence of not knowing the Dutch language, I was unable to give instructions in any science. I determined therefore to return to

Berlin by Hamburg, but found an opportunity of travelling to Hanover by land. In Hanover I went to a wealthy Jew,—a man who does not deserve even to enjoy his riches,—showed him my letter of introduction from Mendelssohn, and represented to him the urgency of my present circumstances. He read Mendelssohn's letter carefully through, called for pen and ink, and, without speaking a word to me, wrote at the foot :—" I also hereby certify that what Herr Mendelssohn writes in praise of Herr Solomon is perfectly correct." And with this he dismissed me.

CHAPTER XXVI.

I return to Hamburg—A Lutheran Pastor pronounces me to be a
scabby Sheep, and unworthy of Admission into the Christian
Fold—I enter the Gymnasium, and frighten the Chief Rabbi
out of his Wits.

I MADE a prosperous journey back to Hamburg, but here
I fell into circumstances of the deepest distress. I lodged
in a miserable house, had nothing to eat, and did not
know what to do. I had received too much education
to return to Poland, to spend my life in misery without
rational occupation or society, and to sink back into the
darkness of superstition and ignorance, from which I had
hardly delivered myself with so much labour. On the
other hand, to succeed in Germany was a result on which
I could not calculate, owing to my ignorance of the
language, as well as of the manners and customs of the
people, to which I had never yet been able to adapt myself properly. I had learnt no particular profession, I
had not distinguished myself in any special science, I
was not even master of any language in which I could
make myself perfectly intelligible. It occurred to me,
therefore, that for me there was no alternative left, but
to embrace the Christian religion, and get myself baptised

in Hamburg. Accordingly I resolved to go to the first clergyman I should come upon, and inform him of my resolution, as well as of my motives for it, without any hypocrisy, in a truthful and honest fashion. But as I could not express myself well orally, I put my thoughts into writing in German with Hebrew characters, went to a schoolmaster, and got him to copy it in German characters. The purport of my letter was in brief as follows :—

"I am a native of Poland, belonging to the Jewish nation, destined by my education and studies to be a rabbi; but in the thickest darkness I have perceived some light. This induced me to search further after light and truth, and to free myself completely from the darkness of superstition and ignorance. In order to this end, which could not be attained in my native place, I came to Berlin, where by the support of some enlightened men of our nation I studied for some years—not indeed after any plan, but merely to satisfy my thirst for knowledge. But as our nation is unable to use, not only such planless studies, but even those conducted on the most perfect plan, it cannot be blamed for becoming tired of them, and pronouncing their encouragement to be useless. I have therefore resolved, in order to secure temporal as well as eternal happiness, which depends on the attainment of perfection, and in order to become useful to myself as well as others, to embrace the Christian religion. The Jewish religion, it is true, comes, in its articles of faith, nearer to reason than Christianity. But in practical use the latter has an advantage over the former ; and since morality, which consists not in opinions but in actions, is the aim of all religion in general, clearly the latter comes nearer than the former to this aim. Moreover, I hold the mysteries of the Christian religion for that which they are, that is, allegorical representations of the truths that are most important for man. By this means I make my faith in them harmonise with reason, but I cannot believe them according to their common meaning. I beg therefore most respectfully an answer to the question, whether after this confession I am worthy of the Christian religion or not. In the former case I am ready to carry my proposal into effect ; but in the latter, I must give up all claim to a religion which enjoins me to lie, that is, to deliver a confession of faith which contradicts my reason."

The schoolmaster, to whom I dictated this, fell into astonishment at my audacity ; never before had he listened to such a confession of faith. He shook his head with much concern, interrupted the writing several times, and became doubtful, whether the mere copying was not itself a sin. With great reluctance he copied it out, merely to get rid of the thing. I went then to a prominent clergyman, delivered my letter, and begged for a reply. He read it with great attention, fell likewise into astonishment, and on finishing entered into conversation with me.

"So," he said, " I see your intention is to embrace the Christian religion, merely in order to improve your temporal circumstances."

" Excuse me, Herr Pastor," I replied, " I think I have made it clear enough in my letter, that my object is the attainment of perfection. To this, it is true, the removal of all hindrances and the improvement of my external circumstances form an indispensable condition. But this condition is not the chief end."

" But," said the pastor, " do you not feel any inclination of the soul to the Christian religion without reference to any external motives?"

" I should be telling a lie, if I were to give you an affirmative answer."

" You are too much of a philosopher," replied the pastor, " to be able to become a Christian. Reason has taken the upper hand with you, and faith must accommodate itself to reason. You hold the mysteries of the Christian religion to be mere fables, and its commands to be mere laws of reason. For the present I cannot be satisfied with your confession of faith. You should therefore pray to God, that He may enlighten you with His grace, and endow you with the spirit of true Christianity; and then come to me again."

" If that is the case," I said, " then I must confess, Herr Pastor, that I am not qualified for Christianity. Whatever light I may receive, I shall always make it luminous with the light of reason. I shall never believe that I have fallen upon new truths, if it is impossible to see their connection with the truths already known to me. I must therefore remain what I am,—a stiffnecked Jew. My religion enjoins me to *believe* nothing, but to *think* the truth and to *practise* goodness. If I find any hindrance in this from external circumstances, it is not my fault. I do all that lies in my power."

With this I bade the pastor goodbye.

The hardships of my journey, coupled with poor food, brought on an ague. I lay on a straw-bed in a garret, and suffered the want of all conveniences and refreshments. My landlord, who took pity on me, called a Jewish physician, who prescribed an emetic which soon cured me of my fever. The doctor found that I was no common man, stayed to converse with me for some hours, and begged me, as soon as I recovered, to visit him.

Meanwhile, however, a young man, who had known me in Berlin, heard of my arrival. He called on me to say that Herr W——, who had seen me in Berlin, was now residing in Hamburg, and that I might very properly call upon him. I did so, and Herr W——, who was a very clever, honourable man, of a benevolent disposition naturally, asked me what I intended to do. I represented to him my whole circumstances, and begged for his advice. He said that in his opinion the unfortunate position of my affairs arose from the fact, that I had devoted myself with zeal merely to the ac-

quisition of scientific knowledge, but had neglected the
study of language, and therefore I was unable to communicate my knowledge to others, or make any use of it.
Meanwhile, he thought, nothing had been lost by delay;
and if I was still willing to accommodate myself to the
circumstances, I could attain my object in the gymnasium
at Altona, where his son was studying, while he would
provide for my support.

I accepted this offer with many thanks, and went home
with a joyful heart. Meanwhile Herr W—— spoke to
the professors of the gymnasium, as well as to the principal, but more particularly to the syndic, Herr G——,
a man who cannot be sufficiently praised. He represented to them, that I was a man of uncommon talents,
who wanted merely some further knowledge of language
to distinguish himself in the world, and who hoped to
obtain that knowledge by a short residence in the gymnasium. They acceded to his request. I was matricu-
lated, and had a room assigned to me, in the institution.

Here I lived for two years in peace and contentment.
But the pupils in such a gymnasium, as may be easily
supposed, make very slow progress; and it was therefore
natural that I, who had already made considerable attainments in science, should find the lessons at times somewhat tedious. Consequently I did not attend them all,
but made a selection to suit my taste. The Director
Dusch I esteemed very highly on account of his profound
scholarship and his excellent character. I therefore at-

tended the most of his lectures. It is true, the philosophy of Ernesti, on which he lectured, could not give me much satisfaction, and just as little did I receive from his lectures on Segner's Mathematical Compendium. But I derived great benefit from his instructions in the English language. The Rector H——, a cheerful old man, though somewhat pedantic, was not altogether pleased with me, because I would not perform his Latin exercises, and would not learn Greek at all. The Professor of History began his lectures *ab ovo* with Adam, and at the end of the year with a great deal of effort reached as far down as the building of the Tower of Babel. The teacher of French used for translation Fenelon's *Sur l'existence de Dieu*,—a work for which I conceived the greatest dislike, because the author, while appearing to declaim against Spinozism, in reality argues in its defence.

During the whole period of my residence in the gymnasium the professors were unable to form any correct idea of me, because they never had an opportunity of forming my acquaintance. By the end of the first year I thought I had attained my object, and laid a good foundation in languages. I had also become tired of this inactive life, and therefore resolved to quit the gymnasium. But Director Dusch ; who began by and by to become acquainted with me, begged me to stay at least another year, and, as I wanted for nothing, I consented.

It was about this time that the following incident in

my life took place. My wife had sent a polish Jew in search of me, and he heard of my residence in Hamburg. Accordingly he came and called on me at the gymnasium. He had been commissioned by my wife to demand, that I should either return home without delay, or send through him a bill of divorce. At that time I was unable to do either the one or the other. I was not inclined to be divorced from my wife without any cause; and to return at once to Poland, where I had not yet the slightest prospect of getting on in the world or of leading a rational life, was to me impossible. I represented all this to the gentleman who had undertaken the commission, and added that it was my intention to leave the gymnasium soon and go to Berlin, that my Berlin friends would, as I hoped, give me both their advice and assistance in carrying out this intention. He would not be satisfied with this answer, which he took for a mere evasion. When he thus found that he could do nothing with me, he went to the chief rabbi, and entered a complaint against me. A messenger was accordingly sent to summon me before the tribunal of the chief rabbi; but I took my stand, that at present I was not under his jurisdiction, inasmuch as the gymnasium had a jurisdiction of its own, by which my case would require to be decided. The chief rabbi made every effort through the Government to make me submit to his wishes, but all his efforts were in vain. When he saw that he could not accomplish his purpose in this way, he sent me an invitation a second time on the pretext that he wished merely to speak with me. To this I willingly consented, and went to him at once.

He received me with much respect ; and when I made known to him my birthplace and family in Poland, he began to lament and wring his hands. " Alas!" said he, " you are the son of the famous Rabbi Joshua ? I know your father well ; he is a pious and learned man. You also are not unknown to me ; I have examined you as a boy several times, and formed high expectations of you. Oh ! is it possible that you have altered so ?" (Here he pointed to my shaven beard). To this I replied, that I also had the honour of knowing him, and that I still remembered his examinations well. My conduct hitherto, I told him, was as little opposed to religion properly understood, as it was to reason. " But," he interrupted " you do not wear a beard, you do not go to the synagogue : is that not contrary to religion ?" " No ! " I replied, and I proved to him from the Talmud that, under the circumstances in which I was placed, all this was allowed. On this point we entered into a lengthy dispute, in which each maintained his right. As he could effect nothing with me by such disputation, he adopted the style of mere sermonising ; but when this also was of no avail, he began to cry aloud, " *Shophar !*
Shophar ! " This is the name of the horn which is blown on New-Year's day as a summons to repentance, and at which it is supposed that Satan is horribly afraid.

While the chief rabbi called out the word, he pointed to a *Shophar* that lay before him on the table, and asked me, " Do you know what that is ? " I replied quite boldly, " Oh yes ! it is a ram's horn." At these words the chief rabbi fell back upon his chair, and began to lament over my lost soul. I left him to lament as long as he liked, and bade him goodbye.

At the end of my second year I began to reflect, that it would be an advantage in view of my future success, as well as fair to the gymnasium, that I should make myself more intimately acquainted with the professors. Accordingly I went to Director Dusch, announced to him that I was soon to leave, and told him that, as I wished a certificate from him, it would be well for him to examine me on the progress I had made, so that his certificate might be as nearly as possible in accordance with the truth. To this end he made me translate some passages from Latin and English works in prose as well as in verse, and was very well pleased with the translation. Afterwards he entered into conversation with me on some subjects in philosophy, but found me so well versed in these, that for his own safety he was obliged to back out. At last he asked me, " But how is it with your mathematics ? " I begged him to examine me in this also. " In our mathematical lessons," he began, " we had advanced to somewhere about the subject of mathematical bodies. Will you work out yourself a proposition not yet taken up in the lessons, for example, that about the relation of the cylinder, the sphere and the cone to one another? You may take some days to do it." I replied that this was unnecessary, and offered to perform the task on the spot. I then demonstrated, not only the proposition prescribed, but several other propositions out of Segner's Geometry. The Director was very much surprised at this, called all the pupils in the gymnasium, and represented to them that the extraordinary progress I had made should make them ashamed of themselves. The most of them did not know what to say to this; but some replied, " Do not suppose, Herr Director, that Maimon made this progress in mathematics here. He has seldom attended the mathematical lessons, and even when he was there he paid no attention to them." They were going to say more, but the Director commanded silence, and gave me an honourable certificate, from which I cannot avoid quoting a few sentences. They became to me afterwards a constant spur to higher attainments, and I hope it will not be considered vainglory in me to cite the opinion of this esteemed man.

" His capacity," says he, " for learning all that is beautiful, good and useful in general, but in particular those sciences which require severe exertion of the mental powers, abstract and profound thought, is, I might almost say, extraordinary. All those sorts of knowledge, which demand in the highest degree one's own mental efforts, appear to him the most agreeable ; and intellectual occupations seem to be his chief, if not his sole, enjoyment. His favourite studies hitherto have been philosophy and mathematics, in which his progress has excited my astonishment, &c."

I now bade good-bye to the teachers and officers of the gymnasium, who unanimously paid me the compliment, that I had done honour to their institution. I then set out once more for Berlin.

CHAPTER XXVII.

Third Journey to Berlin—Frustrated Plan of Hebrew Authorship—
Journey to Breslau—Divorce.

On my arrival in Berlin I called upon Mendelssohn, as
well as some other old friends, and begged them, as I
had now acquired some knowledge of languages, to employ me in some occupation suited to my capacity. They
hit upon the suggestion, that, in order to enlighten the
Polish Jews still living in darkness, I should prepare in
Hebrew, as the only language intelligible to them, some
scientific works, which these philanthropists were to print
at their own expense, and distribute among the people.
His proposal I accepted with delight. But now the
question arose, with what sort of works a beginning
should be made. On this point my excellent friends
were divided in their opinions. One of them thought
that the history of the Jewish nation would be most serviceable for this purpose, inasmuch as the people would
discover in it the origin of their religious doctrines and
of the subsequent corruption which these had undergone,
while they would thus also gain an insight into the fact,
that the fall of the Jewish state, as well as all the subsequent persecution and oppression which they had suf-

S

fered, had arisen from their own ignorance and opposition to all rational arrangements. Accordingly this gentleman recommended that I should translate from French Basnage's *History of the Jews;* he gave me the work for this purpose, and asked me to furnish a copy of my translation. The specimen gave satisfaction to them all, even to Mendelssohn, and I was ready to take the work in hand; but one of our friends thought that we ought to begin with something on natural religion and rational morals, inasmuch as this is the object of all enlightenment. Accordingly he recommended that for this purpose I should translate the *Natural Religion* of Reimarus. Mendelssohn withheld his opinion, because he believed that whatever was undertaken in this line, though it would do no harm, would also be of little use. I myself undertook these works, not from any conviction of my own, but at the request of my friends.

I was too well acquainted with the rabbinical despotism, which by the power of superstition has established its throne for many centuries in Poland, and which for its own security seeks in every possible way to prevent the spread of light and truth. I knew how closely the Jewish theocracy is connected with the national existence, so that the abolition of the former must inevitably bring with it the annihilation of the latter. I saw therefore clearly that my labours in this direction would be fruitless; but I undertook this commission, because, as already stated, my friends would have it so, and because I could think of no other means of subsistence. Accordingly without fixing anything definite about the plan of my labours, my friends resolved to send me to Dessau, where I could carry on my work at leisure.

I reached Dessau in the hope, that after a few days my friends in Berlin would resolve upon something definite about my work : but in this I was deceived ; for, as soon as I turned my back on Berlin, nothing further was thought of the plan. I waited about a fortnight ; but when during that period I received no communication, I wrote to Berlin in the following terms :—" If my friends cannot unite upon a plan, they might leave the settlement of it to my own judgment. For my part I believe that, to enlighten the Jewish nation, we must begin neither with history nor with natural theology and morals. One of my reasons for thinking so is, that these subjects, being easily intelligible, would not be able to instil any regard for science in general among the more learned Jews, who are accustomed to respect only those studies which involve a strain upon the highest intellectual powers. But a second reason is, that, as those subjects would frequently come into collision with religious prejudices, they would never be admitted. Besides, sooth to say, there is no proper history of the Jewish nation : for they have scarcely ever stood in political relation with other civilised nations ; and, with the exception of the Old Testament and Josephus and a few fragments on the persecutions of the Jews in the middle ages, nothing is to be found recorded on the subject.   I believe, therefore, that it would be best to make a beginning with some science which, besides being most favourable for the development of the mind, is also self-evident, and stands in no connection with any religious opinions. Of this sort are the mathematical sciences ; and therefore with this object in view I am willing to write a mathematical text-book in Hebrew."

To this I received the answer, that I might follow my plan.   Accordingly I applied myself with all diligence to the preparation of this text-book, using the Latin work on mathematics by Wolff as its basis ; and in two months it was finished.   I then returned to Berlin, to give an account of my work, but received immediately from one of the gentlemen interested the disappointing information, that, as the work was very voluminous, and as it would entail heavy expenditure especially on account of the copper-plates required, he could not undertake the publication at his own expense, and I might therefore do with my manuscript whatever I chose.   I complained of this to Mendelssohn ; and he thought, that certainly it was unreasonable to let my work go without remuneration, but that I could not require my friends to undertake the publication of a work which could not calculate on any good result in consequence of that aversion to all science, which I myself knew to be prevalent among the Jewish nation.   His advice therefore was, that I should get the book printed by subscription ; and of course I was obliged to content myself with this. Mendelssohn and the other enlightened Jews in Berlin subscribed, and I received for my work merely my manuscript and the list of subscriptions. The whole plan, however, was thought of no more.

On this I fell out again with my friends in Berlin. Being a man with little knowledge of the world, who supposed that human actions must always be determined by the laws of justice, I pressed for the fulfilment of the bargain made. My friends, on the other hand, began, though too late, to see, that their ill-considered project must of necessity collapse, because they had no assurance of a market for such voluminous and expensive works. From the religious, moral and political condition of the Jews up to this time it was easy to foresee that the few enlightened men among them would certainly give themselves no trouble to study the sciences in the Hebrew language, which is very ill-adapted for the exposition of such subjects ; they will prefer to seek science in its original sources. The unenlightened, on the other hand, —and these form the majority,—are so swayed by rabbinical prejudices, that they regard the study of the sciences, even in Hebrew, as forbidden fruit, and persistently occupy themselves only with the Talmud and the enormous number of its commentaries.

All this I understood very well, and therefore I never thought of demanding that the work I had prepared should be printed ; I asked merely remuneration for the labour spent on it in vain. In this dispute Mendelssohn remained neutral, because he thought that both parties had right on their side. He promised to use his influence with my friends, to induce them to provide for my subsistence in some other way. But when even this was not done, I became impatient, and resolved to quit Berlin once more, and go to Breslau. I took with me some letters of introduction, but they were of little service ; for before I reached Breslau myself, letters in the spirit of those which Uriah carried had preceded me, and made a bad impression on the most of those to whom my letters of introduction were addressed. As a natural result, therefore, I was coldly received ; and as I knew nothing of the later letters, I found it impossible to explain my reception, and had made up my mind to quit Breslau.

By chance, however, I became acquainted with the celebrated Jewish poet, the late Ephraim Kuh. This learned and high-minded man took so much interest in me, that, neglecting all his former occupations and enjoyments, he confined himself entirely to my society. To the wealthy Jews he spoke of me with the greatest enthusiasm, and praised me as a very good fellow. But when he found that all his complimentary remarks failed to make any impression on these gentlemen, he took some trouble to find out the cause of this, and at last discovered that the reason lay in those friendly letters from Berlin. Their general tenor was, that I was seeking to spread pernicious opinions. Ephraim Kuh, as a thinking man, at once saw the reason of this charge; but with all the efforts he made, he could not drive it out of the heads of these people. I confessed to him that, during my first sojourn in Berlin as a young man without experience or knowledge of the world, I had felt an irresistible impulse to communicate to others whatever truth I knew; but I assured him that, having for some years become wise by experience, I went to work with great caution, and that therefore this charge was now wholly without foundation.

Irritated by my disheartening situation, I resolved to form the acquaintance of Christian scholars, by whose recommendation I thought I might find a hearing among the wealthy men of my own nation. I could not but fear, however, that my defective language might form an obstacle to the expression of my thoughts; so I prepared a written essay, in which I delivered my ideas on the most important questions of philosophy in the form of aphorisms. With this essay I went to the celebrated Professor Garve, explained to him briefly my intention, and submitted my aphorisms to him for examination. He discussed them with me in a very friendly manner, gave me a good testimonial, and recommended me also orally in very emphatic language to the wealthy banker, Lipmann Meier. This gentleman settled a monthly allowance on me for my support, and also spoke to some other Jews on the subject.

My situation now improved every day. Many young men of the Jewish nation sought my society. Among others the second son of Herr Aaron Zadig took so much pleasure in my humble personality, that he desired to enjoy my instruction in the sciences. This he earnestly begged his father to allow ; and the latter, being a well-to-do enlightened man of great good sense, who wished to give his children the best German education, and spared no expense for that object, willingly gave his consent. He sent for me, and made the proposal that I should live at his house, and for a moderate honorarium should give his second son lessons for two hours a day in physics and *belles lettres*, and also a lesson in arithmetic of an hour a day to his third and youngest son. This proposal I accepted with great willingness ; and, not long after, Herr Zadig asked me, if I would not also consent to give lessons in Hebrew and elementary mathematics to his children who had hitherto had for their teacher in these subjects a Polish Jew, named Rabbi Manoth. But I thought it would be unfair to supplant this poor man, who had a family to support, and who was giving satisfaction at any rate ; and therefore I declined this request. Accordingly Rabbi Manoth continued his lessons, and I entered upon mine.

In this house I was able to carry on but little study for myself. In the first place, there was a want of books ; and, in the second place, I lived in a room with the children, where they were occupied with other masters every hour of the day. Besides, the liveliness of these young people did not suit my character which had already become somewhat stern ; and therefore I had often occasion to get angry at petty outbursts of unruliness. Consequently, as I was obliged to pass most of my time in idleness, I sought society. I often visited Herr Hiemann Lisse, a plump little man of enlightened mind and cheerful disposition. With him and some other jolly companions I spent my evenings in talk and jest and play of every sort. During the day I strolled around among the coffee-houses.

In other families also I soon became acquainted, particularly in those of Herr Simon, the banker, and Herr Bortenstein, both of whom showed me much kindness. All sought to persuade me to devote myself to medicine, for which I had always entertained a great dislike. But when I saw from my circumstances, that it would be difficult for me to find support in any other way, I allowed myself to be persuaded. Professor Garve introduced me to Professor Morgenbesser, and I attended his medical lectures for some time ; but after all I could not overcome my dislike to the art, and accordingly gave up the lectures again. By and by I became acquainted with other Christian scholars, especially with the late Herr Lieberkühn, who was so justly esteemed on account of his abilities, as well as for his warm interest in the welfare of mankind. I also made the acquaintance of some teachers of merit in the Jesuits' College at Breslau.

But I did not give up wholly literary work in Hebrew.
I translated into Hebrew Mendelssohn's *Morgenstunden*.
Of this translation I sent some sheets as a specimen to
Herr Isaac Daniel Itzig in Berlin ; but I received no
answer because this excellent man, owing to his business
being too extensive, cannot possibly give attention to
subjects that are not of immediate interest to him, and
therefore such affairs as the answering of my letter are
easily forgotten. I also wrote in Hebrew a treatise on
Natural Philosophy according to Newtonian principles ;
and this, as well as the rest of my Hebrew works, I still
preserve in manuscript.

At last, however, I fell here also into a precarious
situation. The children of Herr Zadig, in pursuance of
the occupations to which they were destined in life, entered into commercial situations, and therefore required
teachers no longer. Other means of support also gradually failed. As I was thus obliged to seek subsistence
in some other way, I devoted myself to giving lessons ;
I taught Euler's *Algebra* to a young man, gave two children instruction in the rudiments of German and Latin,
&c. But even this did not last long, and I found myself
in a sorrowful plight.

Meanwhile my wife and eldest son arrived from Poland. A woman of rude education and manners, but of
great good sense and the courage of an Amazon, she demanded that I should at once return home with her, not
seeing the impossibility of what she required. I had

now lived some years in Germany, had happily emancipated myself from the fetters of superstition and religious prejudice, had abandoned the rude manner of life in which I had been brought up, and extended my knowledge in many directions. I could not therefore return to my former barbarous and miserable condition, deprive myself of all the advantages I had gained, and expose myself to rabbinical rage at the slightest deviation from the ceremonial law, or the utterance of a liberal opinion. I represented to her, that this could not be done at once, that I should require first of all to make my situation known to my friends here as well as in Berlin, and solicit from them the assistance of two or three hundred thalers, so that I might be able to live in Poland independent of my religious associates. But she would listen to nothing of all this, and declared her resolution to obtain a divorce, if I would not go with her immediately. Here therefore it was for me to choose the less of two evils, and I consented to the divorce.

Meanwhile, however, I was obliged to provide for the lodging and board of these guests, and to introduce them to my friends in Breslau. Both of these duties I performed, and I pointed out, especially to my son, the difference between the manner of life one leads here and that in Poland, while I sought to convince him by several passages in the *Moreh Nebhochim*, that enlightenment of the understanding and refinement of manners are rather favourable than otherwise to religion. I went further : I sought to convince him, that he ought to remain with me ; I assured him, that, with my direction and the support of my friends, he would find opportunities of developing the good abilities with which Nature had endowed him, and would obtain for them some suitable employment. These representations made some impression upon him : but my wife went with my son to consult some orthodox Jews, in whose advice she thought she could thoroughly confide ; and they recommended her to press at once for a divorce, and on no account to let my son be induced to remain with me. This resolution, however, she was not to disclose till she had received from me a sufficient sum of money for household purposes. She might then separate from me for ever, and start for home with her booty.

This pretty plan was faithfully followed. By and by I had succeeded in collecting some score of ducats from my friends. I gave them to my wife, and explained to her that, to complete the required sum, it would be necessary for us to go to Berlin. She then began to raise difficulties, and declared at once pointblank, that for us a divorce was best, as neither could I live happily with her in Poland, nor she with me in Germany. In my opinion she was perfectly right. But it still made me sorry to lose a wife, for whom I had once entertained affection, and I could not let the affair be conducted in any spirit of levity. I told her therefore that I should consent to a divorce only if it were enjoined by the courts.

This was done. I was summoned before the court. My wife stated the grounds on which she claimed a divorce. The president of the court then said, " Under these circumstances we can do nothing but advise a divorce." "Mr. President," I replied, "we came here, not to ask advice, but to receive a judicial sentence." Thereupon the chief rabbi rose from his seat (that what he said might not have the force of a judicial decision, approached me with the codex in his hand, and pointed to the following passage :—" A vagabond, who abandons his wife for years, and does not write to her or send her money, shall, when he is found, be obliged to grant a divorce." "It is not my part," I replied, "to institute a comparison between this case and mine. That duty falls to you, as judge. Take your seat again, therefore, and pronounce your judicial sentence on the case."

The president became pale and red by turns, while the rest of the judges looked at one another. At last the presiding judge became furious, began to call me names, pronounced me a damnable heretic, and cursed me in the name of the Lord. I left him to storm, however, and went away. Thus ended this strange suit, and things remained as they were before.

My wife now saw that nothing was to be done by means of force, and therefore she took to entreaty. I also yielded at last, but only on the condition, that at the judicial divorce the judge, who had shown himself such a master of cursing, should not preside in the court.

After the divorce my wife returned to Poland with my son. I remained some time still in Breslau ; but as my circumstances became worse and worse, I resolved to return to Berlin.*

---

* " Afterwards when he spoke of Poland, he used to be deeply affected in thinking of his wife, from whom he was obliged to separate. He was really very much devoted to her, and her fate went home to his very heart. It was easy when the subject came up in conversation, to read in his face the deep sorrow which he felt ; his liveliness then sensibly faded away, he became by and by perfectly silent, was usually incapable of further entertainment, and went earlier than usual home." *Maimoniana*, p. 177. He seems, however, at a later period, to have at least spoken to his friends about marrying a second time ; but the project was never carried out. *Ibid.*, p. 248.— *Trans.*

CHAPTER XXVIII.

Fourth Journey to Berlin—Unfortunate Circumstances—Help—
Study of Kant's Writings—Characteristic of my own Works.

WHEN I came to Berlin, Mendelssohn was no longer in life,* and my former friends were determined to know nothing more of me. I did not know therefore what to do. In the greatest distress I received a visit from Herr Bendavid, who told me that he had heard of my unfortunate circumstances, and had collected a small sum of about thirty thalers, which he gave to me. Besides, he introduced me to a Herr Jojard, an enlightened and high-minded man, who received me in a very friendly manner, and made some provision for my support. A certain professor, indeed, tried to do me an ill turn with this worthy man by denouncing me as an atheist ; but in spite of this I gradually got on so well, that I was able to hire a lodging in a garret from an old woman.

I had now resolved to study Kant's *Kritik of Pure Reason*, of which I had often heard but which I had never seen yet.† The method, in which I studied this

---

* He died 4th Jan., 1786.—*Trans.*

† Kant's work must still have been quite new, as it appeared in 1781.—*Trans.*

work, was quite peculiar. On the first perusal I obtained a vague idea of each section. This I endeavoured afterwards to make distinct by my own reflection, and thus to penetrate into the author's meaning. Such is properly the process which is called *thinking oneself into a system*. But as I had already mastered in this way the systems of Spinoza, Hume and Leibnitz, I was naturally led to think of a coalition-system. This in fact I found, and I put it gradually in writing in the form of explanatory observations on the *Kritik of Pure Reason*, just as this system unfolded itself to my mind. Such was the origin of my *Transcendental Philosophy*. Consequently this book must be difficult to understand for the man who, owing to the inflexible character of his thinking, has made himself at home merely in one of these systems without regard to any other. Here the important problem, *Quid juris ?* with the solution of which the *Kritik* is occupied, is wrought out in a much wider sense than that in which it is taken by Kant ; and by this means there is plenty of scope left for Hume's scepticism in its full force. But on the other side the complete solution of this problem leads either to Spinozistic or to Leibnitzian dogmatism.

When I had finished this work, I showed it to Marcus Herz.* He acknowledged that he was reckoned among the most eminent disciples of Kant, and that he had

---

* The name is left blank by Maimon, but is known to be that which I have inserted. See Fischer's *Geschichte der neueren Philosophie*, Vol. v., p. 131.—*Trans.*

given the most assiduous application while attending Kant's philosophical lectures, as may indeed be seen from his writings, but that yet he was not in a position to pass a judgment on the *Kritik* itself or on any other work relating to it. He advised me, however, to send my manuscript directly to Kant himself, and submit it to his judgment, while he promised to accompany it with a letter to the great philosopher. Accordingly I wrote to Kant, sending him my work, and enclosing the letter from Herz. A good while passed, however, before an answer came. At length Herz received a reply, in which, among other things, Kant said :—

"But what were you thinking about, my dear friend, when you sent me a big packet containing the most subtle researches, not only to read through, but to think out thoroughly, while I am still, in my sixty-sixth year, burdened with a vast amount of labour in completion of my plan! Part of this labour is to furnish the last part of the *Kritik*,—that, namely, on the Faculty of Judgment,—which is soon to appear ; part is to work out my system of the Metaphysic of Nature, as well as the Metaphysic of Ethics, in accordance with the requirements of the *Kritik*. Moreover, I am kept incessantly busy with a multitude of letters requiring special explanations on particular points ; and, in addition to all this, my health is frail. I had already made up my mind to send back the manuscript with an excuse so well justified on all these grounds ; but a glance at it soon enabled me to

T

recognise its merits, and to show, not only that none of my opponents had understood me and the main problem so well, but that very few could claim so much penetration as Herr Maimon in profound inquiries of this sort. This induced me   .   .   ," and so on.

In another passage of the letter Kant says :—" Herr Maimon's work contains moreover so many acute observations, that he cannot give it to the public without its producing an impression strongly in his favour." In a letter to myself he said :—" Your esteemed request I have endeavoured to comply with as far as was possible for me ; and if I have not gone the length of passing a judgment on the whole of your treatise, you will gather the reason from my letter to Herr Herz. Certainly it arises from no feeling of disparagement, which I entertain for no earnest effort in rational inquiries that interest mankind, and least of all for such an effort as yours, which, in point of fact, betrays no common talent for the profounder sciences."

It may easily be imagined how important and agreeable to me the approbation of this great thinker must have been, and especially his testimony that I had understood him well. For there are some arrogant Kantians, who believe themselves to be sole proprietors of the Critical Philosophy, and therefore dispose of every objection, even though intended, not exactly as a refutation, but as a fuller elaboration of this philosophy, by the mere assertion without proof, that the author has failed to understand Kant. Now these gentlemen were no longer in a position to bring this charge against my book, inasmuch as, by the testimony of the founder himself of the Critical Philosophy, I have a better right than they to make use of this argument.

At this time I was living in Potsdam with a gentleman who was a leather-manufacturer. When Kant's letters arrived, I went to Berlin, and devoted my time to the publication of my *Transcendental Philosophy.* As a native of Poland I dedicated this work to the king, and carried a copy to the Polish Resident ; but it was never sent, and I was put off from time to time with various excuses. *Sapienti sat!*

A copy of the work was also sent, as is usually done, to the editor of the *Allgemeine Litteraturzeitung.* After waiting a good while without any notice appearing, I wrote to the editor, and received the following answer : —"You know yourself how small is the number of those who are competent to understand and judge philosophical works. Three of the best speculative thinkers have declined to undertake the review of your book, because they are unable to penetrate into the depths of your researches. An application has been made to a fourth, from whom a favourable reply was expected ; but a review from him has not yet been received."

I also began to work at this time for the *Journal für Aufklärung.* My first article was on *Truth*, and was in the form of a letter to a friend* in Berlin.   The article was occasioned by a letter which I had received from this friend during my stay in Potsdam, and in which he wrote to me in a humorous vein, that philosophy was no longer a marketable commodity, and that therefore I ought to take advantage of the opportunity which I was enjoying to learn tanning.   I replied, that philosophy is not a coinage subject to the vicissitudes of the exchange ; and this proposition I afterwards developed in my article. Another article in the same periodical was on *Tropes*, in which I show that these imply the transference of a word not from one object to another that is analogous, but from a relative to its correlate.   I wrote also an article on *Bacon and Kant*, in which I institute a comparison between these two reformers of philosophy.   *The Soul of the World* was the subject of another discussion in this journal, in which I endeavoured to make out, that the doctrine of one universal soul common to all animated beings has not only as much in its favour as the opposite doctrine, but that the arguments for it outweigh those on the other side.   My last article in the journal referred to the plan of my *Transcendental Philosophy;* and I explain in it that, while I hold the Kantian philosophy to be irrefutable from the side of the Dogmatist, on the other hand I believe that it is exposed to all attacks from the side of the Scepticism of Hume.

* Samuel Levi, according to *Maimoniana*, p. 78.—*Trans.*

A number of young Jews from all parts of Germany had, during Mendelssohn's lifetime, united to form a society under the designation, *Society for Research into the Hebrew Language.* They observed with truth, that the evil condition of our people, morally as well as politically, has its source in their religious prejudices, in their want of a rational exposition of the Holy Scriptures, and in the arbitrary exposition to which the rabbis are led by their ignorance of the Hebrew language. Accordingly the object of their society was to remove these deficiencies, to study the Hebrew language in its sources, and by that means to introduce a rational exegesis. For this purpose they resolved to publish a monthly periodical in Hebrew under the title of המאסף, *The Collector,* which was to give expositions of difficult passages in Scripture, Hebrew poems, prose essays, translations from useful works, etc.

The intention of all this was certainly good ; but that the end would scarcely be reached by any such means, I saw from the very beginning. I was too familiar with the principles of the rabbis and their style of thought to believe that such means would bring about any change. The Jewish nation is, without reference to accidental modifications, a perpetual aristocracy under the appearance of a theocracy. The learned men, who form the nobility in the nation, have been able, for many centuries, to maintain their position as the legislative body with so much authority among the common people, that they can do with them whatever they please. This high authority is a natural tribute which weakness owes to strength. For since the nation is divided into such unequal classes as the common people and the learned, and since the former, owing to the unfortunate political condition of the nation, are profoundly ignorant, not only of all useful arts and sciences, but even of the laws of their religion, on which their eternal welfare is supposed to depend, it follows that the exposition of Scripture, the deduction of religious laws from it, and the application of these to particular cases, must be surrendered wholly to the learned class which the other undertakes the cost of maintaining. The learned class seek to make up for their want of linguistic science and rational exegetics by their own ingenuity, wit and acuteness. To form an idea of the degree in which these talents are displayed, it is necessary to read the Talmud along with the commentary called *Tosaphoth*, that is, the additions to the first commentary of Rabbi Solomon Isaac.*

The productions of the mind are valued by them, not in proportion to their utility, but in proportion to the talent which they imply. A man who understands Hebrew, who is well versed in the Holy Scriptures, who even carries in his head the whole of the Jewish *Corpus Juris*,—and that is no trifle,—is by them but slightly

---

* See above, p. 41—*Trans.*

esteemed.   The greatest praise that they give to such a man is *Chamor Nose Sepharim*, that is, *An ass loaded with books.*   But if a man is able, by his own ingenuity, to deduce new laws from those already known, to draw fine distinctions, and to detect hidden contradictions, he is almost idolised.   And to tell the truth, this judgment is well founded, so far as it concerns the treatment of subjects that have no ulterior end in view.

It may therefore be easily imagined, that people of this sort will scarcely accord a hearing to an institute which aims merely at the cultivation of taste, the study of language, or any similar object, which to them appears mere trifling.   Yet these are not the few educated men, scattered here and there,—the steersmen of this ship which is driven about in all seas.   All men of enlightened minds, it does not matter how much taste or knowledge they possess, are treated by them as imbeciles.   And why ?   Simply because they have not studied the Talmud to that extent, and in the manner, which they require. Mendelssohn was in some measure esteemed by them on this account, because in point of fact he was a good Talmudist.

I was therefore neither for, nor against, this monthly periodical ; I even contributed to it at times Hebrew articles.   Among these I will mention merely one,—an exposition of an obscure passage in the commentary of Maimonides on the Mishnah, which I interpreted by the Kantian philosophy.   The article was afterwards translated into German, and inserted in the *Berlinische Monats-schrift.*

Some time after this I received from this society, which now calls itself the *Society for the Promotion of all that is Noble and Good*, a commission to write a Hebrew commentary on the celebrated work of Maimonides, *Moreh Nebhochim.* This commission I undertook with pleasure, and the work was soon done. So far, however, only a part of the commentary has as yet appeared. The preface to the work may be considered as a brief history of philosophy.

I had been an adherent of all philosophical systems in succession, Peripatetic, Spinozist, Leibnitzian, Kantian, and finally Sceptic ; and I was always devoted to that system, which for the time I regarded as alone true. At last I observed that all these systems contain something true, and are in certain respects equally useful. But, as the difference of philosophical systems depends on the ideas which lie at their foundation in regard to the objects of nature, their properties and modifications, which cannot, like the ideas of mathematics, be defined in the same way by all men, and presented *a priori*, I determined to publish for my own use, as well as for the advantage of others, a philosophical dictionary, in which all philo-sophical ideas should be defined in a somewhat free method, that is, without attachment to any particular system, but either by an explanation common to all, or by several explanations from the point of view of each.

Of this work also only the first part has as yet appeared.

In the popular German monthly already mentioned, the *Berlinische Monatsschrift*, various articles of mine were inserted, on Deceit, on the Power of Foreseeing, on Theodicy, and other subjects. On Empirical Psychology also I contributed various articles, and at last became associated with Herr Hofrath Moritz in the editorship of the perodical.*

So much with regard to the events which have occurred in my life, and the communication of which, I thought, might be not without use. I have not yet reached the haven of rest ; but—

> " Quo fata trahunt retrahuntque sequamur."

---

* The last few pages have been condensed from the original ; in which the author gives detailed information, which seems no longer of any special interest, about the articles he contributed to periodicals.—*Trans.*

CONCLUDING CHAPTER.

THE closing words of the Autobiography themselves
awaken the desire to know the sequel of the author's
life, and it seems therefore appropriate to finish the
narrative by the sketch of a few facts derived mainly
from the little volume of *Maimoniana*, to which reference
has been made in the preface.

It is perhaps scarcely necessary to state that Maimon's
life to the very end continued to retain the stamp it bore
throughout the whole period described in the preceding
chapters.   That stamp had apparently been impressed
on it even before he left Poland; and the Western
influences, under which he came in Germany, never
altered essentially the character he brought with him
from home.

Even in its external features his life enjoyed no
permanent improvement.   Fate had indeed been somewhat hard upon a man of so much genuine culture and
sensibility.   Still the chronic poverty, which filled the
largest cup of suffering in his life, was due not wholly to
circumstances: it was partly his own nature or habits
that kept him a pauper.   This is all the more remarkable,
that there is perhaps no work of moral or religious

instruction which attaches more importance than the Talmud to industrial pursuits.* Saturated as his mind was with Talmudic lore, and disciplined as his early years had been by Talmudic training, Maimon could not be ignorant of the advantage which the spiritual life derives from financial independence on others; and it might therefore have been expected of him that, like many of the great rabbis, and Spinoza and Mendelssohn too, he would have devoted himself to some remunerative occupation, however humble. This would not have

---

* By the kindness of my friend, the Rev. Meldola de Sola, of the Portuguese Synagogue in Montreal, I am enabled to make an interesting note on this subject. Among the Talmudic passages enjoining industry are the following :—" Rather skin a carcase for pay in the public streets, than be idly dependent on charity," " Rather perform the meanest labour than beg." As a further evidence of the estimation in which labour was held by the sages of the Talmud, it may be mentioned that Hillel, before being admitted to the Great College, earned his livelihood as a woodcutter ; that Rabbi Joshua was a pinmaker ; Rabbi Nehemiah Halsador, a potter ; Rabbi Judah, a tailor ; Rabbi Joshua Hasandler, a shoemaker ; and Rabbi Judah Hanechtan, a baker. "Of all things," says Mr. Deutsch, "the most hated were idleness and asceticism ; piety and learning themselves only received their proper estimation when joined to healthy, bodily work. 'It is well to add a trade to your studies ; you will then be free from sin,' 'The tradesman at his work need not rise before the greatest doctor,' 'Greater is he who derives his livelihood from work than he who fears God'—are some of the most common dicta of the period." (*Literary Remains*, p. 25, where there are some striking stories in condemnation of asceticism). Mr. Deutsch elsewhere quotes, "Rather live on your Sabbath as you would on a week-day than be dependent on others," (*Ibid.*, p. 30).—*Trans.*

been impossible even in Poland, where the Jews were subject to no disability excluding them from the common industries of the country ; and from the Autobiography it appears that, even at an early period of his life, he was more than half aware that his poverty was due, not wholly to the imperious demands of a higher culture, but to a somewhat selfish indolence.*   In Germany, with its more advanced civilisation, it would have been much less difficult for him to make a tolerable living at some employment.   The Autobiography shows that he was very generously received by a large circle of influential friends, who took a great deal of pains to secure for him a position of independence, and that they abandoned their effort only when they found it in vain. From the *Maimoniana* also it appears that some of the most eminent men of his time continued to tender their friendly services.   Among others, Plattner, Schultze (Aenesidemus), and even Goethe, made advances towards Maimon in a way that was not only very flattering, but might have been very helpful, if he had so chosen.†   But he never got rid of the habit, which he had acquired in Poland, of depending on others ; and the low standard of comfort, to which he had accustomed himself, left him without sufficient stimulus to seek an escape from his pauperised condition.

---

* See above, pp. 140-1.

† *Maimoniana,* pp. 196-200.

His condition, therefore, never improved. He continued during his later years to work at various literary employments; but the remuneration he obtained for these was never sufficient for his subsistence. His works appealed to a very limited public. He had consequently often to go a-begging for a publisher, and to content himself with what slight honorarium the reluctant publishers chose to give.* The literary hack-work, of which he was obliged to do a good deal, brought him no better return. That sort of labour was probably as poorly paid in Berlin at the time as in the Grub Street of last century. He was therefore at times reduced to utter beggary. Many of his earlier friends, as appears from the Autobiography, had lost patience with him; and some, who had helped him before, when he was forced by sheer starvation to apply to them afterwards, treated him as a common beggar, dismissing him with a copper in charity (*Zehrpfennig*), and at times with unnecessarily cold, even insulting language.† If we add to this the fact, that his irregular habits often made him the victim of unscrupulous men,‡ it will not seem surprising that he sometimes fell into a bitter tone and harsh judgments about his friends, § or that he was apt occasionally to burst out into pretty strong language of general misanthropy. ‖

---

* *Ibid.* p. 80.   † *Ibid.* pp. 80, 83-4.   ‡ *Ibid.*, p. 95, note.
§ *Ibtd.*, pp. 82-3.   ‖ *Ibid.*, pp. 154, 157.

Perhaps Maimon might have risen out of the chronic destitution, to which he seemed doomed, if he had cultivated in any degree the virtue of thrift. But thriftlessness, as the Autobiography shows, had been an hereditary vice in his family, at least for two generations before him ; and though he gives vivid pictures of its pitiable results in the households of his grandfather and father, he never made any effort to rise above it himself. Whenever he obtained any remuneration for his work, instead of husbanding it economically till he obtained more, he usually squandered it at once in extravagancies, often of a useless, sometimes of a reprehensible kind. * He points out in his first chapter, that his grandfather might have been a rich man if he had kept accounts of income and expenditure. But his friend Wolff, has to confess that, good mathematician as Maimon was, he never seemed to think of the difference between *plus* and *minus* in money-matters. † With such a character one of Maimon's friends was not far from the truth, when on a fresh application for assistance, he dismissed him, too harshly perhaps, with the blunt remark, "People like you there is no use in trying to help." ‡ Certainly help was not to be found in Maimon himself, and it is difficult to see how he could have avoided the chance of a miserable death by actual starvation, had it not been that a generous

---

* *Ibid.*, pp. 80, 95, 104.   † *Ibid.*, p. 84.   ‡ *Ibid.*, p. 105.

home was at last opened to him, where he closed his days in comfort and peace.

A character like that of Maimon implied a general irregularity of life,—an absence of that regulation by fixed rules of conduct, which is essential to wellbeing.   He was not indeed unaware of the importance of such regularity.   " I require of every man of sound mind," he said one day, " that he should lay out for himself a plan of action."   No wonder that this requirement leads his friend to remark, that it seemed to him as if Maimon's only plan of life had been to live without any plan at all.*

The irregularity of his habits is strikingly seen in his want of method even at his literary work.   Nothwith-standing the technical culture he gave himself in early life in drawing, he seems never to have reached any degree of muscular expertness.   Wolff remarked his awkwardness in handling his pen, and his inability to fold a letter with tolerable neatness.†   In other respects also he was careless about those mechanical conveni-ences by which mental work is usually facilitated.   He was commonly to be seen working at a very unsteady desk, one leg of which was supported by a folio volume.‡ He did not even confine himself to any particular place for work.   Apparently he spent more of his day in public taverns than in his private lodging, and he might often

---

* *Ibid.*, p. 159.   † *Ibid.*, pp. 231-2.   ‡ *Ibid.*, p. 96.

be seen amid the distraction of such surroundings writing or revising proofs, while, as a consequence, his papers sometimes were mislaid and lost, and his work had all to be done over again. It was said of the Autobiography itself that it had been written on an alehouse bench.* He could never understand how any man could do intellectual work by rule; and therefore, though he had to make his living as best he could by literature, he never formed the habit of reserving one part of the day for work. He commonly worked in the morning, at least in *his* morning, and that, his friend acknowledges, was not very early;† but this itself was evidently no fixed rule. Probably for the same reason he never adopted the plan, which authors find so serviceable, of first sketching an outline of a work before it is written out in detail. " I have," he said one day, " given up, with good result, the habit of making a draught beforehand. You are not, by a long way, so careful about your work when you know that you are going to write it over again ; you neglect many a thought, do not write it down, because you believe that it will occur to you again in copying out, which frequently does not happen." ‡ It is clear, however, that, his opinion to the contrary notwithstanding, his writings suffered from his unmethodical habits. " The fact," says the most competent of judges on this subject, " that Maimon is

---

far from having attained the recognition which his importance deserves, may be accounted for by the defective condition of his writings. His extraordinary acuteness was designed, but was not sufficiently cultivated, to give to his investigations the light and the force of methodical exposition. He wrote with most pleasure in his Talmudic fashion, commenting and disputing, without proper sifting and arrangement of his materials. To these defects must be added the faults of his style. It is surprising that he learned to write German as he did. In his writings there are passages in which the thought bursts out with really resplendent power, and actually forces the language, even plays with it, in turns of expression that take you by surprise. But a German author he never became; and as a philosophical author he wanted a certain sense of order that is indispensable for exposition. He can sometimes formulate very well, but cannot systematise, and hence his most important opinions, in which the whole meaning of his position rests, are often in the course of his writings found in passages the least lucid and the least prominent." *

It is perhaps only saying the same thing of Maimon in another form, that he had no mechanical memory, that consequently he was apt to forget the names of persons and of places, sometimes could not remember the name of the street where he lived, or the day or even the

---

* Fischer's *Geschichte der neuern Philosophie*, vol. v., pp. 133-4.

month ; and it is not therefore surprising that he often injured himself by neglecting all sort of engagements.[*] It may be readily inferred that he was particularly negligent about all engagements and regulations bearing upon the mere externals of life. That a man of his condition and character must have been unusually careless about his personal appearance, follows as a matter of course, and therefore we may pass over the references of Wolff to peculiarities of Maimon's dress. He was usually to be seen out of doors clad in an overcoat which had evidently not been made for himself, and which, we may suspect, was intended as a convenient covering for the defects of under-garments, his boots bearing the weather-stains of many days, and his beard often showing that for a good while he had forgotten his engagement with his barber. In the latter years of his life he abandoned the use of a wig, as well as of powder in his hair, at a time when these changes must have been regarded as rather daring innovations on prevalent fashion. But in all his surroundings he showed what, for a man of his intellectual attainments, seems a most astonishing disregard of sanitary cleanliness and the comfortable decencies of life. The state of his lodging must have raised a shudder in any one sensitive to disorder or uncleanliness. He acknowledged that he was constantly at war with the housemaid on this subject,

---

[*] *Maimoniana*, pp. 190-6.

as he could never bear to have his room swept and dusted, and he complained of the perpetual annoyance to which he was exposed in Amsterdam from the excessive scruples of the people in regard to tidiness.* It may fairly be suspected that the annoyance was considerably greater, as it was more justifiable, on the other side. His habits in this respect clung to him to the last, and it was evidently difficult to keep his surroundings tolerable even in the comparatively sumptuous home in which he closed his days.

The frank confessions of the Autobiography reveal the fact, that the irregularity, which characterised the life of Maimon, sometimes led to a breach of the weightier matters of the law. The habit, which he began in Poland, of seeking relief from external discomfort and internal wretchedness in alcoholic stimulation, grew upon him afterwards ; and as his health began to fail, he used to treat his various complaints by a liberal allowance of various wines and beers which he supposed adapted to their cure.† The liberal allowance was very apt, especially in the evenings, to exceed all reasonable moderation; and the sleepy inhabitants of Berlin were not infrequently disturbed by the half-tipsy philosopher, as he wended his way unsteadily homewards at unseasonable hours, discoursing on all sorts of speculative themes in disagree-

---

* *Ibid.*, pp. 90-1.   † *Ibid.*, pp. 183-8.

ably loud tones that were occasionally interrupted by the expostulations of a night-watchman.*

The peculiarly undisciplined manners of Maimon were occasionally shown in violent outbursts of various feelings. Too frequently it was an irritable temper that gave way. The slightest provocation, even the loss of a game at chess,† was apt to cause a painful explosion ; and then his language was certainly far from being restrained by those usages which are found essential to the pleasantness of social intercourse.‡   The uncontrollable violence of these outbursts was amusingly exhibited in the fact, that sometimes he could not command the intellectual calm requisite for thinking and expressing himself in his acquired German, and, even though it might be a Gentile with whom he quarrelled, he fell back on his Judæo-Polish mother tongue,which came to him as if by natural instinct.§ It is but fair, however, to add that these outbursts were often merely the unusually forcible, but not altogether unjustifiable, utterances of an honest indignation at wrong. ‖

For this strangely educated man, who in his outward manners seemed to remain a somewhat rude child of nature, was after all ready to yield, not only to an unkindly irritability, but also to the more genial emotions.   It is

---

* *Ibid.*, pp. 101-4.   † *Ibid.*, p. 217.

‡ *Ibid.*, pp. 109-112, 208, 212-3.

§ *Ibid.*, p. 87.   ‖ *Ibid.*, p. 213.

pleasing, for example, to know that he had a particular fondness for animals ; and his pets were allowed in his lodging liberties which, however objectionable to a tidy house-maid, showed at least the essential gentleness of his heart. Tutored as he was himself in the severest school of poverty, it is also pleasing to know that he cherished a kindly sympathy for the poor, and was ever ready to help them as he could, sometimes at the cost of no small sacrifice to himself.* The finer sensibilities of his nature were also easily touched by music. Though he had no musical culture, and used to regret that he had had none, an old Hebrew melody, long after he had broken off all connection with the Jews, could move him so deeply that he was obliged, even in company, to seek relief in tears. † For in the uncontrolled simplicity of his nature he allowed his feelings to find their natural vent without much restraint from circumstances; and therefore he was seen at times in the theatre excited to loud sobbing by a tragedy, or to boisterous laughter over a comedy. ‡

Nor is it to be regarded as an unpleasant feature of his character, but rather as an indication of a wholesome check on the general irregularity of his life, that, even after he had thrown off all the peculiar restraints of his national religion, he clung with evident fondness to many of those rabbinical habits which he had cultivated in his

---

* *Ibid.*, p. 249.   † *Ibid.*, p. 88.
‡ *Ibid.*, p. 230.

earlier years. From Fischer's account of the style of Maimon's works we have seen how his intellectual work was affected by his Talmudic studies. The criticism is evidently just. Maimon himself had met with it, and acknowledged its justice. He protested indeed that it did not affect the truth of his speculations, though he evidently felt its disadvantages, and laboured at times to acquire a more methodical style.*

The rabbinical habits of Maimon, however, were most quaintly seen in peculiarities of outward manner. Gesticulations customary in the study of the Talmud he was seen to adopt not infrequently when he forgot himself in the earnestness of conversation, or when in a company he fell into a brown study, or even in the studies of his retirement. Thus in reading Euler's mathematical works or any other book which required great attention, he would fall into the Talmudic sing-song and rhythmical swing of the body.†

It is noteworthy also, that, with all the unrestrained rudeness which often characterised his manners, Maimon was not without a certain dignified courtesy ; and when the occasion demanded it, he could turn a polite phrase as prettily as the most accomplished gentleman.‡ There was, moreover, in Maimon an intrinsic shyness which must have gone a long way to soften the less amiable

---

* *Ibid.*, pp. 86-7.   † *Ibid.*, p. 89.
‡ See, for example, *Ibid.*, pp. 112, 115, 209, 250-1.

side of his social character.*   Then it is evident that his conversation, in his better moods at least, had a charm which made him a welcome guest in any company. Thus, amid all that may have been repulsive at times, there must have been in Maimon's character a good deal to attract the friendly companionship of others.   The Autobiography itself, as well as Wolff's little book, shows that Maimon enjoyed as much as he desired of the cultured society of his time.   Being naturally shy, indeed, he rather shrank from company in which intercourse is regulated by a somewhat rigid social code ; and the desire of freedom from such restriction often drove him into company of a much more objectionable kind.   He also seems to have entertained a strong dislike to any excessively demonstrative affection.   He himself was rather curt in his expressions of courtesy or friendliness towards others, contenting himself generally, on meeting them, with a familiar nod.   The lifting of the hat appeared to him meaningless, and a deliberate embrace " in cold blood " was intolerable.†   Yet in many instances the attachment of his friends was marked with an unusual degree of warmth, and brought many an hour of sunshine to a life which otherwise would have been shadowed with insufferable gloom.

Among all Maimon's friends, the most conspicuous place must be given to the man by whose generous

---

* *Ibid.*, p.   † *Ibid.*, pp. 165-6.

hospitality he was able to close his chequered life amid the comforts of a luxurious home.   While he was living in a miserable lodging in one of the suburbs of Berlin, he learned from one of his friends that a Silesian noble-man, Graf Kalkreuth, who had formed a high opinion of his writings, was anxious to make his personal acquain-tance.   After a good deal of delay, Maimon was at last induced to call upon the Graf at his residence in Berlin. Fortunately he was very favourably impressed with the character of his noble friend ; and the friendship thus begun led before long to his taking up his abode permanently with the Graf.*   The generous considera-tion which the host displayed for all the eccentricities of his guest, made this arrangement one of the happiest for the poor philosopher, who since his childhood had seldom enjoyed the comforts of a home.

But it is evident that the hardships of his life had at an early period begun to tell upon his constitution, and that this was further shattered by irregular habits in his later years.   Symptoms of serious trouble in the lungs excited his alarm in the winter of 1795, and he was induced to seek medical advice.   Partly from an unwise scepticism in regard to medicine, partly from his usual failure to adhere to any fixed rule in his conduct, the services of his physicians commonly ended with the con-sultation ; he seldom or never acted on their advice.†

---

* *Ibid.*, pp. 201-210.   † *Ibid.*, pp. 183-8.

He lived in indifferent health for five or six years more. When his last illness overtook him, he was living in the house of Graf Kalkreuth at Siegersdorf near Freistadt, in Lower Silesia. The only account of him at this crisis was written by the pastor of Freistadt, for a monthly periodical of the time, entitled *Kronos*. It forms the close of Wolff's little book ; and as it is the only account, it may be of some interest here. The pastor, Herr Tscheggey, had made the acquaintance of Maimon about the year 1795 ; but their intercourse had become much closer about six weeks before Maimon's death, when he used to visit the pastor two or three times a week. On hearing that Maimon had been confined for some days, the good pastor at once went to see him. He found him in a state of great weakness, unable to leave his room, and besought him earnestly, but in vain, to take medical advice. A few days afterwards he called again, and saw that evidently the end was drawing nigh. Curious to know whether Maimon in this situation would remain true to his principles, he gave the following turn to the conversation, which he professes to report word for word.

" I am sorry to find you so ill to-day, dear Maimon," said the pastor.

" There will perhaps be some improvement yet," replied Maimon.

"You look so ill," his friend proceeded, "that I am doubtful about your recovery."

"What matters it after all?" said Maimon. "When I am dead, I am gone."

"Can you say that, dear friend," rejoined the clergyman, with deep emotion. "How? Your mind, which amid the most unfavourable circumstances ever soared to higher attainments, which bore such fair flowers and fruits—shall it be trodden in the dust along with the poor covering in which it has been clothed? Do you not feel at this moment that there is something in you which is not body, not matter, not subject to the conditions of space and time?"

"Ah!" replied Maimon, "these are beautiful dreams and hopes "——

"Which will surely be fulfilled," his friend broke in; and then, after a short pause, added, "You maintained not long ago that here we cannot reach further than to mere *legality*. Let this be admitted; and now perhaps you are about to pass over soon into a condition, in which you will rise to the stage of *morality*, since you and all of us have a natural capacity for it. Why? Should you not wish now to come into the society of one whom you honoured so much as Mendelssohn?"

The zealous pastor says he gave the conversation this turn on purpose, in order to touch this side of the philosopher's heart. After a while the dying man exclaimed, "Ay me! I have been a foolish man, the most foolish among the most foolish—and how earnestly I wished it otherwise!"

"This utterance," observed the pastor, "is also a proof that you are not yet in complete accord with your unbelief. No," he added, taking Maimon by the hand, "you will not all die ; your spirit will surely live on."

"So far as mere faith and hope are concerned, I can go a good way ; but what does that help us?" was Maimon's reply.

"It helps us at least to peace," urged the pastor.

"I am at peace *(Ich bin ruhig),*" said the dying man, completely exhausted.

Here Tscheggey broke off the conversation, as the sufferer was evidently unable to continue it. When he rose to leave, Maimon begged him to stay, or at least to come back again soon. He came back the following morning, but found the patient unconscious. At ten o'clock on the same evening—it was the 22nd of November, 1800—this strangely tossed life had reached its haven.

"He died at peace," says the kindly clergyman, "though I do not venture to say from what source the peace was derived. When a few days afterwards I passed the castle of his noble friend, I looked up with sadness to the window of his former room, and blessed his ashes." It is to be regretted that the generous piety of the friendly minister was not universal, and that the ashes of the unfortunate doubter were only with a grudge allowed to find a decent resting-place.

University of Illinois Press
1325 South Oak Street
Champaign, IL 61820-6903
www.press.uillinois.edu